The Complete

CAST-IRON SKILLET

Cookbook

The Complete
CAST-IRON SKILLET

Cookbook

150 CLASSIC AND CREATIVE RECIPES

ELENA ROSEMOND-HOERR

Photography by Marija Vidal

R

ROCKRIDGE
PRESS

For my three—Dan, Ev, and Sam.
Thanks for being my constant.

For general information on our other products and services or to obtain technical support, please contact our Customer Care Department within the United States at (866) 744-2665, or outside the United States at (510) 253-0500.

Rockridge Press publishes its books in a variety of electronic and print formats. Some content that appears in print may not be available in electronic books, and vice versa.

TRADEMARKS: Rockridge Press and the Rockridge Press logo are trademarks or registered trademarks of Callisto Media Inc. and/or its affiliates, in the United States and other countries, and may not be used without written permission. All other trademarks are the property of their respective owners. Rockridge Press is not associated with any product or vendor mentioned in this book.

Interior and Cover Designer: Regina Stadnik
Art Producer: Meg Baggott
Editor: Annie Choi
Production Editor: Matt Burnett

Photography © 2020 Marija Vidal
Food styling by Elisabet der Nederlanden
Cover: Fig, Prosciutto, and Arugula Pizza; page 101

ISBN: Print 978-1-64611-763-5
eBook 978-1-64611-764-2
R0

CONTENTS

INTRODUCTION xiii

Chapter One: **COVERING THE CAST-IRON BASICS** 1

Chapter Two: **BREAKFAST AND BRUNCH** 11

Blueberry Pancakes 12

French Toast with Strawberry Compote 13

Savory Dutch Baby 14

Bananas Foster Dutch Baby 16

Four-Ingredient Pancakes 18

Andouille and Bell Pepper Breakfast Hash 19

Kohlrabi and Potato Hash 20

Caramelized Cream-Fried Eggs over Parmesan Grits 21

Fried Bologna and Egg Sandwich 22

Roasted Red Pepper and Goat Cheese Frittata 23

French Toast Casserole 24

Walnut and Cranberry Baked Oatmeal 25

Spinach and Mushroom Breakfast Casserole 26

Croque Madame 27

Carrot Cake Pancakes with Cream Cheese Frosting 29

Chapter Three: **BREADS AND BISCUITS** 31

Chocolate Zucchini Bread 32

Rosemary Buttermilk Biscuits 33

Sourdough Bread 35

Buttered Dinner Rolls 38

Jalapeño-Cheddar Drop Biscuits 40

Blueberry Scones 41

Caramel-Pecan Cinnamon Rolls 42

Green Chile Corn Bread with Whipped Honey Butter 44

Banana Nut Bread 45

Ham and Cheese Stuffed Biscuits 46

Caramelized Onion and
Tomato Focaccia 47

Mozzarella-Stuffed Garlic Knots 49

Irish Soda Bread with Marmalade 51

Braided Cinnamon Bread 53

Swirled Herb Bread 55

Chapter Four: APPETIZERS AND SIDES 59

Sausage and Cheddar Balls 60

Goat Cheese and Bacon
Stuffed Mushrooms 61

Buffalo Wings 62

Spinach and Artichoke Dip 63

Vegetable Tempura 64

Crispy Chipotle Chickpeas 65

Boudin Balls 66

Cheese and Bacon Smashed
Potatoes 67

Skillet Greens 69

Fried Pickles 70

Sriracha Brussels Sprouts 71

Roasted Cauliflower 72

Garlic Butter Green Beans 73

Turmeric Roasted Beets 74

Hasselback Potatoes 75

Buttermilk Fried Okra 76

Herb Butter Roasted Pattypan 77

Panzanella 78

Charred Zucchini 79

Roasted Artichokes 80

Chapter Five: SANDWICHES AND PIZZA 83

Beef and Mint Lettuce Wraps 84

Turkey Melt 85

Fried Chicken Biscuits 86

Bacon, Arugula, Tomato, and
Pesto Sandwiches 88

Sourdough Toast with Avocado,
Bacon, Tomato, and a Runny Egg 89

Croque Monsieur 91

Cheeseburgers 93

Skillet Calzone 94

Hot Italian Sandwich 95

Beet and Goat Cheese Pizza 96

Pepperoni Pizza with Hot Honey 98

Pesto and Sausage Pizza 100

Fig, Prosciutto, and Arugula Pizza 101

Chapter Six: VEGETARIAN MAINS 103

Spring Pea and Mushroom Risotto 104

Butter Halloumi 106

Broccoli and Carrot Stuffed Shells 107

Eggplant Lasagna 109

Lentil Bolognese 111

Enchilada Casserole 113

Vegetarian Stir-Fry 115

Ricotta-Stuffed Zucchini Boats 116

Macaroni and Cheese 117

Sweet Potato Frittata 119

Skillet Nachos 120

Carrot and Zucchini Fritters 121

Curried Pea and Mushroom Shepherd's Pie 122

Potato and Cheese Pierogis 124

Spiced Buttery Lentils 126

Chiles Rellenos 128

Chapter Seven: POULTRY 131

Chicken and Zucchini Curry 132

Sweet and Sour Chicken 134

Turkey Burgers 136

Miso Chicken Thighs 137

French Onion Chicken 138

Biscuit-Topped Chicken Potpie 140

Pickle-Brined Fried Chicken 142

Chicken Quesadillas 144

Turkey and Sage Meatballs 145

Chicken and Green Bean Stir-Fry 146

Buttermilk Roast Chicken 147

Jerk Chicken Naked Wings 149

Roasted Turkey Breast 150

Chicken Marsala 151

Blackened Chicken Thighs with Pineapple Salsa 153

Chicken Biryani 155

Chapter Eight: SEAFOOD 159

Jalapeño and Shallot Crab Cakes 160

Seared Lobster Tails 161

Brown Butter and Garlic Wahoo 162

Shrimp and Grits 163

Blackened Mahi-Mahi Tacos with Mango Salsa 165

Buttermilk Grouper Bites 167

Shrimp Burgers with Chipotle Mayonnaise 169

Bacon-Wrapped Scallops 170

Seared Ahi Tuna 171

Lobster Mac and Cheese 172

Salmon Cakes 173

Shrimp and Scallop Scampi 174

Sweet and Spicy Catfish 175

Maple-Glazed Salmon 176

Seafood Jambalaya 177

Chapter Nine: BEEF, PORK, AND LAMB 179

Steak with Grilled Fennel Salad 180

Bacon and Kohlrabi over Creamy Grits 181

Herb and Garlic Meatloaf 183

London Broil with Spring Onion Pesto 185

Classic Lamb Shepherd's Pie 186

One-Skillet Steak and Potatoes 188

Herb-Crusted Pork Loin 189

Oven-Roasted Ribs 190

Pork-Stuffed Bell Peppers 191

Apple Cider Vinegar Pork Chops 192

Roasted Sausage and Potatoes with Chipotle Cream Sauce 193

Breaded Pork Medallions 194

Lamb Chops with Herb Butter 195

Seared Short Ribs with Lime Cabbage Slaw 196

Pork Belly and Kimchi Bowl 197

Thai Basil Beef 198

Garlic Lamb and Vegetable Pasta 199

Beef Ragù with Pappardelle 200

Carne Asada Tacos 201

Chipotle Beef Tostada 202

Chapter Ten: DESSERTS 205

Shoofly Pie 206

Chocolate-Strawberry Bread Pudding 208

Blood Orange Rhubarb Crumble 209

Buttermilk Pie 210

Crispy Marshmallow Bars 211

Pear and Pecan Pie 212

Mountain Pie 214

Caramel Fried Green Tomatoes
and Ice Cream 215

Bourbon White Peach and
Nectarine Pie 217

Apple Cider Donuts 218

Baked Apple Crisp 220

Beignets 221

Carrot Cake with Whipped
Cream Cheese Frosting 223

Iced Lemon Pound Cake 225

Gooey Chocolate Skillet Cake 226

Strawberry and Goat
Milk Cobbler 228

Iced Cranberry and Orange Cake 229

Chocolate Chip Skillet Cookie 230

Chocolate-Peppermint Brownies 231

Gingerbread Cake 232

MEASUREMENT CONVERSIONS 235

INDEX 236

INTRODUCTION

Every day, sometimes for three meals a day, I reach for my cast-iron skillet. In our house, the question is not, "What should we cook in cast iron?" but, instead, "What can't we cook in cast iron?" Just this week, I have used cast iron to make Chicken and Zucchini Curry (page 132), Enchilada Casserole (page 113), Cheeseburgers (page 93), Sourdough Bread (page 35), a Turkey Melt (page 85), and Mountain Pie (page 214). And, as always, an endless stream of fried eggs.

Cast iron has been used in my family for as long as I can remember, both in my parents' house and in my grandma's house. It was always at the ready—the first skillet reached for. My dad's cast-iron collection was his pride and joy, which includes cast iron he took great pains to restore. His greatest restoration project was a 40-quart cauldron my great-grandmother Sybil used for making enormous quantities of Brunswick stew. By the time it reached my dad, it had a hole in it and was covered in rust and scale. The process of restoration took most of a year, but, in the end, it was as good as new. My dad's restoration efforts inspired me to restore my first skillet, which is the same 12-inch skillet I now cook with every day. For me, cast iron is more than a type of pan; it's a connection to home, to family, to my personal history.

In this book, you'll find a selection of recipes that are accessible for beginners and inspirational for more experienced cast-iron users. Beginners will want to take their time with the first chapter, which explains how to season, care for, and cook with cast iron. Those already familiar with cast iron may want to review chapter 1 but can also dive directly into recipes, which begin in chapter 2 (see page 11).

No matter where you are on your cast-iron journey, I hope this book adds something to your experience. These recipes were developed with the modern family in mind. Many are family favorites that I grew up eating and now prepare for my own family. Some are weekday meals that you can pull together quickly (even with "helpful" children underfoot), and a few are special-occasion meals to take your time with. All are made better because of the beauty of cast iron.

Chapter One

COVERING THE CAST-IRON BASICS

Welcome to the wonderful world of cast iron! This chapter is your personal guide to the ins and outs of cooking with and caring for cast iron. If you're feeling intimidated, I'm here to reassure you. I will teach you the techniques to set you up for success. Before you know it, your cast-iron skillet will become your go-to kitchen tool.

The Cast-Iron Skillet, Then and Now

Cast iron is an iron alloy made by reducing iron ore in a blast furnace. It was first created in China in the 5th century BCE and used to make plowshares, pots, and weapons. Slowly, its production and use spread westward. In 1707, Englishman Abraham Darby patented a method of iron casting that enabled him to make pots and cauldrons light and thin enough for everyday cooking. Before long, cast-iron cookware was readily available, and its use became widespread.

When nonstick pots and pans became popular in the late 20th century, people stopped cooking with cast iron; however, in an era when the internet allows food trends to spread like wildflowers, cast iron has been given another moment in the sun. Increasingly, people are bringing cast iron into their homes, in part because it is far more environmentally friendly than Teflon-based nonstick options, but also because of its versatility and durability.

Cast iron has always been an important part of how I cook, and it's integral to the Southern food culture I grew up in. Now, as a mother who cares about the health of my family, cast iron is the logical choice, and I love that my own cast iron will help nourish generations to come.

Buying Your First Cast-Iron Skillet

When I moved into my first apartment, my father made sure my kitchen was stocked with the essentials, including a 10-inch cast-iron skillet. For years, this skillet was the perfect size for me, and then for myself and my husband. Eventually, I added a 12-inch skillet to my collection, which has become the most useful piece of cookware in our daily life, especially since our oldest son was born.

Buying your first cast-iron skillet can be intimidating. I recommend starting with either a 10-inch or 12-inch skillet, which are the sizes used for the recipes in this book. Both sizes are affordable and easy to find. If your budget allows, you may want one of each.

Of the original cast-iron cookware manufacturers in the United States, only Lodge is still manufacturing under its own brand name. Because of their experience and reliable quality, Lodge remains one of the most well-known and widely used cast-iron brands on the market. I have several Lodge pans, and when I purchase a skillet as a gift, I generally stick with Lodge.

If you're buying a skillet, it will likely be advertised as "pre-seasoned." Think of this as a base coat seasoning and know you'll want to work to build up the seasoning before using the skillet (see page 3). If you've settled on buying a secondhand or vintage skillet, the process of cleaning and seasoning may be more intensive (see page 7) but still worthwhile.

TO GO ENAMEL OR NOT TO GO ENAMEL

There is a difference between enameled and traditional cast-iron skillets. Enameled cast iron does not need to be seasoned and is not vulnerable to rust in the same way a traditional cast-iron skillet is. However, enameled cast iron does not have the same nonstick qualities as traditional cast iron.

Both traditional and enameled cast iron have value, and each is useful for cooking different things. Although the 12-inch skillet is my go-to traditional piece, I also use my enameled Dutch oven regularly. I have a traditional Dutch oven, but the enameled Dutch oven allows more flexibility when cooking soups and stews and eliminates the concern of rust developing or having to maintain the patina.

Seasoning Your First Cast-Iron Skillet

The primary way to care for cast iron is to protect and reinforce the patina by keeping your skillet seasoned. The patina is a thin layer of fat that has polymerized and bonded with the iron, protecting it from rust and damage. To maintain the patina, cook foods that add to the seasoning, clean your cast iron properly after each use, and regularly inspect the patina for damage. Acidic ingredients can be taxing to the patina and may cause dry spots in the skillet. If this happens, a thorough coating of oil after you clean the skillet will refortify the seasoning.

Both new, "pre-seasoned" cast iron and salvaged cast iron can benefit from an initial seasoning. Follow these steps to apply a basic seasoning to your new or vintage skillet.

1. Preheat the oven to 450°F.

2. Pour ½ cup coarse sea salt into the skillet and give it a good scrub with a towel. This will remove any surface grime.

3. Wash the skillet with mild dish soap and hot water.

4. Place the skillet on the stovetop over medium heat until it is completely dry, then turn off the heat and, using oven mitts, remove the skillet from the stove.

5. While the skillet is warm, pour in 1 tablespoon of vegetable oil, olive oil, coconut oil, or peanut oil and spread it over the skillet with a clean rag. Use more oil, as necessary, to thoroughly coat the top, bottom, sides, and handle. Drain off any excess.

6. Place the cast iron into the oven for 30 minutes.

7. Turn off the heat and let the skillet cool in the oven. Repeat this oiling and baking process three or four times until the skillet is pitch black and slick.

You'll know your skillet is well seasoned when it:

- Fries an egg without sticking

- Has a dark black sheen

- Has no dry spots

- Is not sticky or greasy to the touch

Re-seasoning Your First Cast-Iron Skillet

As you learn to cook with your skillet, you'll find the balance between foods that feed your seasoning and foods that take away from it, and it will become second nature to keep the seasoning healthy through day-to-day cooking and care. Occasionally, however, you will need to re-season your skillet.

The first step to re-season a skillet depends on the damage.

- **For a dry spot**, follow steps 5 through 7 of the seasoning process on page 4.

- **For rust**, you'll need to first remove the damage using steel wool or sandpaper, then begin with step 1 of the seasoning process on page 4.

- **For more serious damage** (happens to the best of us!), follow the process for rescuing a skillet (see page 7), then begin with step 1 of the seasoning process on page 4. You may have to repeat the process a few times before the optimal patina is achieved.

I always christen a newly seasoned skillet by cooking dishes that add oil and, therefore, build the seasoning, like Potato and Cheese Pierogis (page 124) or Boudin Balls (page 66).

A Well-Stocked Kitchen

This book is centered on cast iron, but no one piece of kitchen equipment can truly stand alone. The following tools will come in handy when cooking with this book:

- **Flexible spatula:** I like a spatula that can get under what you're flipping but that also has a little spring to it.

- **Food processor:** This tool is not required, but a food processor can make a lot of things in the kitchen easier, from mixing sauces to making pie dough.

- **Mixing bowls:** You will be instructed to use mixing bowls (small, medium, and large) to make many of the recipes in this book.

- **Saucepan:** Many recipes will ask you to prepare an element of the dish in a saucepan. A 3-quart stainless-steel saucepan works great and is handy for the types of cooking that cast iron doesn't do well, namely boiling.

- **Sharp knives:** A good sharp knife is an extension of your hand in the kitchen; it makes everything easier. A dull or thin knife will slow you down, frustrate you, and make everything harder—and more dangerous.

- **Wooden spoons:** Using a metal spoon is a quick way to damage your cast iron's seasoning, so I rely on wooden spoons to keep my skillets safe.

Cast Iron Care

My standard wedding present is a 12-inch cast-iron skillet. In the accompanying card, I make the point that, if treated with love, respect, kindness, and care, a skillet and a marriage can both last a lifetime. And the fact of the matter is that a well cared for cast-iron skillet will last for many lifetimes—sometimes generations.

The Definitive Cleaning Regimen

Next to keeping your cast iron seasoned, the most important thing you can do is clean your skillet immediately after cooking with it every time you use it. Letting it sit dirty can damage the seasoning. (It's also usually much easier to clean while still warm.) The one exception to this rule is after frying, in which case let the oil cool completely before pouring it off and cleaning the skillet.

Although people argue about whether using salt, a potato, or hot water is the best way to scour cast iron, most everyone agrees the cardinal rule is to avoid using soap. I clean my skillet with hot water and a bristle brush, occasionally using a nonmetal scouring pad for tougher jobs. If you feel uncomfortable with the idea of not using soap, rest assured that the polymer coating formed in the seasoning keeps the skillet free of harmful bacteria. Keeping the seasoning intact keeps the skillet safe to use.

Once you've thoroughly cleaned your cast iron, it's vital to dry and oil it to prevent it from rusting. Return the wet skillet to the stovetop over low heat until it has completely dried. Once it's cool enough to handle, coat the skillet with a thin layer of vegetable oil.

RESCUING A RUSTY SKILLET

My biggest pride and joy is the 12-inch skillet I rescued from a friend's backyard, rusted beyond belief. What makes restoring cast iron so enjoyable is that it is almost always possible to do; in fact, it's rare for a piece of cast iron to be damaged beyond repair. So, as long as you're willing to put in the time and elbow grease, you can bring something from utter disrepair to gleaming glory.

The first step in restoring any piece of cast iron is cleaning it and removing the debris and rust. You can do this with steel wool, sandpaper, or an electric sander. Depending on the amount of damage and the tools you use, this restoration stage may take time.

Once you've stripped the skillet of all rust, debris, and scaling, it's time to rebuild the seasoning. Following steps 5 through 7 for seasoning a cast-iron skillet (see page 4), alternate oiling and baking the skillet. Through repeating these steps, the patina will darken until a true, glossy seasoning is achieved.

It's important to remember that the amount of sanding your skillet required during restoration will directly affect the process of rebuilding the seasoning. The skillet I rescued from my friend's yard took about a year of regular cooking and care to achieve the deep, black patina that is the goal.

About the Recipes

This book contains a collection of recipes that touches on different types of foods and cooking techniques. All of the recipes were developed for a 10-inch or 12-inch skillet. There is, of course, some flexibility between the two sizes, and most things can be scaled up or down 25 percent to fit a different skillet size.

Some recipes are easy to modify or scale. For instance, frying is easy to do in any size skillet by adjusting the amount of oil and how many things you fry at once. Other recipes will require some math to increase or decrease the amount of each ingredient to fit your skillet; just take care to keep the ratios the same, especially when baking.

Additionally, each recipe includes one or more labels to give you some quick insight into the recipe. These labels include:

CLASSIC: These recipes were traditionally made in cast iron, such as apple pies.

GLUTEN-FREE: These recipes do not contain wheat.

OVEN-COOKED: These recipes involve transferring a heavy skillet full of ingredients in and out of the oven, which may be challenging for some.

VEGAN: These recipes do not contain any animal ingredients.

VEGETARIAN: These recipes do not contain meat, poultry, or fish. They may include dairy, eggs, or honey.

WEEKDAY: These recipes take 1 hour or less to make, from start to finish.

THE GOLDEN RULES OF CAST-IRON COOKING

These rules, if followed consistently, will have you and your skillet cooking in harmony for years to come.

◆ Always clean, dry, and oil your skillet after each use. You won't have to fully re-season your cast iron very often if it is well maintained.

◆ Never use harsh or abrasive chemicals while cleaning your skillet, and never put it in the dishwasher. Cast iron is porous, so don't put anything on it that you wouldn't want on your eggs.

◆ Balance the types of food you cook in your skillet to help keep the seasoning strong. If you've cooked a lot of acidic foods in your skillet recently, cook a few with fats that will replenish the patina.

◆ Be careful handling your skillet! A cast-iron skillet is not to be under-estimated. They are large and heavy, and when they're hot, the whole skillet is hot, including the handle. This is particularly important to remember when transferring the skillet in and out of the oven.

◆ Trust the process and try not to move food around too much; the food will release when it's cooked and ready to be flipped.

◆ Store your cast iron in a cool, dry place. Too much time in a hot or damp environment will rust your skillet, and you'll need to re-season it.

FRENCH TOAST WITH STRAWBERRY COMPOTE, PAGE 13

Chapter Two

BREAKFAST
AND BRUNCH

BLUEBERRY PANCAKES

CLASSIC, VEGETARIAN, WEEKDAY

SERVES 4

Prep time: 10 minutes | **Cook time:** 15 minutes | **Cast iron:** 12-inch skillet

Every cook has an Achilles' heel. For me, it's pancakes. I can make so many wonderful things in the kitchen, but pancakes take me to task every time, which is to say, this is my husband, Dan's, recipe for pancakes. He is our resident pancake chef, and his pancakes are always light, fluffy, and golden brown.

2 cups all-purpose flour

3 tablespoons sugar

1½ teaspoons baking powder

1½ teaspoons baking soda

2 large eggs

1½ cups buttermilk

4 tablespoons (½ stick) salted butter, plus more for cooking and serving

1 cup fresh blueberries

Maple syrup or honey, for serving

1. In a large bowl, stir together the flour, sugar, baking powder, and baking soda.

2. In another large bowl, whisk the eggs, buttermilk, butter, and blueberries.

3. Gently fold the egg mixture into the flour mixture.

4. In the skillet over medium heat, melt 1 pat of butter. Working in batches, pour ½-cup portions of batter into the hot skillet. Cook for 2 to 3 minutes, or until bubbles form in the center of the batter. Flip and cook for 1 to 2 minutes more, or until golden brown. Transfer the pancakes to a plate and loosely cover them with a clean kitchen towel to keep them warm. Repeat with the remaining batter, using more butter as needed.

5. Serve with butter and syrup.

TIP: Substitute chocolate chips, diced fresh strawberries, or chopped pecans for the blueberries.

FRENCH TOAST WITH STRAWBERRY COMPOTE

VEGETARIAN, WEEKDAY

SERVES 4

Prep time: 15 minutes | **Cook time:** 40 minutes | **Cast iron:** 12-inch skillet

French toast is on my short list of breakfasts fancy enough to feel special but simple enough to make before I've had a full cup of coffee. This version is great for spring and early summer, when you have extra strawberries in the refrigerator that need to be used. Cooking them with honey and a little lemon zest gives the berries new life and raises your French toast game to the next level.

2 cups fresh strawberries, quartered, plus more for serving

2 tablespoons honey, plus more for serving

Zest of 1 lemon, grated

Pinch sea salt

4 large eggs

½ cup whole milk

1 tablespoon light brown sugar

1 teaspoon vanilla extract

1 teaspoon ground cinnamon

4 tablespoons (½ stick) salted butter, divided

1 loaf crusty bread, cut into ¾-inch to 1-inch slices

1. In a medium saucepan over medium heat, combine the strawberries, honey, lemon zest, and salt. Bring to a gentle boil, stirring occasionally. Reduce the heat to low and simmer for 5 minutes, stirring frequently. Set the compote aside to cool.

2. In a large shallow bowl, whisk the eggs, milk, brown sugar, vanilla, and cinnamon to blend.

3. In the skillet over medium-high heat, melt 1 tablespoon of butter.

4. Dredge 1 slice of bread in the egg mixture, then turn it over to coat it fully. Place the coated bread in the hot skillet. Cook for 2 to 3 minutes per side, or until browned. Transfer the French toast to a plate and cover it loosely with a clean kitchen towel to keep it warm. Repeat with the remaining bread slices and egg mixture.

5. Serve topped with strawberry compote, a drizzle of honey, and fresh strawberries.

SAVORY DUTCH BABY

OVEN-COOKED, WEEKDAY

SERVES 2

Prep time: 20 minutes | **Cook time:** 25 minutes | **Cast iron:** 10-inch and 12-inch skillets

Although pancakes are my culinary Achilles' heel, I have a wonderful success rate with their German cousin, the Dutch baby. A Dutch baby is a big, fluffy, eggy, full-skillet pancake that bubbles and puffs up in the most magical way. This version is a savory twist on the classic, with fresh herbs and Parmesan, topped with fried eggs, prosciutto, and arugula.

For the Dutch baby

1 cup buttermilk

3 large eggs

1 tablespoon fresh rosemary leaves, minced

1 tablespoon fresh thyme leaves, minced

1 tablespoon fresh oregano leaves, minced

1 tablespoon fresh basil leaves, minced

½ teaspoon sea salt

¼ cup grated Parmesan cheese

¾ cups all-purpose flour

5 tablespoons salted butter

For the toppings

1 tablespoon salted butter

2 large eggs

Pinch sea salt

3 or 4 slices prosciutto

Handful fresh arugula

1. **To make the Dutch baby:** Preheat the oven to 425°F. Adjust an oven rack to the middle position and place the 10-inch skillet on it while the oven preheats.

2. In a medium bowl, whisk the buttermilk, eggs, rosemary, thyme, oregano, basil, salt, and Parmesan cheese to combine. Gently fold in the flour until blended. Let the batter rest for 5 minutes.

3. Using an oven mitt, remove the skillet from the oven. Melt the butter into the skillet, then swirl the skillet to coat.

4. Pour the batter into the skillet and immediately place it into the oven. Bake for 15 to 20 minutes, or until the Dutch baby is golden brown and the sides have risen.

5. **To make the toppings:** When the Dutch baby still has about 5 minutes to cook, melt the butter in the 12-inch skillet over medium heat.

6. Crack the eggs into the skillet so they are evenly spaced. Sprinkle salt over the yolks. Cook for about 4 minutes, or until the whites have cooked through. Carefully flip the eggs so as not to break the yolks, and cook for 1 minute more.

7. Remove the Dutch baby from the oven. Top it with the fried eggs, prosciutto, and arugula, and serve.

TIP: You can make this dish using dried herbs: Reduce the amount to 1½ teaspoons each.

BANANAS FOSTER DUTCH BABY

OVEN-COOKED, VEGETARIAN, WEEKDAY

SERVES 2

Prep time: 30 minutes | **Cook time:** 25 minutes | **Cast iron:** 10-inch and 12-inch skillets

Having only ever lived in places with limited storage space, it's crucial that the tools we have serve multiple purposes. This is exactly the reasoning my husband used when he talked me into buying a blow torch. Not just for metal work—it could also be used to brûlée in the kitchen!

For the Dutch baby

1 cup buttermilk
3 large eggs
2 tablespoons granulated
  sugar
1 teaspoon vanilla extract
Pinch sea salt
¾ cups all-purpose flour
5 tablespoons salted butter

For the bananas Foster

6 tablespoons (¾ stick)
  salted butter
¾ cup packed light brown
  sugar
1 teaspoon vanilla extract
½ teaspoon ground
  cinnamon
2 tablespoons banana
  liqueur or creme
  de banana
2 ripe bananas, sliced
¼ cup dark rum

1. **To make the Dutch baby:** Preheat the oven to 425°F. Adjust an oven rack to the middle position and place the 10-inch skillet on it while the oven preheats.

2. In a medium bowl, whisk the buttermilk, eggs, granulated sugar, vanilla, and salt to blend. Gently fold in the flour until blended. Let the batter rest for 5 minutes.

3. Using an oven mitt, remove the skillet from the oven. Melt the butter into the skillet, then swirl the skillet to coat.

4. Pour the batter into the skillet and immediately place it into the oven. Bake for 15 to 20 minutes, or until the Dutch baby is golden brown and the sides have risen.

5. **To make the bananas Foster:** While the Dutch baby bakes, melt the butter in the 12-inch skillet or a large saucepan over medium heat. Stir in the brown sugar, vanilla, and cinnamon and cook until the brown sugar dissolves.

For the whipped cream

1 cup heavy (whipping) cream

2 tablespoons granulated sugar

1 teaspoon vanilla extract

6. Stir in the liqueur and bananas. Mix well and let it bubble for 1 to 2 minutes, or until thickened.

7. Add the rum, taking care not to drip it onto the hot stovetop. Using oven mitts, transfer the skillet to a heatproof surface. Use a stick lighter or torch to carefully light the bananas Foster, then watch from a safe distance as the alcohol burns off.

8. As the flames die down, return the skillet to the heat and resume stirring. Let the sauce thicken for 2 to 3 minutes. Remove from the heat.

9. **To make the whipped cream:** In the bowl of a stand mixer fitted with the whisk attachment or a large bowl using an electric mixer, combine the cream, granulated sugar, and vanilla. Beat on high speed until stiff peaks form.

10. Remove the Dutch baby from the oven. Top it with the bananas Foster and whipped cream, and serve.

TIP: If you can't find banana liqueur, use 2 tablespoons of heavy (whipping) cream instead.

FOUR-INGREDIENT PANCAKES

VEGETARIAN, WEEKDAY

SERVES 2

Prep time: 5 minutes | **Cook time:** 15 minutes | **Cast iron:** 10- or 12-inch skillet

These banana pancakes were an absolute favorite when my son was a baby, and they're still a staple in our home because they're quick and simple.

1 banana

2 large eggs

½ cup old-fashioned rolled oats

1 teaspoon ground cinnamon

1 tablespoon salted butter

1. In a medium bowl, use a fork to mash the banana, then mix in the eggs, oats, and cinnamon.

2. In the skillet over medium heat, melt the butter. Spoon the batter into the skillet to form 2 pancakes. Cook for 2 to 3 minutes, or until the centers of the pancakes bubble. Flip, and cook for 1 to 2 minutes more. Transfer the pancakes to a plate and loosely cover them with a clean kitchen towel to keep them warm. Repeat with the remaining batter.

ANDOUILLE AND BELL PEPPER BREAKFAST HASH

CLASSIC, GLUTEN-FREE, WEEKDAY

SERVES 4

Prep time: 15 minutes | **Cook time:** 35 minutes | **Cast iron:** 12-inch skillet

Hash is one of the most flexible brunch options. If you have a handful of potatoes to start, you can add endless combinations of vegetables, cheeses, spices, and meats to change the flavor. One of my favorites features andouille sausage, bell pepper, and seasoning that give this dish a distinctly Cajun flair.

8 ounces andouille sausage

1 tablespoon olive oil, for cooking

2 tablespoons salted butter

1 white onion, chopped

2 garlic cloves, minced

2 cups cubed red potatoes

1½ teaspoons Cajun seasoning

½ teaspoon sea salt

1 red bell pepper, cut into strips

1 green bell pepper, cut into strips

4 ounces Cheddar cheese, shredded

1. Warm the skillet over medium heat. When it's hot, add the sausage and oil. Cook for 8 to 10 minutes, or until browned and crisp. Transfer the sausage to a plate, cut it into ½-inch slices, and set aside.

2. Put the butter, onion, and garlic into the skillet. Cook for 3 to 4 minutes, until the onion begins to soften. Add the potatoes, Cajun seasoning, and salt and stir thoroughly. Distribute the potatoes evenly in the skillet. Cook for 7 to 10 minutes, stirring occasionally, until they are browned and crisp.

3. Stir in the red and green bell peppers and cook for 5 to 7 minutes, until the potatoes are cooked through.

4. Stir the sausage slices into the potatoes. Remove the hash from the heat, sprinkle with the Cheddar cheese, and serve.

TIP: Try this dish with fried or poached eggs and a splash of Tabasco.

KOHLRABI AND POTATO HASH

CLASSIC, GLUTEN-FREE, VEGETARIAN, WEEKDAY

⊙————— SERVES 4 —————⊙

Prep time: 20 minutes | **Cook time:** 15 minutes | **Cast iron:** 12-inch skillet

The first time I made this hash, I was massively pregnant with my first child. It was late spring, and our weekly Community Supported Agriculture (CSA) box was loaded with kohlrabi. This recipe includes late-spring greens that we get in our area, like baby broccoli and garlic scapes, but could easily be adapted to include zucchini, pattypan squash, fresh tomatoes, or any other vegetables you enjoy.

2 tablespoons salted butter, plus more as needed

1 white onion, chopped

1 white kohlrabi, grated

5 or 6 small new potatoes, grated

½ teaspoon sea salt

¼ teaspoon freshly ground black pepper

¼ teaspoon red pepper flakes

1 cup minced kohlrabi greens

3 garlic cloves, minced

1 purple kohlrabi, grated

1 bunch baby broccoli, roughly chopped

5 or 6 garlic scapes, roughly chopped

1. In the skillet over medium heat, melt the butter. Add the onion and cook for 1 to 2 minutes, or until it begins to soften.

2. Stir in the white kohlrabi, potatoes, salt, black pepper, and red pepper flakes, then spread the mixture into an even layer in the skillet. Cook for 3 to 4 minutes, then use a spatula to flip the mixture in as close to one big piece as possible to preserve the crispy edges (don't worry if it's not perfect). Cook for 3 to 4 minutes more.

3. Stir in the kohlrabi greens, garlic cloves, purple kohlrabi, and broccoli. If the hash is beginning to stick, add another pat of butter. Cook for 3 to 5 minutes, until the potatoes are browned and crisp.

4. Stir in the garlic scapes and serve.

TIP: It's best to let the hash sit in the skillet and brown without stirring it too much. Flipping it every once in a while allows the cooking to be even, but stirring it too much will prevent it from crisping.

CARAMELIZED CREAM-FRIED EGGS OVER PARMESAN GRITS

GLUTEN-FREE, VEGETARIAN, WEEKDAY

⊝———————— SERVES 2 ————————⊝

Prep time: 10 minutes | **Cook time:** 20 minutes | **Cast iron:** 12-inch skillet

When I first read about eggs fried in cream from the food blog *Food52*, I was skeptical. When I made them, I realized immediately they weren't going to replace my tried-and-true fried eggs in butter, but they would be a heavenly companion to a bowl of cheesy grits.

1 cup stone-ground grits

3 cups water

1½ cups heavy (whipping) cream, divided

1 tablespoon sea salt, plus ½ teaspoon

1 tablespoon salted butter

½ cup grated Parmesan cheese

4 large eggs

1. In a medium saucepan over high heat, stir together the grits, water, 1 cup of cream, and 1 tablespoon of salt until well combined. Bring to a boil. Reduce the heat to low, cover the saucepan, and simmer for about 20 minutes, until the grits have thickened. Stir in the butter and Parmesan cheese.

2. Once the grits have cooked for 10 minutes, pour the remaining ½ cup of cream into the skillet. Crack the eggs into the cream and season them with the remaining ½ teaspoon of salt.

3. Place the skillet over medium-high heat and cook for 6 to 7 minutes, or until the whites have set and the cream has begun to brown (the eggs will cook as the cream caramelizes). Remove the skillet from the heat, cover it, and let sit for 1 to 2 minutes to let the whites firm up.

4. Divide the grits into 2 serving bowls. Top each serving with 2 eggs and a spoonful of cream and serve.

FRIED BOLOGNA AND EGG SANDWICH

Prep time: 10 minutes | **Cook time:** 15 minutes | **Cast iron:** 12-inch skillet

Growing up in the South, I never questioned the prominence of bologna in our diet. As I've gotten older, I've realized that people from other parts of the country have *feelings* about bologna. And I'm just here to say, get over it. Fried bologna and eggs on white bread with mayonnaise makes a breakfast sandwich to die for.

2 slices bologna

1 tablespoon salted butter

2 large eggs

Pinch sea salt

4 slices bread

1 tablespoon mayonnaise

1. Heat the skillet over medium heat. Place the bologna in the hot skillet and cook for 2 to 3 minutes per side, until well browned. Transfer the bologna to a plate and loosely cover it with a clean kitchen towel to keep it warm. Set aside.

2. Still at medium heat, melt the butter in the skillet. Crack the eggs into the skillet so they are evenly spaced. Sprinkle salt over the yolks. For over-easy eggs, cook for about 4 minutes, until the whites have cooked through (about 5 minutes for over-medium, and about 6 minutes for over-well), flip the eggs while the yolks are still liquid, being careful not to break them. Cook for 1 minute more and remove from the heat.

3. While the eggs cook, toast the bread.

4. Spread the mayonnaise evenly on each slice of bread and assemble each sandwich with 1 egg and 1 piece of bologna.

ROASTED RED PEPPER AND GOAT CHEESE FRITTATA

GLUTEN-FREE, OVEN-COOKED, VEGETARIAN

SERVES 6

Prep time: 10 minutes | **Cook time:** 55 minutes | **Cast iron:** 12-inch skillet

I love the flavor combination of roasted red peppers and goat cheese. Roasting red peppers softens and sweetens their flavor, and the tang of the goat cheese plays beautifully against that sweetness. The simplicity of a frittata allows these flavors to shine—a combination of light, fluffy eggs, creamy goat cheese, and soft peppers.

2 red bell peppers, halved and seeded

1 tablespoon olive oil

2 tablespoons salted butter

1 white onion, chopped

2 garlic cloves, minced

6 large eggs

¼ cup heavy (whipping) cream

½ teaspoon sea salt

1 cup goat cheese, crumbled

1. Preheat the oven to 400°F.

2. Place the pepper halves into the skillet and drizzle them with oil. Roast for 20 minutes, until the peppers begin to brown. Flip the peppers and roast for 10 minutes more, then remove them from the oven. Keep the oven at 400°F. Roughly chop the peppers and set aside.

3. In the skillet over medium heat, melt the butter. Add the onion and cook for 5 to 7 minutes, stirring occasionally, until softened. Add the garlic and cook for 2 minutes, or until fragrant.

4. Meanwhile, in a large bowl, whisk the eggs, cream, and salt to blend. Stir in the roasted red peppers and goat cheese. Pour the mixture into the skillet and cook for 1 to 2 minutes, or until the eggs just begin to set.

5. Transfer the skillet to the oven. Bake for 10 to 12 minutes, or until the frittata is cooked through.

FRENCH TOAST CASSEROLE

OVEN-COOKED, VEGETARIAN, WEEKDAY

—————— SERVES 6 TO 8 ——————

Prep time: 20 minutes | **Cook time:** 40 minutes | **Cast iron:** 12-inch skillet

Like so many people, I started making Sourdough Bread (page 35) during the initial COVID 19 quarantine. Because there is only so much bread one person can eat, I frequently ended up with stale bread. And a great use for stale bread is French toast casserole, as it holds up better to the moisture of the filling. You can even assemble this dish the night before and keep it refrigerated so it's ready put into the oven when you wake up.

1 stale loaf French or
    sourdough bread
6 large eggs
1½ cups whole milk
1 cup heavy (whipping)
    cream
1 cup packed light brown
    sugar, divided
2 teaspoons vanilla extract
1½ teaspoons ground
    cinnamon, divided
8 tablespoons (1 stick)
    salted butter, melted
½ cup chopped pecans
¼ cup all-purpose flour
Maple syrup, for serving

1. Preheat the oven to 350°F.

2. Cut the bread into bite-size pieces, then spread them evenly across the skillet.

3. In a large bowl, whisk the eggs, milk, cream, ½ cup of brown sugar, vanilla, and 1 teaspoon of cinnamon. Pour the mixture over the bread.

4. In a small bowl, stir together the butter, the remaining ½ cup of brown sugar and ½ teaspoon of cinnamon, the pecans, and the flour. Spread the topping over the casserole.

5. Bake for 40 minutes, or until the casserole is cooked through and browned on top. Serve with a drizzle of maple syrup.

WALNUT AND CRANBERRY BAKED OATMEAL

OVEN-COOKED, VEGETARIAN, WEEKDAY

○———————— **SERVES 4** ————————○

Prep time: 10 minutes | **Cook time:** 45 minutes | **Cast iron:** 12-inch skillet

In an ongoing effort to feed my child whole foods that nourish his mind and body before school each morning, I rely on things I can put together with minimal effort and maximum impact. Baked oatmeal is simple, delicious, and can be made ahead and doled out throughout the week, making weekday breakfast a breeze.

2 cups old-fashioned rolled oats

1 cup chopped walnuts

1 cup dried unsweetened cranberries

1 tablespoon light brown sugar

1 teaspoon baking powder

½ teaspoon sea salt

2 large eggs

1½ cups whole milk

¼ cup honey

3 tablespoons salted butter, at room temperature

Plain full-fat yogurt, for serving (optional)

1. Preheat the oven to 350°F.

2. In a large bowl, stir together the oats, walnuts, cranberries, brown sugar, baking powder, and salt.

3. In a medium bowl, whisk the eggs, milk, honey, and butter to combine.

4. Fold the milk mixture into the oat mixture, then transfer the oatmeal to the skillet.

5. Bake for 40 to 45 minutes, or until crisp around the edges and cooked through. Serve with a generous dollop of yogurt (if using).

SPINACH AND MUSHROOM BREAKFAST CASSEROLE

OVEN-COOKED, VEGETARIAN

SERVES 6

Prep time: 20 minutes | **Cook time:** 1 hour 15 minutes | **Cast iron:** 12-inch skillet

Breakfast casseroles are an important part of our family's Christmas tradition. We always make two: one featuring sausage and cheese, and another loaded with vegetables. We've tried different vegetables over the years, but my favorite combination is spinach and mushroom.

8 large eggs

1½ cups whole milk

1 teaspoon red pepper flakes

1 cup crumbled feta cheese

1 teaspoon sea salt

1 tablespoon salted butter

1 white onion, diced

3 garlic cloves, minced

2 cups sliced cremini mushrooms

2 cups fresh spinach

4 cups cubed bread

1. Preheat the oven to 375°F.

2. In a large bowl, whisk the eggs, milk, red pepper flakes, feta, and salt to combine.

3. In the skillet over medium heat, melt the butter. Add the onion and garlic and cook for 5 to 7 minutes, stirring occasionally, until the onion begins to soften.

4. Add the mushrooms and cook for 5 minutes, or until the mushrooms soften.

5. Add the spinach, tossing a few times with the other vegetables, and cook for 1 minute. Remove the skillet from the heat, add the bread, and toss to combine.

6. Pour the egg mixture over the top.

7. Bake for 50 to 60 minutes, or until the eggs are cooked through and puffed.

TIP: Assemble this casserole the night before and keep it refrigerated so it's ready to pop into the oven when you wake up.

CROQUE MADAME

Prep time: 15 minutes | **Cook time:** 20 minutes | **Cast iron:** 10-inch and 12-inch skillets

The croque madame is a breakfast variation of the classic French Croque Monsieur (page 91), a ham and Gruyère sandwich that is as delicious as it is excessive. The croque madame is also the fancy cousin of the Fried Bologna and Egg Sandwich (page 22). Sourdough bread is loaded with ham and mustard, then topped with Mornay sauce and a fried egg. It is as indulgent a breakfast sandwich as they come.

4 tablespoons (½ stick) salted butter, divided

1 tablespoon all-purpose flour

¾ cup whole milk

½ teaspoon sea salt, plus more for seasoning

½ cup shredded Gruyère cheese, divided

2 teaspoons Dijon mustard

4 thick slices sourdough bread

6 or 8 slices thick-cut ham

2 large eggs

Freshly ground black pepper

1. Preheat the oven to 350°F.

2. In a small saucepan over medium-high heat, melt 1 tablespoon of butter. Whisk in the flour and cook, whisking, for 1 minute. Add the milk, a little at a time, whisking rapidly to combine. Add the salt and cook for 2 to 3 minutes, whisking constantly, until the sauce thickens. Remove the Mornay sauce from the heat and stir in ¼ cup of Gruyère cheese.

3. Spread ½ teaspoon of mustard on each slice of bread. Divide the ham and the remaining ¼ cup of cheese evenly between 2 slices of bread. Top each with 1 tablespoon of Mornay sauce and cover each sandwich with one of the remaining bread slices, mustard-side down. Spread about 1½ teaspoons of butter on the outside of each bread slice.

4. Heat the 12-inch skillet over medium-high heat and place the sandwiches into it. Cook for 2 to 3 minutes, or until the bread has browned. Flip and cook for 2 to 3 minutes more.

CONTINUED

5. Evenly top each sandwich with half the remaining Mornay sauce and transfer the skillet to the oven while you cook the eggs.

6. In the 10-inch skillet over medium heat, melt the remaining 1 tablespoon of butter. When hot, crack the eggs into the skillet, making sure they are evenly spaced. Season with salt and pepper. For over-easy eggs, cook for about 4 minutes, until the whites have cooked through (about 5 minutes for over-medium, and about 6 minutes for over-well), flip the eggs while the yolks are still liquid, being careful not to break them. Cook for 1 minute more and remove from the heat.

7. Using oven mitts, remove the skillet from the oven, transfer the sandwiches to plates, top each with a fried egg, and serve.

TIP: If you are working with only one skillet, transfer the sandwiches to a baking sheet before topping them with Mornay sauce and putting them into the oven.

CARROT CAKE PANCAKES WITH CREAM CHEESE FROSTING

VEGETARIAN, WEEKDAY

SERVES 4

Prep time: 20 minutes | **Cook time:** 20 minutes | **Cast iron:** 12-inch skillet

Nothing makes a pancake brunch (or dinner!) special like a carrot cake twist and a nice serving of freshly whipped cream cheese frosting.

For the frosting

4 tablespoons (½ stick) salted butter, at room temperature

4 ounces cream cheese, at room temperature

2 cups powdered sugar

½ teaspoon vanilla extract

For the pancakes

2 cups all-purpose flour

3 tablespoons granulated sugar

1½ teaspoons baking powder

1½ teaspoons baking soda

2 large eggs

1½ cups buttermilk

4 tablespoons (½ stick) salted butter, melted, plus more for cooking and serving

1 cup grated carrot

1 cup chopped walnuts

Maple syrup, for serving

1. **To make the frosting:** In the bowl of a stand mixer fitted with the paddle attachment or a medium bowl using an electric mixer, whip the butter, cream cheese, powdered sugar, and vanilla until soft peaks form. Set aside.

2. **To make the pancakes:** In a large bowl, stir together the flour, granulated sugar, baking powder, and baking soda.

3. In another large bowl, whisk the eggs, buttermilk, melted butter, and carrot until blended.

4. Gently fold the wet ingredients into the dry ingredients.

5. In the skillet over medium heat, melt a pat of butter. Working in batches, pour ½-cup portions of batter into the hot skillet. Cook for 2 to 3 minutes, or until bubbles form in the center of the batter. Flip and cook for 1 to 2 minutes more, or until golden brown. Transfer the pancakes to a plate and loosely cover them with a clean kitchen towel to keep them warm. Repeat with remaining butter and batter.

6. Plate the pancakes and top each stack with a generous serving of cream cheese frosting, a sprinkle of walnuts, and a drizzle of maple syrup.

SWIRLED HERB BREAD. PAGE 55

Chapter Three

BREADS AND BISCUITS

CHOCOLATE ZUCCHINI BREAD

OVEN-COOKED, VEGETARIAN

SERVES 4 TO 6

Prep time: 20 minutes | **Cook time:** 1 hour | **Cast iron:** 12-inch skillet

I am a huge proponent of supporting the local economy by signing up for CSA boxes, and in late summer, we always get *a lot* of zucchini. I put it in Carrot and Zucchini Fritters (page 121) and make Ricotta-Stuffed Zucchini Boats (page 116). But there are always at least two zucchini left in my refrigerator that I can't work into my dinner plan. This simple chocolate zucchini bread is my go-to solution for using those last zucchini. It's incredibly moist and tastes divine.

8 tablespoons (1 stick) butter, at room temperature, plus more for greasing

¼ cup coconut oil

1 cup granulated sugar

1 cup packed light brown sugar

½ teaspoon vanilla extract

2 large eggs

2 cups all-purpose flour

½ cup cocoa powder

2 teaspoons baking powder

1 teaspoon ground cinnamon

Pinch sea salt

3 cups grated zucchini

½ cup powdered sugar

1. Preheat the oven to 325°F. Grease the skillet with butter.

2. In a large bowl using an electric mixer, beat the butter, oil, granulated sugar, brown sugar, and vanilla to combine. Add the eggs, one at a time, beating well after each addition.

3. In another large bowl, combine the flour, cocoa powder, baking powder, cinnamon, and salt. Make a well in the center of the dry ingredients, then pour the butter mixture into it. Stir until combined.

4. Fold the zucchini into the batter, making sure it is evenly distributed. Evenly spread the batter into the prepared skillet.

5. Bake for 1 hour, or until a toothpick inserted into the center of the bread comes out clean. Let it cool completely.

6. Dust the bread with powdered sugar and serve.

ROSEMARY BUTTERMILK BISCUITS

OVEN-COOKED, VEGETARIAN, WEEKDAY

○——————— SERVES 6 ———————○

Prep time: 15 minutes | **Cook time:** 25 minutes | **Cast iron:** 10-inch skillet

Buttermilk biscuits are the first recipe my son Everett learned to make by himself. After watching and helping over the course of many Sundays, the spring before his fourth birthday, he informed me that he did not need my help (not a surprise), and then proceeded to make them mostly on his own (definitely a surprise).

3 tablespoons salted butter, divided, plus 8 tablespoons (1 stick) cold salted butter, cubed

2 cups all-purpose flour, plus more for working the dough

1 teaspoon baking soda

2 teaspoons baking powder

1 tablespoon fresh rosemary leaves, finely chopped

1 teaspoon sea salt

1 cup buttermilk

1. Preheat the oven to 425°F. Grease the skillet with 1 tablespoon of butter.

2. In a medium bowl, stir together the flour, baking soda, baking powder, rosemary, and salt.

3. Using a fork or your clean hands, work the butter cubes into the flour mixture until the texture resembles coarse cornmeal. Stir in the buttermilk until a rough dough forms.

4. Flour a work surface and place the dough on it. Pat the dough into a large rectangle. Fold the dough in half, turn it, and pat the dough into a large rectangle again. Repeat this process 3 or 4 times, folding and rotating the dough each time. Add flour as you work to keep the dough from sticking.

5. Pat the dough 1½ to 2 inches thick. Use a 3-inch biscuit cutter or jar lid to cut the biscuits into rounds. Arrange the rounds in the skillet so they are nice and snug.

CONTINUED

6. Melt the remaining 2 tablespoons of butter and brush it over the top of the biscuits.

7. Bake for 20 to 25 minutes, or until the biscuits are fluffy and golden brown.

TIP: If the dough gets warm while you're working it, pop the cut biscuits back into the refrigerator for 10 minutes so they go into the oven cold. The steam created by the butter melting in the oven is one of the things that gives biscuits their rise.

SOURDOUGH BREAD

CLASSIC, OVEN-COOKED, VEGAN

MAKES 1 SOURDOUGH STARTER AND 2 ROUND LOAVES

Prep time: 45 minutes

Inactive time: 5 days to make the starter, plus 24 hours to start the dough (the night before baking) and let it rest and rise | **Cook time:** 1 hour per loaf | **Cast iron:** 12-inch skillet with lid

Like many people, I started baking sourdough during the spring 2020 quarantine. It wasn't my first time dabbling with a starter, but it has been the longest I've kept one alive. The slow, steady progress of the starter and the resulting homemade bread was exactly the comfort and anchor I needed during that time—and I know I wasn't alone!

For the sourdough starter

5 cups all-purpose flour, divided

3¾ cups warm water, divided

For the bread

1 cup sourdough starter

3 cups warm water, divided

4 cups all-purpose flour, divided, plus more for kneading

1 tablespoon sea salt

Ice cubes, for baking

1. **To make the sourdough starter:** On day 1, in a large bowl, stir together 1 cup of flour and ¾ cup of warm water until fully incorporated. Lightly cover the bowl with a clean kitchen towel and put it in a warm, dark place in your kitchen.

2. On days 2 through 4, once each day, divide the starter in half and discard half. Add 1 cup of flour and ¾ cup of warm water. Mix well, making sure there are no clumps of flour remaining. Loosely cover it and keep it on your counter.

3. On day 5, the starter should be double in size, bubbling, and getting fluffy. Divide the starter in half, setting aside half to use in step 4 to make the bread. Feed the other half as normal (1 cup of flour and ¾ cup of warm water) and transfer it to a quart-size jar. Loosely cover the jar with a lid and refrigerate. From now on, your starter can be divided and fed once a week.

CONTINUED

4. **To make the bread:** The night before you're ready to bake your bread, in a large bowl, combine the sourdough starter, 1 cup of warm water, and 1 cup of flour. Mix well, cover, and refrigerate overnight.

5. In the morning, in the bowl of a stand mixer fitted with a dough hook or a large bowl using a wooden spoon, mix in the remaining 3 cups of flour, 2 cups of warm water, and the salt, mixing until the ingredients are fully incorporated and a dough ball forms.

6. Flour a work surface and turn the dough out onto it. Cover it with a damp kitchen towel and let it rest for 30 minutes.

7. Flour the surface of the dough and, with your hands, stretch it out, fold it on itself, and turn it. Repeat this process for 5 minutes. Let the dough rest for 30 minutes, then knead it again for 5 minutes. Knead the dough every 30 minutes for 2½ hours, dusting it with flour, as needed, to prevent sticking.

8. After you've shaped the dough and allowed it to rest for 5 intervals, cover it and let it rise for 30 minutes.

9. Flour a work surface and turn the dough out onto it. Divide the dough and carefully shape it into 2 balls, pulling the dough so it's tight and pinched at the bottom. Line 2 mixing bowls with clean dish towels and dust them thoroughly with flour. Transfer 1 round loaf into each bowl, wrap it with the towel, and let it rise undisturbed for 3 to 4 hours, or until doubled in size.

10. Preheat the oven to 475°F. Place the skillet into the oven to preheat.

11. Lay parchment paper on a work surface and dust it with flour. Transfer 1 round of dough onto the parchment paper, seam-side down. Using a dull knife, score the dough, creating a line on a slight angle across the top.

12. Using oven mitts, remove the skillet from the oven and transfer the dough, with the parchment paper, into the skillet.

13. Slide an ice cube between the parchment paper and the skillet, then quickly cover the skillet.

14. Bake for 20 minutes. Remove the lid and bake for 40 minutes more, or until the crust is golden brown. Transfer the bread to a cooling rack. Repeat from step 11 for the second loaf.

15. Let the bread cool *completely* before slicing and serving.

TIP: Make the starter and bread gluten-free by substituting King Arthur's Gluten-Free Measure-for-Measure flour for the all-purpose flour, adding ¼ cup of xanthan gum, and keeping the lid on for the full hour while baking.

BUTTERED DINNER ROLLS

CLASSIC, OVEN-COOKED, VEGETARIAN

SERVES 10

Prep time: 30 minutes | **Inactive time:** 2 hours
Cook time: 40 minutes | **Cast iron:** 12-inch skillet

I will never make or serve dinner rolls without thinking of my grandma. She was deeply devoted to a handful of recipes that seemed quintessentially 1950s, like Russian dressing, ambrosia salad, and a covered basket full of steaming dinner rolls. These tender, buttery, pull-apart rolls taste like comfort and family.

Olive oil, for coating

1 cup whole milk

2 tablespoons sugar

2 tablespoons shortening

½ teaspoon sea salt, plus more for sprinkling

½ cup warm water

1 tablespoon active dry yeast

1 large egg, beaten

2 cups bread flour, plus more for kneading

5 tablespoons salted butter, plus more for greasing

1. Coat a large bowl with oil and set it aside.

2. In a medium saucepan over medium-high heat, scald the milk by bringing it almost to a boil, then remove it from the heat.

3. Stir in the sugar, shortening, and salt. Continue stirring until the sugar and shortening dissolve. Let the milk mixture cool to room temperature.

4. In a small bowl, whisk the warm water and yeast until the yeast dissolves. Stir the yeast into the milk mixture.

5. Add the beaten egg, whisking well. Stir in the flour, ½ cup at a time, until it forms a soft dough.

6. Flour a work surface and turn the dough out onto it, dusting with flour as needed to prevent sticking. Knead the dough by stretching it out, folding it on itself, and turning it. Repeat this process for 10 minutes.

7. Transfer the dough to the oiled bowl, turn it once, and loosely cover it with a damp kitchen towel. Let the dough rise for 1 hour.

8. Grease the skillet with butter.

9. Divide the dough into 10 equal pieces. Form each piece into a ball by pulling the dough taut and pinching it together at the base of the sphere. Nestle the dough balls together in the prepared skillet. Cover it and let the dough rise for 1 hour.

10. Preheat the oven to 350°F.

11. In a small saucepan over medium-low heat, melt the butter. Brush the butter over the dough. Sprinkle with salt.

12. Bake for 30 to 35 minutes, or until the rolls are puffy and golden brown.

JALAPEÑO-CHEDDAR DROP BISCUITS

OVEN-COOKED, VEGETARIAN, WEEKDAY

SERVES 6

Prep time: 15 minutes | **Cook time:** 25 minutes | **Cast iron:** 12-inch skillet

When I need a fast turnaround, drop biscuits are my favorite quick bread. Simply mix the ingredients, and then, just like it sounds, drop the batter into the skillet and bake. Drop biscuits are light and fluffy but also crumbly and buttery—a lovely combination.

3 tablespoons unsalted butter, divided

8 tablespoons (1 stick) cold salted butter, cubed

2 cups all-purpose flour

2 teaspoons baking powder

1 teaspoon baking soda

1 teaspoon sea salt

1 cup shredded Cheddar cheese

1 jalapeño pepper, seeded and minced

1½ cups buttermilk

1. Preheat the oven to 425°F. Grease the skillet with 1 tablespoon of unsalted butter.

2. In a medium bowl, stir together the flour, baking powder, baking soda, and salt.

3. Using a fork or your clean hands, work the salted butter cubes into the flour mixture until the texture resembles coarse cornmeal. Mix in the Cheddar cheese and jalapeño. Stir in the buttermilk until a rough dough forms. Drop the dough by large spoonfuls into the prepared skillet, nestling them together slightly to fill the pan.

4. Melt the remaining 2 tablespoons of unsalted butter and brush it over the biscuits.

5. Bake for 20 to 25 minutes, or until fluffy and golden brown.

BLUEBERRY SCONES

OVEN-COOKED, VEGETARIAN, WEEKDAY

SERVES 8

Prep time: 25 minutes | **Cook time:** 25 minutes | **Cast iron:** 12-inch skillet

My devotion to scones comes, in large part, from my devotion to The Great British Bake Off. Normally, I don't bother with scones because I have my biscuit method down pat—and why stray from perfection? But a little time with Mary Berry oohing and aahing over buttery scones and, well, fire up the oven!

3 cups all-purpose flour, plus more for working the dough

½ cup granulated sugar

2 teaspoons baking powder

½ teaspoon baking soda

¼ teaspoon salt

8 tablespoons (1 stick) cold salted butter, cubed

1 cup fresh blueberries

1 cup buttermilk

2 large egg yolks

2 tablespoons melted salted butter

1 cup powdered sugar

2 tablespoons water

1. In a large bowl, mix together the flour, granulated sugar, baking powder, baking soda, and salt.

2. Using a fork or your clean hands, work the butter cubes into the flour mixture until the texture resembles coarse cornmeal. Stir in the blueberries.

3. In a small bowl, whisk the buttermilk and egg yolks until blended. Pour the wet ingredients into the dry ingredients and, using a wooden spoon, stir until a loose dough forms.

4. Flour a work surface and turn the dough out onto it. Working carefully to avoid overmixing the dough, form a disk 12 inches in diameter. Cut the dough, like a pie, into 8 wedges and transfer them to the skillet. Refrigerate for 15 minutes.

5. Preheat the oven to 400°F.

6. Brush the scones with the melted butter and transfer the skillet to the oven.

7. Bake for 22 to 25 minutes, until fluffy and golden brown. Transfer the scones to a rack to cool to room temperature

8. In a small bowl, whisk the powdered sugar and water (or lemon juice) until smooth. Use a spoon to drizzle the glaze over the cooled scones.

CARAMEL-PECAN CINNAMON ROLLS

OVEN-COOKED, VEGETARIAN

SERVES 8

Prep time: 45 minutes | **Inactive time:** 1 hour 30 minutes
Cook time: 40 minutes | **Cast iron:** 12-inch skillet

When I was pregnant with my younger child, there was a time when people kept showing me their love and appreciation by sending cinnamon rolls; I constantly had a box in the kitchen. I got used to having them around, and it was hard when the supply ran out. Thankfully, I started testing recipes for this book soon after we stopped receiving these sweet deliveries. So, other than the possibility that my child is 80 percent cinnamon rolls, all's right with the world.

For the dough

Olive oil, for coating
¼ cup warm water
2½ teaspoons active
   dry yeast
½ cup granulated sugar,
   plus a pinch
½ cup whole milk
3 tablespoons salted butter,
   plus more for greasing
1 large egg, lightly beaten
1 teaspoon sea salt
3½ cups all-purpose flour,
   divided, plus more
   for kneading

1. **To make the dough:** Coat a large bowl with oil and set it aside.

2. In another large bowl, whisk the warm water, yeast, and a pinch of granulated sugar until the yeast dissolves.

3. In a small saucepan over low heat, combine the milk and butter and heat until the butter melts. Whisk the milk mixture into the yeast mixture.

4. Add the remaining ½ cup of granulated sugar, the egg, salt, and 2 cups of flour. Stir well. Add the remaining 1½ cups of flour, ½ cup at a time, stirring until a dough forms.

5. Flour a work surface and turn the dough out onto it. Knead the dough by stretching it, folding it, and turning it. Repeat this process for 5 minutes.

6. Form the dough into a loose sphere. Transfer the dough to the oiled bowl, turn it once, and loosely cover it with a damp kitchen towel. Let the dough rise in a warm place for 1 hour.

For the caramel sauce

1 cup granulated sugar

½ cup heavy (whipping) cream

8 tablespoons (1 stick) salted butter

Pinch sea salt

2 teaspoons vanilla extract

For the filling

8 tablespoons (1 stick) salted butter, melted

½ cup packed dark brown sugar

½ cup packed light brown sugar

2 tablespoons ground cinnamon

1 teaspoon vanilla extract

1 cup chopped pecans

7. **To make the caramel sauce:** In the skillet over medium heat, combine the granulated sugar, cream, butter, and salt. Cook for 4 to 6 minutes, stirring constantly, until the sauce thickens. Stir in the vanilla and cook for 1 to 2 minutes. Pour the sauce into a jar and set aside.

8. Rinse the skillet and put it on the stovetop over medium heat to dry. Once dry, grease the skillet with butter and set aside.

9. **To make the filling:** In a medium bowl, stir together the melted butter, light and dark brown sugars, cinnamon, vanilla, and pecans until well combined. Set aside.

10. **To assemble the cinnamon rolls:** Flour a work surface and turn the risen dough out onto it. Roll the dough into a 12-by-16-inch rectangle, about ½ inch thick.

11. Spread the filling evenly over the dough.

12. Starting at a long side, roll the dough onto itself to form a tight spiral. Cut the dough into 8 equal slices and arrange them in the skillet, cut-side down. Cover loosely and let the dough rise for 30 minutes.

13. Preheat the oven to 350°F.

14. Bake the rolls for 25 to 30 minutes, or until bubbling and golden brown. Remove the cinnamon rolls from oven and drizzle them with the caramel sauce.

TIP: Try adding some toasted pecans to the topping for extra crunch. In a small skillet over medium heat, toast ½ cup of pecans in 1 tablespoon of butter for 3 to 5 minutes, then sprinkle them on top.

GREEN CHILE CORN BREAD WITH WHIPPED HONEY BUTTER

OVEN-COOKED, VEGETARIAN, WEEKDAY

⊙————— SERVES 4 TO 6 —————⊙

Prep time: 20 minutes | **Cook time:** 25 minutes | **Cast iron:** 12-inch skillet

This corn bread is not sweet, but it has a little kick from the Anaheim pepper and is served with a whipped honey butter that plays off the pepper's heat.

For the corn bread

1 Anaheim pepper
2 cups coarse yellow
 cornmeal
1 teaspoon sea salt
1 teaspoon baking powder
1 teaspoon baking soda
1½ cups buttermilk
6 tablespoons (¾ stick)
 salted butter, melted,
 divided
1 large egg

For the whipped butter

8 tablespoons (1 stick)
 salted butter, at room
 temperature
¼ cup honey

1. **To make the corn bread:** Adjust the oven rack to the top position and turn the broiler to high.

2. Place the Anaheim pepper into the skillet and put it under the broiler for 2 minutes, until the skin begins to blacken. Remove it from the oven and set it aside to cool. Once cooled, seed and dice the pepper.

3. Using oven mitts, adjust the oven rack back to the middle position. Preheat the oven to 400°F and place the skillet into the oven to preheat.

4. In a large bowl, stir together the cornmeal, salt, baking powder, baking soda, and the diced Anaheim pepper.

5. In a small bowl, whisk the buttermilk, 4 tablespoons of melted butter, and the egg until well combined.

6. Using oven mitts, remove the skillet from the oven and brush it with the remaining 2 tablespoons of melted butter. Pour the batter into the preheated skillet and bake for 20 minutes, or until browned on top.

7. **To make the whipped butter:** In the bowl with a stand mixer fitted with the whisk attachment, or in a medium bowl and using an electric mixer, whip the butter and honey until light and fluffy. Serve the corn bread warm with the whipped butter.

BANANA NUT BREAD

OVEN-COOKED, VEGETARIAN

SERVES 4

Prep time: 20 minutes | **Cook time:** 1 hour | **Cast iron:** 12-inch skillet

Banana bread is one of the ultimate comfort foods. I usually have most of the ingredients on hand, including a few blackened bananas in my freezer. Nothing is more gratifying than getting a craving for banana bread and being able to satisfy it in little more than an hour.

2 large eggs

1 cup sugar

3 ripe bananas, fresh or frozen, diced

1 teaspoon baking soda

1 teaspoon ground nutmeg

1 teaspoon ground cinnamon

½ cup buttermilk

1 teaspoon vanilla extract

½ cup chopped walnuts

1 teaspoon sea salt

2 cups all-purpose flour

1 tablespoon salted butter

1. Preheat the oven to 400°F.

2. In a large bowl, whisk the eggs, sugar, and bananas.

3. One at a time and whisking after each addition, add the baking soda, nutmeg, cinnamon, buttermilk, vanilla, walnuts, and salt.

4. Fold in the flour, taking care to work out any clumps.

5. Grease the skillet with the butter, then pour in the batter and spread it evenly.

6. Bake for 1 hour, or until the bread is cooked through and browned around the edges.

TIP: Peeling a banana that has been frozen is one of my least favorite chores. Save yourself the headache and peel and slice browning bananas before you put them in the freezer, which will make them significantly easier to use.

HAM AND CHEESE STUFFED BISCUITS

OVEN-COOKED, WEEKDAY

SERVES 8

Prep time: 20 minutes | **Cook time:** 30 minutes | **Cast iron:** 12-inch skillet

These little pockets of heaven are buttery, flaky, cheesy, salty, and divine. A simple buttermilk biscuit with ham and cheese is perfection.

3 tablespoons salted butter, divided, plus 8 tablespoons (1 stick) cold salted butter, cubed

2 cups all-purpose flour, plus more for working the dough

1 tablespoon fresh rosemary leaves, finely chopped

2 teaspoons baking powder

1 teaspoon baking soda

1 teaspoon sea salt

1 cup buttermilk

4 or 6 slices thick-cut ham

1 cup shredded Cheddar cheese

1. Preheat the oven to 425°F. Grease the skillet with 1 tablespoon of butter.

2. In a medium bowl, stir together the flour, rosemary, baking powder, baking soda, and salt.

3. Using a fork or your clean hands, work the butter cubes into the flour mixture until the texture resembles coarse cornmeal. Stir in the buttermilk until a rough dough forms.

4. Flour a work surface and turn the dough out onto it. Pat the dough into a large rectangle. Fold the dough in half, turn it, and pat it again into a large rectangle. Repeat this process 3 or 4 times, folding and rotating the dough each time. Add flour as you work to keep the dough from sticking.

5. Pat the dough into a rectangle about ½ inch thick. Arrange the ham and cheese on one half of the dough. Fold the biscuit dough over the filling. Cut the dough into 8 square biscuits. Pinch the edges of each biscuit to seal in the stuffing. Nestle the biscuits into the prepared skillet.

6. Melt the remaining 2 tablespoons of butter and brush it on the biscuits.

7. Bake for 25 to 30 minutes, or until fluffy and golden brown.

CARAMELIZED ONION AND TOMATO FOCACCIA

OVEN-COOKED, VEGETARIAN

SERVES 4 TO 6

Prep time: 30 minutes | **Inactive time:** 2 hours
Cook time: 1 hour | **Cast iron:** 12-inch skillet

Focaccia is a great beginner yeasted bread. It's also sublime—all crisp edges drenched in olive oil and salt, something that disappears all too quickly. This focaccia is made with caramelized onions and cherry tomatoes, which give it a hint of sweetness that plays well against the salt and oil.

6 tablespoons olive oil, divided

1 cup warm water

1 tablespoon active dry yeast

1½ teaspoons sea salt, divided

2½ cups all-purpose flour, plus more for kneading

2 tablespoons salted butter

2 large white onions, slivered

½ pint cherry tomatoes, halved

1 tablespoon roughly chopped fresh rosemary leaves

3 garlic cloves, chopped

1. Coat a large bowl with 1 tablespoon of oil and set it aside.

2. In another large bowl, whisk the warm water, yeast, 2 tablespoons of oil, and 1 teaspoon of salt until well combined and frothy. Let it sit for 10 minutes.

3. Using a wooden spoon, stir in the flour, a little at a time, until a rough ball forms.

4. Flour a work surface and turn the dough out onto it. Knead the dough by stretching it out, folding it, and turning it. Repeat this process for 15 minutes.

5. Transfer the dough to the oiled bowl, turn it once, and loosely cover it with a damp kitchen towel. Let the dough rise for 1 hour, or until it has doubled in size.

6. Meanwhile, in the skillet, melt the butter over low heat. Add the onions and cook for 25 to 30 minutes, stirring frequently, or until golden brown. Transfer the onions to a bowl and set it aside.

CONTINUED

7. Punch down the dough, then roll it into a 12-inch round.

8. Coat the skillet with 2 tablespoons of oil, then transfer the dough to the skillet. Loosely cover it and let it rise for 45 minutes.

9. Preheat the oven to 400°F.

10. Dimple the dough with your fingers.

11. Press the tomatoes into the dough and spread the onions, rosemary, garlic, and remaining ½ teaspoon of salt and 1 tablespoon of oil evenly over the top.

12. Bake for 15 to 30 minutes, or until the focaccia is a light golden brown. Let it cool slightly before serving.

MOZZARELLA-STUFFED GARLIC KNOTS

OVEN-COOKED, VEGETARIAN

—————— SERVES 4 TO 6 ——————

Prep time: 40 minutes | **Inactive time:** 1 hour 45 minutes
Cook time: 30 minutes | **Cast iron:** 12-inch skillet

Garlic knots will always remind me of the 1990s, watching movies at sleepovers, and more marinara sauce than I would ever consume today. These pull-apart knots, with their melted cheese and garlic butter glaze, are perfect for sharing on the couch in front of a movie, just like at a '90s sleepover.

1½ tablespoons olive oil, plus more for greasing

1 tablespoon active dry yeast

1 tablespoon sea salt, plus 1 teaspoon

¾ cup warm water

2½ cups bread flour, plus more for kneading

12 ounces fresh mozzarella cheese, cut into 16 pieces

8 tablespoons (1 stick) salted butter, melted

3 garlic cloves, minced

½ cup grated Parmesan cheese

1 tablespoon dried oregano

1. Coat a large bowl with oil and set it aside.

2. In another large bowl, whisk the oil, yeast, 1 tablespoon of salt, and the warm water until well combined and frothing. Let it sit for 10 minutes.

3. Using a wooden spoon, stir in 1¼ cups of flour. Add the remaining 1¼ cups of flour and use your hands to knead it together until a rough dough forms.

4. Flour a work surface and turn the dough out onto it. Knead the dough by stretching it out, folding it, and turning it. Repeat this process for 10 minutes until the dough ball is smooth and pliable. Transfer the dough to the oiled bowl, turn it once, and loosely cover it with a damp kitchen towel. Let the dough rise in a warm place for 1 hour, or until the dough has doubled in size.

5. Punch the dough down, then let it rise for 15 minutes.

CONTINUED

6. Flour a work surface and gently turn the dough out onto it. Knead the dough for 5 to 7 minutes, or until it is pliable and stretches nicely without tearing. Divide the dough into 16 equal pieces. Roll each piece into a 6-inch cylinder. Tie each cylinder into a simple knot and tuck a piece of mozzarella inside the knot. Tuck the ends of the knot into the bottom, making sure the mozzarella is fully covered. Add flour as needed to keep the dough from sticking. Nestle the knots into the skillet. Loosely cover them and let them rise for 15 minutes.

7. Preheat the oven to 400°F.

8. In a small bowl, stir together the melted butter, garlic, and remaining 1 teaspoon of salt. Brush the garlic butter over the knots. Sprinkle the knots with Parmesan cheese and oregano.

9. Bake for 25 to 30 minutes, or until golden brown. Let the knots cool slightly before serving.

TIP: Serve this with a marinara dipping sauce: Heat 1 tablespoon of olive oil in a medium saucepan over medium heat. Add ⅓ cup of minced onion and 2 garlic cloves, minced. Sauté for 5 minutes, then add 1 (15-ounce) can of crushed tomatoes, a pinch of salt, and 1 teaspoon of dried basil. Simmer, stirring frequently, for 30 minutes.

IRISH SODA BREAD WITH MARMALADE

OVEN-COOKED, VEGETARIAN

SERVES 6

Prep time: 30 minutes | **Cook time:** 1 hour 10 minutes | **Cast iron:** 12-inch skillet

Irish soda bread is a simple, quick bread leavened by the chemical reaction between the baking soda and buttermilk. It's easy to overwork this dough, so handle it only enough to bring the ingredients together and form the dough ball. It's best eaten warm, slathered with good quality Irish butter and a generous dollop of easy homemade marmalade.

For the marmalade

3 medium navel oranges

Juice of 1 lemon

1½ cups sugar

¼ cup water

2 tablespoons pectin

For the soda bread

Salted butter, for greasing

4 cups all-purpose flour, plus more for working the dough

1 teaspoon baking soda

1 teaspoon sea salt

1½ cups buttermilk

Irish butter, for serving

1. **To make the marmalade:** Zest the oranges into a small bowl. Remove the pith and any remaining peel, then roughly chop the pulp and flesh, pulling out as much of the membrane as you can and reserving the juice.

2. In a medium saucepan over medium heat, combine the orange pulp and flesh, orange juice, orange zest, lemon juice, and sugar. Cook for 3 to 4 minutes, stirring frequently, until the sugar dissolves.

3. Bring the marmalade to a slow boil, then stir in the water and pectin. Cook for 20 to 25 minutes, stirring, as the pectin dissolves and the jam thickens. Once the marmalade is thick enough to coat the back of a spoon, transfer it to a small bowl or jam jar and let it cool.

4. **To make the soda bread:** Preheat the oven to 375°F. Grease the skillet with butter.

CONTINUED

5. In a large bowl, stir together the flour, baking soda, and salt. Slowly stir in the buttermilk until a shaggy dough ball forms.

6. Flour a work surface and turn the dough out onto it. Pat the dough out flat and fold it a few times, eventually forming a ball roughly the size of the skillet. Using a sharp knife, cut an X into the top of the dough, then transfer the dough to the skillet.

7. Bake for 35 to 40 minutes, or until golden brown.

8. Slice and serve the bread with Irish butter and marmalade.

TIP: Irish soda bread is often made with raisins. For a sweeter twist, add 1 cup of raisins and 2 tablespoons of sugar in step 5.

BRAIDED CINNAMON BREAD

OVEN-COOKED, VEGETARIAN

SERVES 4 TO 6

Prep time: 40 minutes | **Inactive time:** 3 hours 10 minutes
Cook time: 40 minutes | **Cast iron:** 12-inch skillet

I find breadmaking incredibly peaceful. With a braided bread especially, the process of forming a beautiful pattern and allowing it to rise, bake, and become something new is captivating.

Olive oil, for coating

1 cup warm water

1 tablespoon active
  dry yeast

2 tablespoons sugar,
  plus a pinch

4 cups bread flour, plus
  more for kneading

Pinch sea salt

1 teaspoon ground
  cinnamon

2 large eggs, beaten, plus
  1 large egg, separated

3 tablespoons shortening

Butter, for greasing

1. Coat a large bowl with oil and set it aside.

2. In a small bowl, whisk the warm water and yeast until the yeast dissolves. Add a pinch of sugar, stir well, and let it sit for 10 minutes.

3. In a large bowl, stir together the flour, salt, cinnamon, and 2 tablespoons of sugar. Stir in the beaten eggs, then the yolk from the separated egg, then the shortening.

4. Slowly add the yeast mixture to the flour mixture, a little at a time, mixing well with a wooden spoon until a rough dough forms.

5. Flour a work surface and turn the dough out onto it. Knead the dough by stretching it out, folding it, and turning it. Repeat this process for 8 to 10 minutes, adding flour as needed if the dough gets sticky. When the dough is smooth and soft, transfer it to the oiled bowl, turn it once, and loosely cover it with a damp kitchen towel. Let the dough rise for 2 hours, or until it has doubled in size.

CONTINUED

6. Flour a work surface and turn the dough out onto it. Divide the dough into 3 equal pieces. Pull each piece into a 12-inch-long rope, then lay the ropes parallel to each other on the counter. Join the ropes at the top and braid them, joining them again at the bottom.

7. Loop the braid onto itself so it forms a circle, tucking the ends underneath.

8. Grease the skillet with butter and set it aside. Place the braided loaf inside the prepared skillet and cover it with a damp towel. Let the loaf rise for 1 hour.

9. Preheat the oven to 350°F.

10. Brush the top of the bread with the white from the separated egg.

11. Bake for 35 to 40 minutes, or until browned. Let the braided loaf cool on a rack before serving.

TIP: This is a beautiful bread for a fall harvest celebration, especially if you add ½ teaspoon each of nutmeg, ginger, and cloves to the cinnamon in step 3.

SWIRLED HERB BREAD

OVEN-COOKED, VEGETARIAN

○———— SERVES 4 TO 6 ————○

Prep time: 45 minutes | **Inactive time:** 2 hours
Cook time: 40 minutes | **Cast iron:** 12-inch skillet

This spring, we finally got around to putting in the front yard garden beds we've been planning since we bought our house a few years ago. With full, beautiful sunlight, it's the perfect place for growing herbs. One of my favorite uses for herbs is to add them to a simple yeasted bread, which infuses it with the savory flavor and aroma of a summer garden.

For the herb filling

2 tablespoons olive oil

4 tablespoons (½ stick) salted butter, at room temperature

¼ cup fresh oregano leaves, minced

¼ cup fresh basil leaves, minced

¼ cup fresh sage leaves, minced

2 tablespoons fresh rosemary leaves, minced

2 tablespoons fresh thyme leaves, minced

3 garlic cloves, minced

For the bread

Olive oil, for coating, plus more for brushing

1 cup whole milk

2 tablespoons sugar

1. **To make the herb filling:** In a small bowl, stir together the oil, butter, oregano, basil, sage, rosemary, thyme, and garlic until well mixed. Set aside.

2. **To make the bread:** Coat a large bowl with oil and set it aside.

3. In a medium saucepan over medium-high heat, scald the milk by bringing it almost to a boil, then remove it from the heat. Stir in the sugar, shortening, and salt, stirring until the sugar and shortening dissolve. Let it cool to room temperature.

4. In a small bowl, whisk the warm water and yeast until the yeast dissolves. Add the yeast mixture to the milk mixture and stir well to combine. Whisk in the egg. Stir in the flour, ½ cup at a time, until a soft dough forms.

CONTINUED

2 tablespoons shortening

1 teaspoon sea salt, plus
   more for sprinkling

½ cup warm water

1 tablespoon active
   dry yeast

1 large egg, beaten

4 cups bread flour, plus
   more for kneading

5 tablespoons salted butter,
   plus more for greasing

5. Flour a work surface and turn the dough out onto it. Knead the dough by stretching it out, folding it, and turning it. Repeat this process for 10 minutes. Transfer the dough to the oiled bowl, turn it once, and loosely cover it with a damp kitchen towel. Let the dough rise for 1 hour.

6. Flour a work surface and turn the dough out onto it. Roll the dough into a ½-inch-thick rectangle. Spread half the herb butter over the rectangle and fold the dough onto itself, turn it, and fold it again.

7. Gently pat the dough into a ½-inch-thick rectangle. Evenly spread the remaining herb butter over the dough. Starting at a long end, roll the dough onto itself, forming a log.

8. Beginning 2 inches from one end of the log, slice the log lengthwise all the way through to the other end. Twist the two sides around each other, then curl the twist onto itself, forming a spiral.

9. Grease the skillet with butter and set it aside. Place the dough spiral inside the prepared skillet and loosely cover it with a damp kitchen towel. Let it rise for 1 hour.

10. Preheat the oven to 350°F.

11. Brush the dough with oil and sprinkle with salt.

12. Bake for 35 to 40 minutes, or until the bread is golden brown. Serve warm with salted butter.

TIP: To make herbed rolls instead of a loaf, cut the dough log into 3-inch slices, nestle them all in the greased skillet, and proceed as directed from step 10.

PANZANELLA, PAGE 78

Chapter Four

APPETIZERS AND SIDES

SAUSAGE AND CHEDDAR BALLS

CLASSIC, OVEN-COOKED, WEEKDAY

⊙———————— SERVES 6 TO 8 ————————⊙

Prep time: 15 minutes | **Cook time:** 25 minutes | **Cast iron:** 12-inch skillet

Sausage balls are a Christmas classic—a holiday appetizer so delicious I will happily plant myself in front of the platter and eat my way through them. Although sausage balls are often made with biscuit mix, this recipe uses flour and baking powder, which gives you more control over the ingredients.

2 cups all-purpose flour

3 teaspoons baking powder

½ teaspoon sea salt

¼ teaspoon red pepper flakes

1 pound ground sausage

4 cups freshly shredded Cheddar cheese

4 tablespoons (½ stick) salted butter, melted

1. Preheat the oven to 375°F.

2. In a large bowl, combine the flour, baking powder, salt, and red pepper flakes.

3. Stir in the sausage, cheese, and butter. Mix together with your hands, until the flour is fully incorporated. Form the mixture into 20 to 24 (1-inch) sausage balls and arrange them in the skillet.

4. Bake for 15 minutes. Remove the skillet from the oven and flip the sausage balls. Return to the oven for 10 minutes more, until crispy and golden brown. Let them cool slightly before serving.

TIP: If you have a stand mixer, combine all the ingredients in the bowl and use the paddle attachment to mix on low speed until combined.

GOAT CHEESE AND BACON STUFFED MUSHROOMS

GLUTEN-FREE, OVEN-COOKED, WEEKDAY
SERVES 2 TO 4

Prep time: 10 minutes | **Cook time:** 40 minutes | **Cast iron:** 10- or 12-inch skillet

Stuffed mushrooms are one of my favorite appetizers because they are scrumptious, easy, and the perfect finger food. The goat cheese and herbs in this recipe make these mushroom bites creamy and fresh—the perfect match for the salty bacon and earthy mushroom.

3 bacon strips

½ cup goat cheese, at room temperature

1 tablespoon fresh rosemary leaves, minced

1 tablespoon fresh oregano leaves, minced

Pinch sea salt

24 small cremini mushrooms, stemmed

1. In the skillet, arrange the bacon strips so they do not touch. Place the skillet over medium-low heat and cook the bacon for about 10 minutes, or until it begins to crisp around the edges. Flip the bacon, increase the heat to medium-high, and cook for 7 to 8 minutes more, or until browned and crisp. Remove the bacon from the pan. Drain off the drippings and let the skillet cool before wiping it out.

2. Preheat the oven to 350°F.

3. Crumble the bacon into a small bowl, then stir in the goat cheese, rosemary, oregano, and salt. Spoon the filling into each mushroom cap and arrange them in the skillet.

4. Bake for 20 to 22 minutes, or until the mushrooms are cooked through and the filling begins to turn golden brown.

TIP: Make these stuffed mushrooms vegetarian by nixing the bacon and stirring in 3 tablespoons of salted shelled sunflower seeds instead.

BUFFALO WINGS

WEEKDAY

SERVES 4

Prep time: 20 minutes | **Cook time:** 40 minutes | **Cast iron:** 12-inch skillet

In all my pregnancies, I've had a complicated relationship with chicken. Once during the dreaded first trimester, I decided I *very much* wanted chicken wings, and then, when they came, I decided it was too much chicken. Thankfully, after the end of the first trimester, I regained my enthusiasm for chicken and, with my younger, found that chicken wings became a craving. Especially buffalo wings.

For the sauce

1 cup (2 sticks) salted butter
2 (5-ounce) bottles
 hot sauce
2 tablespoons
 Worcestershire sauce
1 tablespoon garlic powder

For the wings

2 large eggs
2 tablespoons apple cider
 vinegar
1 cup all-purpose flour
1 cup bread crumbs
1 tablespoon garlic powder
1 tablespoon sea salt
1 tablespoon red pepper
 flakes
Peanut oil, for frying
12 chicken wings and
 drumsticks, patted dry

1. **To make the sauce:** In a medium saucepan over medium-low heat, melt the butter. Whisk in the hot sauce, Worcestershire sauce, and garlic powder. Reduce the heat to low and simmer the sauce for 20 to 25 minutes, stirring occasionally.

2. **To make the wings:** On a work surface, line up 2 small bowls. In the first bowl, whisk the eggs and vinegar.

3. In the second bowl, stir together the flour, bread crumbs, garlic powder, salt, and red pepper flakes.

4. Heat 1 inch of oil to 375°F in the skillet over high heat.

5. Working one piece at a time, dip the chicken into the egg mixture, and then into the flour mixture. Working in batches of 3 or 4 at a time, carefully place the chicken in the hot oil and fry for 2 to 3 minutes per side, until cooked through and the juices run clear.

6. Using tongs, remove the chicken from the skillet and dunk it in the hot sauce. Transfer the wings to a wire rack to cool slightly before serving.

SPINACH AND ARTICHOKE DIP

GLUTEN-FREE, OVEN-COOKED, VEGETARIAN, WEEKDAY

SERVES 4

Prep time: 15 minutes | **Cook time:** 40 minutes | **Cast iron:** 12-inch skillet

I never pass up spinach and artichoke dip on an appetizer menu. My family loves this dip served with tortilla chips, but it is also delicious with crusty French bread or pita bread.

1½ teaspoons olive oil

4 cups fresh spinach

3 garlic cloves, minced

2 cups artichoke hearts, frozen or canned and drained

8 ounces cream cheese, at room temperature

½ cup mayonnaise

¼ cup sour cream

½ cup grated Parmesan cheese

½ cup shredded white Cheddar cheese

¼ teaspoon sea salt

¼ teaspoon red pepper flakes

Tortilla chips, for serving

1. Preheat the oven to 375°F.

2. Heat the oil in the skillet over medium heat. Add the spinach and cook for 5 to 7 minutes, stirring frequently.

3. Add the garlic and cook for 2 to 3 minutes. Transfer the spinach to a large bowl.

4. Add the artichoke hearts, cream cheese, mayonnaise, sour cream, Parmesan cheese, Cheddar cheese, salt, and red pepper flakes to the spinach. Mix well. Spoon the dip into the skillet, spreading it evenly.

5. Bake for 25 to 30 minutes, or until the dip is bubbling and browned around the edges.

TIP: Substitute 2 cups of frozen spinach, thawed and drained, for the fresh spinach.

VEGETABLE TEMPURA

VEGETARIAN, WEEKDAY

SERVES 4 TO 6

Prep time: 20 minutes | **Cook time:** 15 minutes | **Cast iron:** 12-inch skillet

The success of tempura hinges on the combination of hot oil and cold batter. Having all your ingredients prepared and laid out is as important as ever with this recipe. Keep the ingredients for the batter chilled until you are ready for them, or even consider putting the batter bowl in an ice bath to ensure it stays cool.

For the dipping sauce

1 cup dashi broth

¼ cup soy sauce

3 tablespoons mirin

1½ teaspoons sugar

For the tempura

Vegetable oil, for frying

1 cup all-purpose flour, divided

Pinch sea salt

1 large egg, cold

1 cup cold water

1 sweet potato, cooked and thinly sliced

1 zucchini, thinly sliced into circles

1 cup oyster mushrooms, cut into strips

1 Japanese eggplant, thinly sliced into circles

1. **To make the dipping sauce:** In a small saucepan over medium-high heat, combine the dashi, soy sauce, mirin, and sugar. Bring it to a boil, stir well, then remove it from the heat to cool.

2. **To make the tempura:** Heat 1 inch of oil to 350°F in the skillet over medium-high heat.

3. In a large bowl, combine the flour and salt. Carefully whisk in the egg, then the cold water, taking care not to overwhisk. A few lumps are fine.

4. Working in batches, dip the sweet potato, zucchini, mushrooms, and eggplant into the batter, coating completely, then place them into the skillet, making sure the vegetables aren't touching as you fry them. Fry for 2 to 3 minutes, flip, and fry for 1 minute more. Transfer the fried vegetables to a rack to cool slightly and repeat until all the vegetable are fried.

5. Serve warm with the dipping sauce.

TIP: Dashi broth is a common ingredient in Japanese cooking. It can be found in the broth aisle of many grocery stores or online.

CRISPY CHIPOTLE CHICKPEAS

GLUTEN-FREE, VEGAN, WEEKDAY

⊖ ───────── **SERVES 2 TO 4** ───────── ⊖

Prep time: 10 minutes | **Cook time:** 35 minutes | **Cast iron:** 12-inch skillet

I first had crispy chickpeas at a restaurant here in our little coastal town. They are also easy to whip up at home, and they're an appetizer the whole family will love.

⅓ cup vegetable oil

2 (15-ounce) cans chickpeas, drained and patted dry

1 teaspoon chipotle powder

1 teaspoon garlic powder

½ teaspoon cayenne

Pinch sea salt

Handful fresh parsley leaves, minced

1. Heat the oil in the skillet over medium-high heat.

2. Working in batches, fry half the chickpeas for 15 to 17 minutes, stirring frequently, until crisp. Transfer them to a paper towel to drain and repeat with the remaining chickpeas.

3. In a large bowl, combine the fried chickpeas, chipotle powder, garlic powder, cayenne, and salt. Toss well to coat. Sprinkle with fresh parsley and serve.

TIP: If you'd rather try a baked version, simply toss the chickpeas in 2 tablespoons of olive oil and roast them in the skillet at 400°F for 25 to 30 minutes.

BOUDIN BALLS

GLUTEN-FREE, WEEKDAY

SERVES 6

Prep time: 20 minutes | **Cook time:** 30 minutes | **Cast iron:** 12-inch skillet

Boudin—a Cajun, smoked, pork sausage—is one of the many gifts my Baton Rouge-raised brother-in-law, Bradley, has brought to our family. This recipe uses ground pork and a food processor to combine the meat instead of a grinder, and yields perfect bite-size meatballs.

1 pound ground pork

8 ounces pork liver, rinsed and cubed

5 garlic cloves, minced

2 celery stalks, diced

1 small white onion, chopped

1 small green bell pepper, chopped

Vegetable or canola oil, for frying

3 teaspoons sea salt

2 teaspoons cayenne

1 teaspoon freshy ground black pepper

3 cups cooked rice

Handful fresh parsley leaves, chopped

Handful chopped scallion

1. In a food processor, combine the ground pork, liver, garlic, celery, onion, and bell pepper. Pulse until well blended.

2. Heat 1 tablespoon of oil in the skillet over medium heat. Add the pork mixture, salt, cayenne, and black pepper. Cook for 8 to 10 minutes, stirring frequently, or until the pork has browned. Transfer to a large bowl.

3. Add the cooked rice, parsley, and scallion to the pork. Mix well.

4. Form 1-inch balls of the boudin mixture.

5. Wipe out the skillet, place it over high heat, and heat 1 inch of oil to 375°F.

6. Working in batches, fry the meatballs for 2 to 3 minutes, flip, and fry 2 to 3 minutes more. Transfer the boudin balls to a rack to cool slightly before serving.

TIP: To use a meat grinder, simmer for 1 hour: 1½ pounds of chopped pork shoulder, the pork liver, 1 quart of water, and half the vegetables. Drain the liquid and put the mixture through a grinder fitted with a ¼-inch die. Pass the remaining vegetables and parsley through the grinder. Combine with the ground meat, spices, and rice. Refrigerate for 2 hours. Follow the recipe from step 5.

CHEESE AND BACON SMASHED POTATOES

GLUTEN-FREE, OVEN-COOKED

SERVES 4

Prep time: 20 minutes | **Cook time:** 1 hour 35 minutes | **Cast iron:** 12-inch skillet

Smashed potatoes are, in my opinion, the rock star of the potato world. They're flashy and scrumptious and endlessly adaptable. They work with all sorts of companion foods, from brunch to a nice steak dinner.

8 ounces thick-cut bacon strips

7 to 10 small or medium red potatoes

3 tablespoons olive oil, divided

1 teaspoon sea salt, divided

1 teaspoon red pepper flakes, divided

4 tablespoons (½ stick) salted butter, cubed

2 garlic cloves, minced

1 cup shredded Cheddar cheese

1. In the skillet, arrange the bacon strips so they do not touch. Place the skillet over medium-low heat and cook the bacon for about 10 minutes, or until it begins to crisp around the edges. Flip the bacon, increase the heat to medium-high, and cook for 7 to 8 minutes more, or until brown and crisp. Remove the bacon from the skillet and chop it coarsely. Drain the drippings, reserving 1 tablespoon in the skillet.

2. Preheat the oven to 350°F.

3. Put the potatoes into the skillet. Add 1 tablespoon of oil, ½ teaspoon of salt, and ½ teaspoon of red pepper flakes. Toss well to coat.

4. Transfer the skillet to the oven and roast the potatoes for 30 minutes, or until they can be easily pierced with a fork.

5. Using oven mitts, remove the skillet from the oven and increase the temperature to 425°F.

CONTINUED

6. Using a fork or meat tenderizer, smash the potatoes flat. Return the smashed potatoes to the oven and roast for 25 minutes. Remove the skillet from the oven. Flip the potatoes and top them with the remaining 2 tablespoons of oil, ½ teaspoon of salt, ½ teaspoon of red pepper flakes, and the bacon.

7. Return the skillet to the oven and roast for 15 to 20 minutes, or until brown and crisp.

8. Top with Cheddar cheese and serve.

TIP: Throw on a handful of minced fresh herbs (oregano, thyme, rosemary) before serving for a fresh contrast to the cheese and bacon.

SKILLET GREENS

CLASSIC, GLUTEN-FREE, VEGAN, WEEKDAY

○──────── SERVES 2 TO 4 ────────○

Prep time: 10 minutes | **Cook time:** 40 minutes | **Cast iron:** 12-inch skillet

Skillet greens are one of my go-to vegetable sides. They're simple, and I pretty much always have some sort of green in my refrigerator. These greens are the ideal companion to meals, from runny eggs to mashed potatoes. My preferred bitter green is collards, but this recipe works beautifully with turnip greens, kale, escarole, bok choy, and kohlrabi greens.

1 bunch collard greens, cleaned and deveined (see tip)

1 tablespoon olive oil

1 small yellow onion, chopped

3 garlic cloves, minced

¼ cup apple cider vinegar

1 teaspoon sea salt

1. Roughly chop the greens into bite-size pieces.

2. Heat the oil in the skillet over medium heat. Add the onion and cook for 5 to 7 minutes, stirring occasionally, or until softened.

3. Add the garlic and chopped greens to the skillet. Toss to coat, then add the vinegar and salt. Reduce the heat to medium-low and cook for about 30 minutes, stirring occasionally, until the greens are tender.

4. Serve drizzled with the juice from the skillet.

TIP: Deveining collards can be quick and easy once you get the hang of it. Fold the leaf in half and run a knife along the main stem vein to remove it.

FRIED PICKLES

SERVES 4 TO 6

Prep time: 15 minutes | **Cook time:** 15 minutes | **Cast iron:** 12-inch skillet

There are a few things my husband, Dan, cannot pass up when he sees them on a menu, and fried pickles are at the top of that list. He's become a connoisseur of fried pickles, ranking them based on the type of pickle (dill is at the top), shape (he prefers slices to spears), breading, and dipping sauce. Everyone needs a special-occasion food, and for Dan, it's fried pickles.

1 cup all-purpose flour, plus
   2 tablespoons

1 teaspoon paprika, divided

1 teaspoon sea salt, divided

1 teaspoon red pepper
   flakes, divided

2 large eggs

¼ cup apple cider vinegar

1 cup cornmeal

Peanut oil or safflower oil,
   for frying

2 cups dill pickle slices,
   drained and patted dry

1. On a work surface, line up 3 small bowls. In the first bowl, stir together 1 cup of flour, ½ teaspoon of paprika, ½ teaspoon of salt, and ¾ teaspoon of red pepper flakes.

2. In the second bowl, whisk the eggs and vinegar to combine.

3. In the third bowl, stir together the cornmeal and the remaining 2 tablespoons of flour, ½ teaspoon of paprika, ½ teaspoon of salt, and ¼ teaspoon of red pepper flakes.

4. Heat 1 inch of oil to 375°F in the skillet over high heat.

5. Dredge the pickle slices in the flour mixture, then in the egg mixture, and finally in the cornmeal mixture.

6. Working in batches, fry the pickles for 2 to 3 minutes per side, or until browned and crisp. Transfer them to a wire rack to cool slightly before serving.

SRIRACHA BRUSSELS SPROUTS

SERVES 4

Prep time: 10 minutes | **Cook time:** 30 minutes | **Cast iron:** 12-inch skillet

Brussels sprouts, especially roasted, are one of my favorite vegetables. They're a wonderful canvas for a huge variety of sauces and flavor profiles. This recipe tosses the sprouts in a hot honey mixture—a sweet-and-spicy combination that plays nicely off the crisply roasted leaves.

2 tablespoons honey

1 tablespoon sriracha or red chile paste

¼ cup soy sauce

15 to 20 Brussels sprouts, stemmed and halved

1. Preheat the oven to 400°F.

2. In a small bowl, whisk the honey, sriracha, and soy sauce to blend.

3. In the skillet, combine the Brussels sprouts and sauce and toss well to coat.

4. Roast for 20 minutes, stir well, and return to the oven. Turn the broiler to high and broil for 5 to 7 minutes, or until crispy.

5. Serve with your favorite entrée.

ROASTED CAULIFLOWER

GLUTEN-FREE, OVEN-COOKED, VEGAN, WEEKDAY

SERVES 4

Prep time: 10 minutes | **Cook time:** 25 minutes | **Cast iron:** 12-inch skillet

Cauliflower has been having a moment, popping up in all sorts of dishes as a replacement for perfectly good carbs. This, of course, is ridiculous because mashed potatoes and pizza were already perfect, and cauliflower was also already a delicious vegetable when it stayed in its lane—roasted until perfectly browned around the edges, then doused with lemon juice. This is the glory that cauliflower deserves.

1 head cauliflower, cut
   into florets
2 tablespoons olive oil
1 teaspoon sea salt
Juice of 1 lemon

1. Preheat the oven to 450°F.

2. In the skillet, combine the cauliflower, oil, and salt and toss well to coat.

3. Roast for 20 to 25 minutes, or until the cauliflower is tender and browned.

4. Sprinkle it with lemon juice and serve.

GARLIC BUTTER GREEN BEANS

GLUTEN-FREE, VEGETARIAN, WEEKDAY

SERVES 2 TO 4

Prep time: 10 minutes | **Cook time:** 10 minutes | **Cast iron:** 10-inch skillet

This recipe really shines in cast iron because the skillet allows the green beans to brown while they cook. Cooking them this way gives the beans a crunch and depth of flavor that is irresistible and a far cry from the green bean mush that can result from cooking them in other types of pans.

3 tablespoons salted butter

1 pound fresh green beans, ends removed

2 garlic cloves, minced

Pinch sea salt

1. In the skillet over medium heat, melt the butter. Add the green beans and cook for 3 to 5 minutes, stirring occasionally.

2. Add the garlic and the salt, stir well, and cover the skillet. Cook for 5 minutes.

3. Serve with your favorite entrée.

TIP: I like my green beans slightly more al dente than the rest of my family, so when I'm cooking these for myself, I reduce the cooking time to 2 minutes after adding the garlic.

TURMERIC ROASTED BEETS

GLUTEN-FREE, OVEN-COOKED, VEGAN
SERVES 4

Prep time: 15 minutes | **Cook time:** 40 minutes | **Cast iron:** 12-inch skillet

One of my favorite books that I read in 2019 was *Indian Instant Pot® Cookbook* by Urvashi Pitre. It has also left me with the conviction that beets and turmeric are perfect companions. This dish is simple, just roasted beets and spices, but the earthy and slightly bitter flavor of the turmeric combines beautifully with the sweetness of the roasted beets.

4 large beets, peeled
 and chopped
2 tablespoons olive oil
¼ teaspoon ground turmeric
Pinch sea salt

1. Preheat the oven to 400°F.
2. In the skillet, combine the beets, oil, turmeric, and salt and toss well to coat.
3. Roast for 35 to 40 minutes, or until the beets are cooked through.
4. Serve warm or chilled.

HASSELBACK POTATOES

GLUTEN-FREE, OVEN-COOKED, VEGETARIAN

SERVES 4 TO 6

Prep time: 15 minutes | Cook time: 1 hour | Cast iron: 12-inch skillet

Hasselback potatoes, also known as accordion potatoes, are potatoes sliced almost all the way through. This allows the butter, garlic, and salt to creep down between each slice, making them irresistibly crisp.

5 Yukon gold potatoes

8 tablespoons (1 stick) salted butter, cubed

4 garlic cloves, minced

1½ teaspoons sea salt

½ teaspoon red pepper flakes

Olive oil, for brushing

¼ cup grated Parmesan cheese

2 tablespoons fresh parsley leaves, minced

1. Preheat the oven to 425°F.

2. Without cutting through the bottom skin, cut the potatoes crosswise into ½-inch slices. Arrange the potatoes in the skillet and sprinkle them with the butter, followed by the garlic, salt, and red pepper flakes.

3. Roast for 30 minutes.

4. Brush the potatoes with oil and bake for 30 minutes more.

5. Sprinkle the potatoes with Parmesan cheese and fresh parsley.

TIP: If you accidentally cut through the skin on the base of the potato, it's okay! Just use the side of the skillet to wedge the potato back together.

BUTTERMILK FRIED OKRA

VEGETARIAN, WEEKDAY

⊙ ——————— SERVES 4 TO 6 ——————— ⊙

Prep time: 15 minutes | **Cook time:** 15 minutes | **Cast iron:** 12-inch skillet

If Fried Pickles (page 70) are Dan's appetizer must-have, mine is fried okra. I love okra in all its forms, from pickles to curries, but fried okra is something special. It has a double crunch—the first from the breading, and the second from the seeds.

2 cups all-purpose flour, divided

1 teaspoon sea salt, divided

1 teaspoon cayenne, divided

1 teaspoon garlic powder, divided

1 cup buttermilk

1 tablespoon apple cider vinegar

1 tablespoon hot sauce

½ cup bread crumbs

Peanut oil, for frying

12 okra, cut into ½-inch slices

1. On a work surface, line up 3 small bowls. In the first bowl, stir together 1 cup of flour, ½ teaspoon of salt, ½ teaspoon of cayenne, and ½ teaspoon of garlic powder.

2. In the second bowl, whisk the buttermilk, vinegar, and hot sauce to combine.

3. In the third bowl, stir together the bread crumbs and the remaining 1 cup of flour, ½ teaspoon of salt, ½ teaspoon of cayenne, and ½ teaspoon of garlic powder.

4. Heat 1 inch of oil to 375°F in the skillet over high heat.

5. Dredge the okra slices in the seasoned flour, dip them in the buttermilk, and coat them in the seasoned bread crumbs.

6. Working in batches, fry the okra for 2 to 3 minutes per side, or until browned and crisp. Transfer to a wire rack to cool slightly before serving.

TIP: Try this fried okra with a spicy aioli dipping sauce. In a medium bowl, whisk 1 cup of mayonnaise, the juice of 1 lemon, a generous pinch chipotle powder, and a glug or two of hot sauce.

HERB BUTTER ROASTED PATTYPAN

GLUTEN-FREE, OVEN-COOKED, VEGETARIAN, WEEKDAY

SERVES 4

Prep time: 10 minutes | **Cook time:** 15 minutes | **Cast iron:** 12-inch skillet

Pattypan squash are little UFO-shaped bundles of joy. I like to slice the pattypan so they retain their shape and so there is maximum surface area for the herbs and butter to cover.

4 or 5 pattypan squash, stemmed and cut into ½-inch slices

1 tablespoon olive oil

3 garlic cloves, minced

1 tablespoon fresh oregano leaves, minced

1 tablespoon fresh rosemary leaves, minced

1 tablespoon fresh thyme leaves, minced

4 tablespoons (½ stick) salted butter, cubed

1. Preheat the oven to 400°F.

2. In the skillet, combine the squash, oil, garlic, oregano, rosemary, and thyme. Toss to coat. Top the squash with the butter cubes.

3. Roast for 7 minutes, stir well, and return to the oven for 7 to 8 minutes more, until soft and browned around the edges.

TIP: Roasted pattypan halves are also delightful. Simply halve the squash and roast for 10 minutes, flip, and roast for 8 to 10 minutes more.

PANZANELLA

VEGETARIAN, WEEKDAY

SERVES 4

Prep time: 15 minutes | **Cook time:** 15 minutes | **Cast iron:** 12-inch skillet

Panzanella is my favorite early summer salad, with herbs from my garden, leftover Sourdough Bread (page 35), ripe tomatoes, and garlic from my CSA box. It tastes like summer and the comforts of home.

½ cup olive oil, divided

4 cups cubed baguette or sourdough bread

1 teaspoon sea salt, divided

3 garlic cloves, minced

2 shallots, thinly sliced

1 teaspoon Dijon mustard

2 tablespoons Champagne vinegar

2 pounds cherry tomatoes, halved

6 ounces fresh mozzarella cheese, cubed

½ cup fresh basil leaves, roughly chopped

1. Heat ¼ cup of oil in the skillet over medium-low heat. Add the bread cubes and ½ teaspoon of salt. Cook for 10 to 12 minutes, tossing frequently, or until the bread is browned and crisp.

2. In a small bowl, whisk the remaining ¼ cup of oil, along with the garlic, shallots, mustard, and vinegar until frothy.

3. In a large bowl, combine the bread, tomatoes, and mozzarella. Toss with the vinaigrette and top with basil and the remaining ½ teaspoon of salt. Serve immediately.

TIP: Either red wine vinegar or white vinegar can be used in place of Champagne vinegar.

CHARRED ZUCCHINI

GLUTEN-FREE, OVEN-COOKED, VEGAN, WEEKDAY

SERVES 4

Prep time: 5 minutes | **Cook time:** 20 minutes | **Cast iron:** 12-inch skillet

My primary bone to pick with zucchini is that if it is even slightly overcooked, it becomes mush. This is not a vegetable that you can be loosey-goosey with; you need to watch it carefully so you can capture it at the perfect moment when crisp and charred on the edges and not too soft inside.

2 large zucchini, halved lengthwise

2 tablespoons olive oil

½ teaspoon sea salt, divided

¼ teaspoon freshly ground black pepper, divided

1. Preheat the oven to 450°F.

2. Brush the zucchini on both sides with oil. Lay the zucchini, skin-side up, in the skillet and sprinkle with ¼ teaspoon of salt and ⅛ teaspoon of pepper.

3. Roast for 10 minutes, flip the zucchini, then roast for 5 to 7 minutes more, or until the zucchini are browned but still firm. Sprinkle with the remaining ¼ teaspoon of salt and ⅛ teaspoon of pepper and serve.

TIP: For firmer zucchini, roast for 8 minutes, flip, and roast for 3 to 4 minutes more. For softer zucchini, adjust the initial roast time to 12 minutes.

ROASTED ARTICHOKES

GLUTEN-FREE, VEGAN

SERVES 2 TO 4

Prep time: 20 minutes | **Cook time:** 45 minutes | **Cast iron:** 12-inch skillet

Overall, the artichoke can be a rather intimidating vegetable. However, roasting artichokes is both simple to execute and mouthwateringly good to eat.

2 large artichokes, trimmed,
    halved, and chokes
    removed (see tip)
¼ cup olive oil
4 garlic cloves, crushed
Juice of 2 lemons, divided
½ teaspoon salt

1. Preheat the oven to 400°F.

2. Lay the artichokes in the skillet. Brush both sides with oil and arrange them, cut-side up, in the skillet.

3. Fill the cavity of each artichoke half with 1 garlic clove. Flip the artichoke halves, cut-side down, taking care to keep the garlic nestled in the cavity.

4. Squeeze the juice of 1 lemon over the artichokes and sprinkle them with salt.

5. Roast the artichokes, uncovered, for 15 minutes. Cover the skillet with a lid or aluminum foil and bake for 25 to 30 minutes more, or until the artichokes are cooked through and tender.

6. Transfer the artichokes to a serving dish, and present them cut-side up, taking care to transfer the garlic with the artichokes. Top with the remaining juice of 1 lemon and serve.

TIP: To clean the artichokes, use a knife to cut off the bottom inch of the artichoke, including the stem. Remove the top inch, along with any loose leaves. Rinse well in cold water. Halve the artichokes vertically and use a spoon to scoop out the choke, which is fuzzy and located at the base. Trim off the pointy ends of the leaves, and you're ready to roast!

FRIED CHICKEN BISCUITS, PAGE 86

Chapter Five

SANDWICHES AND PIZZA

BEEF AND MINT LETTUCE WRAPS

WEEKDAY

○————— SERVES 2 TO 4 —————○

Prep time: 20 minutes | Cook time: 10 minutes | Cast iron: 12-inch skillet

I love the combination of beef and mint, especially how the freshness of the mint lifts the savory beef. These lettuce wraps enclose a simple ground beef and red pepper stir-fry, served with a fresh and spicy mint dressing.

For the mint dressing

1 cup fresh mint leaves
½ jalapeño pepper, seeded
2 garlic cloves, peeled
Juice of 1 lime
2 tablespoons soy sauce
2 tablespoons sesame oil
1 tablespoon honey
1 teaspoon fish sauce

For the wraps

1 teaspoon sesame oil
1 tablespoon vegetable oil
1 pound 85% lean ground
   beef
1 red bell pepper, cut into
   thin strips
1 tablespoon soy sauce
1 head Bibb lettuce
1 cup shredded red cabbage
1 large carrot, shredded

1. **To make the mint dressing:** In a food processor, combine the mint, jalapeño, garlic, lime juice, soy sauce, sesame oil, honey, and fish sauce. Puree until smooth and set aside.

2. **To make the wraps:** Heat the sesame oil and vegetable oil in the skillet over medium heat. Add the ground beef and cook for 7 to 9 minutes, stirring frequently, or until browned.

3. Add the bell pepper and soy sauce to the skillet, toss, and cook for 1 to 2 minutes.

4. Make a platter with the beef and red pepper, lettuce, red cabbage, carrot, and dressing.

5. To assemble a lettuce wrap, combine the different components on a piece of lettuce, layering the meat at the bottom and topping with the vegetables and dressing, then wrap and enjoy.

TIP: Bibb lettuce is also known as butter lettuce or Boston lettuce. It's the perfect lettuce for wraps because it is sturdy and tender.

TURKEY MELT

OVEN-COOKED, WEEKDAY

SERVES 2

Prep time: 10 minutes | **Cook time:** 10 minutes | **Cast iron:** 12-inch skillet

Turkey melts are turkey sandwiches that have been baked, and with the right additions, it's easy to take them to the next level of fancy sandwiches. I love a combination of sriracha, Cheddar cheese, avocado, and mayonnaise, but it's a recipe you can play with based on what's on hand and what you like.

4 thick slices bread

1 tablespoon butter

2 tablespoons mayonnaise, divided

8 slices turkey

4 slices Cheddar cheese

1 tablespoon sriracha

1 avocado, peeled, halved, pitted, and sliced

Handful salad greens (spinach, kale, or arugula)

1. Preheat the oven to 350°F.

2. Spread one side of each bread slice with about ¾ teaspoon of butter. Spread the other side of each bread slice with about ¾ teaspoon of mayonnaise.

3. Lay all 4 slices of bread, butter-side down, in the skillet. On 2 slices, layer the turkey and cheese.

4. Bake the sandwiches for 10 minutes, until the cheese is bubbling, then remove them from the oven.

5. Meanwhile, in a small bowl, stir together the sriracha and the remaining 1 tablespoon of mayonnaise.

6. Spread the spicy mayo on the 2 top pieces of bread. Layer avocado and greens on each sandwich, cover with the top slices of bread, mayo-side down. Transfer the sandwiches to plates and serve.

TIP: For one glorious week, I had a box of croissants in my house and made some delicious next-level turkey melts. I *highly* recommend swapping the bread for a fresh croissant if you can.

FRIED CHICKEN BISCUITS

OVEN-COOKED, WEEKDAY

SERVES 4

Prep time: 15 minutes | **Cook time:** 40 minutes | **Cast iron:** 10-inch and 12-inch skillets

Biscuits are how I welcome someone to my home. I always make buttermilk biscuits for my guests, and when the stars align, I try to up the ante and make chicken biscuits. Because nothing says, "Please visit all the time and stay as long as you'd like because we love you," like a chicken biscuit brunch.

For the biscuits

4 tablespoons (½ stick) cold salted butter, cubed, plus more for greasing and brushing

2 cups all-purpose flour, plus more for kneading

1 teaspoon baking powder

1 teaspoon baking soda

1 teaspoon sea salt

1 cup buttermilk

1. **To make the biscuits:** Preheat the oven to 425°F. Grease the 10-inch skillet with butter.

2. In a medium bowl, stir together the flour, baking powder, baking soda, and salt.

3. Using a fork or your clean hands, work the butter into the flour mixture until the texture resembles coarse cornmeal. Stir in the buttermilk until a rough dough forms.

4. Flour a work surface and turn the dough out onto it. Pat the dough into a large rectangle. Fold the dough in half, turn it, and pat it again into a large rectangle. Repeat this process 3 or 4 times, folding and rotating the dough each time. Add flour as you work to keep the dough from sticking.

5. Pat the dough 1½ to 2 inches thick. Use a 3-inch biscuit cutter or jar lid to cut 4 biscuits rounds. Arrange the rounds in the prepared skillet so they are snug. Melt 1 tablespoon of butter and brush it over the biscuits.

6. Bake for 20 to 25 minutes, or until fluffy and golden brown.

For the fried chicken

Peanut oil, for frying

1 cup all-purpose flour, divided

1 teaspoon red pepper flakes, divided

1 teaspoon cayenne, divided

1 teaspoon garlic powder, divided

1 teaspoon sea salt, divided

2 large eggs

1 tablespoon apple cider vinegar

1 tablespoon stone-ground grits

4 boneless, skin-on chicken thighs

For the sandwiches

2 tablespoons mayonnaise

2 tablespoons spicy brown mustard

Dill pickle slices, for topping

7. **To make the fried chicken:** While the biscuits bake, heat 1 inch of oil to 375°F in the 12-inch skillet over high heat.

8. On a work surface (near the skillet), line up 3 small bowls. In the first bowl, stir together ½ cup of flour, ½ teaspoon of red pepper flakes, ½ teaspoon of cayenne, ½ teaspoon of garlic powder, and ½ teaspoon of salt.

9. In the second bowl, whisk the eggs and vinegar to blend.

10. In third bowl (closest to the skillet), stir together the grits, along with the remaining ½ cup of flour, ½ teaspoon of red pepper flakes, ½ teaspoon of cayenne, ½ teaspoon of garlic powder, and ½ teaspoon of salt.

11. Dredge the chicken into the flour mixture, dip them in the egg mixture, and coat them in the flour and grits mixture.

12. Fry the chicken in the hot oil for 6 to 7 minutes per side, or until cooked through, golden brown, and crisp. Transfer to a rack to cool.

13. **To assemble the sandwiches:** When the biscuits come out of the oven, let them cool for 2 to 3 minutes, then split them horizontally. Spread mayonnaise on one cut side of each biscuit and mustard on the other. Add a piece of fried chicken and few pickle slices to each sandwich, then serve.

TIP: Although I love mustard and pickles on my chicken biscuits, I also find the salty/sweet combination of honey on a chicken biscuit to be delightful.

BACON, ARUGULA, TOMATO, AND PESTO SANDWICHES

WEEKDAY

○——————— SERVES 2; MAKES 1 CUP PESTO ———————○

Prep time: 20 minutes | **Cook time:** 15 minutes | **Cast iron:** 12-inch skillet

This year, I learned how to make Sourdough Bread (page 35) and, as a result, had fresh sourdough every week. We quickly fell into the habit of making two loaves, one for the week and one for Sunday night BLT sandwiches. These sandwiches are magnificent when tomatoes and basil are in season, but you can enjoy them with conventional tomatoes year round. A drizzle of Hot Honey (page 98) pairs well with the pesto.

For the pesto

2 cups fresh basil leaves

½ cup grated Parmesan cheese

½ cup shelled sunflower seeds

2 garlic cloves, peeled

Pinch salt, plus more as needed

½ cup olive oil

For the sandwiches

8 bacon strips

2 tablespoons pesto

4 slices sourdough bread

1 tablespoon mayonnaise

1 large ripe tomato, sliced

Handful fresh arugula

1. **To make the pesto:** In a food processor or blender, combine the basil, Parmesan cheese, sunflower seeds, garlic, and salt. Add a drizzle of oil and turn on the food processor. Using the feed hole in the lid, drizzle in the oil while the processor runs. Taste and adjust the seasoning, if desired. Transfer the pesto to a jar with a lid and store any leftover pesto in the refrigerator for up to 1 week.

2. **To make the sandwiches:** In the skillet, arrange the bacon strips so they do not touch. Place the skillet over medium-low heat and cook the bacon for about 10 minutes, or until it begins to crisp around the edges. Flip the bacon and cook for 3 to 4 minutes more, until brown and crisp. Transfer to a wire rack to drain.

3. Spread the pesto on 2 slices of bread and the mayonnaise on the other 2 slices. Layer 4 bacon slices, tomato slices, and arugula on each pesto slice. Top with the remaining bread. Transfer the sandwiches to plates and serve.

SOURDOUGH TOAST WITH AVOCADO, BACON, TOMATO, AND A RUNNY EGG

WEEKDAY

SERVES 1

Prep time: 10 minutes | Cook time: 30 minutes | Cast iron: 12-inch skillet

There's a lot of baggage surrounding avocado toast. You love it, or you hate it, or you think that if an entire generation weren't eating it, they would be able to afford houses instead. I'm not above it, y'all. Because here's the thing—it is delicious. This version features salty bacon, creamy avocado, buttery toast, a runny egg, cherry tomatoes, and everything seasoning, and it's one of my favorite meals.

4 bacon strips

2 tablespoons salted butter, divided

2 slices Sourdough Bread (page 35)

2 large eggs

Sea salt

1 avocado, peeled, halved, pitted, and cubed

4 cherry tomatoes, halved

1 teaspoon everything seasoning

1. In the skillet, arrange the bacon strips so they do not touch. Place the skillet over medium-low heat and cook the bacon for about 10 minutes, or until it begins to crisp around the edges. Flip the bacon and cook for 3 to 4 minutes more, until brown and crisp. Transfer the bacon to a wire rack to drain. Pour off the bacon grease but do not clean the skillet.

2. In the same skillet over medium heat, melt 1 tablespoon of butter. Place the bread into the skillet and toast it for 2 minutes per side, or until browned and crisp. Remove the bread from the skillet and set aside.

CONTINUED

3. Crack the eggs into the same skillet and season with salt. For over-easy eggs, cook for about 4 minutes, until the whites have cooked through (about 5 minutes for over-medium, and about 6 minutes for over-well), flip the eggs while the yolks are still liquid, being careful not to break them. Cook for 1 minute more and remove from the heat.

4. Mash half the avocado onto each slice of bread. Top each slice with 2 bacon strips, 1 egg, a pinch of salt, tomatoes, and ½ teaspoon of everything seasoning. Serve open face.

TIP: If you can't find everything seasoning at the store, it's easy to make and something you can use in a lot of different ways. In a small bowl, stir together equal amounts of white sesame seeds, poppy seeds, garlic flakes, onion flakes, and black sesame seeds. Add sea salt, gauging the quantity based on your salt preferences, or leave it out and add your own salt when seasoning.

CROQUE MONSIEUR

OVEN-COOKED, WEEKDAY

SERVES 2

Prep time: 15 minutes | Cook time: 15 minutes | Cast iron: 10-inch and 12-inch skillets

Thanks to both its name (which roughly translates to "crunchy mister," a delightful name for a sandwich) and the inclusion of béchamel sauce, the croque monsieur is a very fancy sandwich. It's slightly more effort than your average ham sandwich, but well worth it.

For the béchamel sauce

1 tablespoon salted butter
1 tablespoon all-purpose
  flour
¾ cup whole milk
½ teaspoon sea salt

For the sandwiches

2 teaspoons Dijon mustard
4 thick slices sourdough
  bread
6 or 8 slices thick-cut ham
¼ cup shredded Gruyère
  cheese
2 tablespoons salted butter

1. Turn the broiler to high.

2. **To make the béchamel sauce:** In a saucepan over medium heat, melt the butter. Stir in the flour and cook for 1 minute, whisking. Add the milk, a little at a time, whisking rapidly to combine. Add the salt and cook for 2 to 3 minutes, whisking constantly, or until the sauce thickens. Remove from the heat.

3. **To make the sandwiches:** Spread ½ teaspoon of mustard on each slice of bread.

4. Evenly divide the ham and cheese between 2 slices of bread and top with 1 tablespoon of béchamel sauce.

5. Cover each sandwich with one of the remaining slices of bread (mustard-side down).

6. Spread about 1½ teaspoons of butter on the outside of each slice of bread.

7. Heat the 12-inch skillet over medium heat.

8. Place the sandwiches into the skillet and top them with the 10-inch skillet to press them. Cook for 5 minutes.

CONTINUED

9. Remove the 10-inch skillet, flip the sandwiches, and re-top them with the 10-inch skillet.

10. Cook for 2 to 3 minutes more, or until both sides of the sandwiches are brown and the cheese is bubbling.

11. Top each sandwich with half the remaining béchamel sauce.

12. Transfer the skillet to the oven and broil for 1 to 2 minutes.

13. Plate the sandwiches and serve.

TIP: If you don't have two skillets to work with, cook the sandwiches grilled cheese–style without a press.

CHEESEBURGERS

Prep time: 10 minutes | **Cook time:** 20 minutes | **Cast iron:** 12-inch skillet

Lately, I have been particularly craving hamburgers grilled to perfection and loaded with toppings from our summer garden. Fresh juicy tomatoes, tender lettuce, homemade dill pickles—it's the stuff of dreams.

1 pound 85% lean ground beef

2 garlic cloves, minced

½ teaspoon sea salt

1 tablespoon olive oil

4 slices Cheddar cheese

Unsalted butter, for toasting the buns (optional)

4 hamburger buns

¼ cup mayonnaise

2 tablespoons spicy brown mustard

Dill pickles slices, for topping

1 ripe tomato, sliced

½ red onion, thinly sliced

1 cup fresh greens (arugula, spinach, or lettuce)

1. In a medium bowl, combine the ground beef, garlic, and salt. Mix well to distribute the seasonings. Divide the mixture into 4 balls and form each into a patty.

2. Heat the oil in the skillet over medium-high heat. Place the patties into the skillet and cook for 5 to 7 minutes. Flip the patties, top each with 1 slice of cheese, and cook for 5 to 7 minutes more.

3. If you prefer a toasted bun, while the burgers cook, preheat the oven to 350°F. Spread a thin layer of butter (if using) on the inside of each bun half and toast them in the oven for 5 to 7 minutes.

4. Plate the buns and spread mayonnaise and mustard evenly on the insides of each bun.

5. Layer the cheeseburger, pickles, tomato, onion, and greens on the bottom bun, cover with the top bun, and serve.

TIP: To make refrigerator pickles, in a pint-size jar, combine 1 sliced cucumber, 1½ teaspoons of mustard seeds, 1½ teaspoons of red pepper flakes, 1½ teaspoons of dill seeds, 1½ teaspoons of dill weed, and a few garlic cloves. Fill the jar halfway with apple cider vinegar and halfway with warm water. Add 1 tablespoon of kosher salt. Seal the lid, shake well, and refrigerate for at least 24 hours before serving.

SKILLET CALZONE

SERVES 1 TO 2

Prep time: 20 minutes | **Cook time:** 30 minutes | **Cast iron:** 12-inch skillet

I recently binge-watched *Parks and Recreation*, and I feel, deep in my soul, that show is a national treasure. One of the many fun and silly bits in the show is that Ben Wyatt loves calzones while everyone else thinks they're a ridiculous insult to pizza. I would be lying if I said I didn't decide to put a calzone recipe in this book because of the constant calzone jokes on *Parks and Recreation*. So, Ben Wyatt, this one is dedicated to you.

All-purpose flour, for rolling the dough

Pizza dough (see Beet and Goat Cheese Pizza, page 96)

½ cup pizza sauce

½ cup ricotta

8 ounces fresh mozzarella cheese, cut into ¼-inch slices

Sea salt

2 tablespoons olive oil

1. Preheat the oven to 500°F.

2. Flour a work surface and place the pizza dough on it. Roll the dough into a 12-inch round.

3. In the center of the round, spread a 6-inch circle of pizza sauce. Top the sauce with ricotta and mozzarella cheese. Season with a pinch of salt. Fold the dough on itself so it forms a pocket.

4. Brush the edges of the dough with water, then pinch the edges together. Using your clean fingers, crimp the edges of the dough and roll it slightly onto itself to seal.

5. Place the calzone into the skillet, brush the top and sides with oil, and sprinkle it with salt. Use a knife to cut 2 or 3 small slits in the top so steam can vent.

6. Bake for 25 to 30 minutes, or until the calzone is browned and bubbling.

TIP: My husband's favorite calzone is the meat lover's variety: Put ¼ cup each of pepperoni, cooked sausage, and cooked bacon on top of the mozzarella cheese in step 3 before folding.

HOT ITALIAN SANDWICH

OVEN-COOKED, WEEKDAY

SERVES 1

Prep time: 15 minutes | **Cook time:** 10 minutes | **Cast iron:** 12-inch skillet

Food is *everything* to my mom's Sicilian side of the family. Every phone conversation I have with Grammy is spent mostly talking about what we have both recently cooked and eaten. I have strong emotional ties to certain foods that I only eat when I'm with that side of the family, like pork roll sandwiches, lasagna, and Italian subs. One bite of this sandwich can transport me to my aunt's kitchen table with my big chaotic family all around me. That is the power of food.

2 thick slices Italian bread

1 tablespoon mayonnaise

2 slices Genoa salami

2 slices ham

4 slices pepperoni

4 strips roasted red pepper

2 slices provolone cheese

1 tablespoon olive oil

¼ cup shredded lettuce

¼ cup slivered red onion

1 tablespoon Italian dressing

1. Preheat the oven to 350°F.

2. On a work surface, lay out the bread slices and spread ½ tablespoon of mayonnaise on each one. Top the bottom slice with the salami, ham, and pepperoni. Add a layer of roasted red peppers and top with provolone cheese.

3. Pour the oil into the skillet and put both halves of the sandwich into the skillet. Transfer to the oven and bake for 10 minutes, until the cheese is bubbling.

4. While the sandwich bakes, in a small bowl, combine the lettuce, onion, and Italian dressing. Mix well to coat.

5. Using oven mitts, remove the skillet from the oven and plate the sandwich. Top with the coated lettuce and onion, close the sandwich, and serve.

TIP: If you prefer more of a hoagie-style sandwich, swap the Italian bread for a sub roll.

BEET AND GOAT CHEESE PIZZA

SERVES 4

Prep time: 20 minutes | **Inactive time:** 1 hour 15 minutes
Cook time: 15 minutes | **Cast iron:** 12-inch skillet

Beets may be my favorite vegetable. They're so versatile, and when they're roasted, they have the perfect sweetness. It's no secret they're one half of a power couple, and goat cheese is the other half. In this recipe, these two amazing flavors are complemented by spicy sausage and salty, crunchy pizza dough.

For the dough

1½ tablespoons olive oil,
    plus more for greasing
1 tablespoon active
    dry yeast
1 tablespoon sea salt
1 tablespoon fresh rosemary
    leaves, minced
¾ cup warm water
2½ cups bread flour, plus
    more for kneading and
    rolling the dough

1. **To make the dough:** Coat a large bowl with oil and set it aside.

2. In another large bowl, whisk the oil, yeast, salt, rosemary, and warm water until well combined and frothy.

3. Add 1¼ cups of flour and stir until incorporated. Add the remaining 1¼ cups of flour and stir until a rough dough ball forms.

4. Flour a work surface and turn the dough out onto it. Knead the dough by pulling it into a circle, folding it onto itself, and turning it. Repeat this process for 10 minutes.

5. Transfer the dough to the oiled bowl, turn it once, and loosely cover it with a damp kitchen towel. Let the dough rise for 1 hour. Punch down the dough, then let it rise for 15 minutes more.

For the pizza

4 ounces goat cheese

1 large beet, peeled and
   thinly sliced

2 spicy pork sausages,
   cooked and sliced

Olive oil, for seasoning

Sea salt

Handful beet greens or
   kale, rinsed

6. **To make the pizza:** Preheat the oven to 500°F.

7. Flour a work surface and place the dough on it. Roll
   the dough into a 12-inch round and place it into the
   skillet. Spread the goat cheese evenly over the top.
   Add the beets and sausage. Drizzle with oil and
   sprinkle with salt.

8. Bake for 12 to 15 minutes, or until the dough is
   cooked through and crisp around the edges.

9. Top with fresh greens, slice, and serve.

PEPPERONI PIZZA WITH HOT HONEY

OVEN-COOKED

SERVES 4; MAKES 1 CUP HOT HONEY

Prep time: 30 minutes | Cook time: 1 hour 10 minutes | Cast iron: 12-inch skillet

I was first introduced to hot honey at Vivian Howard's pizza restaurant, Benny's Big Time Pizzeria. It's the perfect combination of sweet and spicy, and when drizzled on cheesy, salty, crunchy, gooey pizza, it makes it irresistible.

For the hot honey

1 cup honey
1 teaspoon red pepper flakes

For the sauce

1 tablespoon olive oil
½ cup tomato paste
1 tablespoon minced garlic
1 tablespoon fresh oregano leaves
1 tablespoon fresh thyme leaves
1 tablespoon fresh rosemary leaves
½ teaspoon red pepper flakes
½ teaspoon sea salt
1 (15-ounce) can crushed tomatoes

For the pizza

All-purpose flour, for rolling the dough

1. **To make the hot honey:** In a small saucepan over medium-low heat, combine the honey and red pepper flakes. Bring to a simmer and cook for 10 minutes. Transfer to a glass jar. Let it cool completely.

2. **To make the sauce:** Heat the oil in a medium saucepan over medium heat. Add the tomato paste, garlic, oregano, thyme, rosemary, red pepper flakes, and salt. Cook, stirring vigorously, until the tomato paste absorbs the oil. Add the crushed tomatoes and stir until the sauce is a consistent texture. Reduce the heat to low and let simmer for 45 to 60 minutes, stirring occasionally.

3. **To make the pizza:** Preheat the oven to 500°F.

4. Flour a work surface and place the dough on it. Roll the dough into a 12-inch round and place it into the skillet. Spread the sauce in an even layer over the dough. Top with the mozzarella cheese, then the pepperoni.

Pizza dough (see Beet
and Goat Cheese Pizza,
page 96)

2 cups shredded
mozzarella cheese

10 or 12 pepperoni slices

5. Bake for 10 to 12 minutes, or until the pizza is cooked through and crisp around the edges.

6. Drizzle hot honey over the pizza, slice, and serve.

TIP: If you prefer a thin-crust pizza, split the dough in half before rolling it into a 12-inch round, and either make two pizzas (you'll need to stretch or double the toppings) or freeze half the dough for up to 1 year.

PESTO AND SAUSAGE PIZZA

OVEN-COOKED

SERVES 4

Prep time: 20 minutes | Cook time: 25 minutes | Cast iron: 12-inch skillet

My son Everett's favorite dinner is pesto pasta—to the point where there are frequently weeks where he asks *every single day* if we're having pesto pasta for dinner. We try to meet him halfway and work it into the menu once a week. This recipe hits all the high notes of pesto pasta: pesto, spicy Italian sausage, and mozzarella cheese. It's a win for the whole family.

1 teaspoon olive oil, plus more for greasing

8 ounces ground spicy Italian sausage

All-purpose flour, for rolling the dough

Pizza dough (see Beet and Goat Cheese Pizza, page 96)

1 recipe Pesto (see Bacon, Arugula, Tomato, and Pesto Sandwiches, page 88)

2 cups shredded mozzarella cheese

Pinch sea salt

Pinch red pepper flakes

1. Heat the oil in the skillet over medium heat. Add the sausage and cook for 7 to 10 minutes, stirring occasionally, or until the sausage is cooked through and no longer pink. Transfer the sausage to a bowl and set it aside.

2. Clean and re-oil the skillet.

3. Preheat the oven to 500°F.

4. Flour a work surface and place the dough on it. Roll the dough into a 12-inch round and place it into the skillet. Spread the pesto in an even layer over the dough and top it with 1 cup of mozzarella cheese. Evenly spread the cooked sausage over the pizza, then top it with the remaining 1 cup of mozzarella. Sprinkle with the salt and red pepper flakes.

5. Bake for 10 to 12 minutes, or until dough is cooked through and crisp around the edges. Slice and serve.

TIP: For everyday pesto, I use sunflower seeds because they are significantly more affordable than pine nuts and have a similar texture. I've also had success with walnuts and cashews.

FIG, PROSCIUTTO, AND ARUGULA PIZZA

OVEN-COOKED, WEEKDAY

SERVES 4

Prep time: 20 minutes | Cook time: 15 minutes | Cast iron: 12-inch skillet

One of the big selling points of our house for me was the two fig trees in the backyard. We eat them fresh from the tree (Everett's favorite) and make fig jam, but my favorite is having them on fresh fig pizza with salty prosciutto and peppery arugula.

All-purpose flour, for rolling the dough

Pizza dough (see Beet and Goat Cheese Pizza, page 96)

¼ cup olive oil

4 garlic cloves, minced

8 ounces fresh mozzarella cheese, sliced

3 ripe figs, sliced

6 slices prosciutto

Pinch sea salt

2 cups fresh arugula

1. Preheat the oven to 500°F.

2. Flour a work surface and place the dough on it. Roll the dough into a 12-inch round and place it into the skillet. Brush the dough thoroughly with oil and top it with the garlic. Arrange the mozzarella slices and figs evenly over the dough, then top it with the prosciutto. If you don't want the prosciutto cooked, drape over the hot pizza after it's done baking. Sprinkle with salt.

3. Bake for 10 to 12 minutes, or until the dough has cooked through and crisped around the edges.

4. Top with fresh arugula, slice, and serve.

TIP: If you don't have access to fresh figs, this pizza works well with fig jam. Just spread a thin layer of fig jam on the dough underneath the mozzarella.

BROCCOLI AND CARROT STUFFED SHELLS, PAGE 107

Chapter Six

VEGETARIAN
MAINS

GLUTEN-FREE, VEGETARIAN

SERVES 4

Prep time: 15 minutes | **Cook time:** 1 hour 10 minutes | **Cast iron:** 12-inch skillet

Despite having an aura of mystery and challenge to it, risotto is easy to make. The catch is that it needs constant attention. So, you're on the hook for 30 minutes or so of standing next to the stove stirring nonstop. I discovered this is the perfect dish for children to help with because their desire to over-stir is unparalleled, and, here, it's actually helpful!

4 tablespoons (½ stick) salted butter, divided

2 cups sliced button mushrooms

3 garlic cloves, minced

3 cups vegetable broth

1 tablespoon olive oil

1 white onion, minced

Sea salt

1 cup Arborio rice

½ cup dry white wine

Juice of 1 lemon

¼ cup grated Parmesan cheese

1 cup shelled peas, fresh or frozen, thawed to room temperature

1. In the skillet over medium heat, melt 1 tablespoon of butter. Add the mushrooms and cook for 4 to 5 minutes, stirring occasionally, or until the mushrooms are browned and tender. Stir in the garlic and cook for 1 minute. Transfer the mushrooms and garlic to a small bowl and set it aside.

2. In a medium saucepan over high heat, bring the broth to a boil, then reduce the heat to low and let simmer for 20 minutes.

3. In the skillet over medium heat, combine the oil and 1 tablespoon of butter. Add the onion and a pinch of salt and cook for 2 to 3 minutes, stirring occasionally, until the onion begins to soften.

4. Add the rice to the skillet. Stir to thoroughly coat the rice with the oil and butter. Sauté for 1 to 2 minutes, stirring frequently to keep the rice from browning.

5. Stir in the wine and cook, stirring, for 3 to 4 minutes, or until the wine is fully absorbed.

6. Add 1 ladleful of warm broth to the rice, stirring constantly until the broth is absorbed. Repeat this process, adding broth one ladleful at a time and stirring while it fully absorbs, until all the broth has been added, which should take 25 to 30 minutes.

7. Stir in the remaining 2 tablespoons of butter, the lemon juice, and Parmesan cheese.

8. Add the cooked mushrooms and garlic and peas. Cook for 2 to 3 minutes. Taste and adjust the seasoning, if desired.

TIP: Although the skillet is a wonderful tool for risotto, it is a taxing recipe for the seasoning. Be sure to clean and oil the skillet properly after cooking this so your skillet does not dry out.

GLUTEN-FREE, VEGETARIAN

SERVES 4

Prep time: 15 minutes | **Cook time:** 55 minutes | **Cast iron:** 10-inch and 12-inch skillets

In a continued effort to make environmentally responsible choices for my family, I try to keep the majority of dinners vegetarian. For this dish, I took one of my favorite weekday meals, butter chicken, and substituted halloumi cheese for the chicken. Pan-cooked halloumi, which is a Greek cheese also known as bread cheese, becomes salty and crispy and is amazing combined with spiced tomato sauce and fluffy rice.

8 tablespoons (1 stick) butter, divided

¼ cup tomato paste

6 garlic cloves

1 tablespoon peeled, minced fresh ginger

1½ teaspoons garam masala

1 teaspoon ground turmeric

1 teaspoon ground cumin

1 teaspoon ground coriander

1 teaspoon sea salt

½ teaspoon cayenne

½ teaspoon paprika

1 (14-ounce) can diced tomatoes, drained

1 cup heavy (whipping) cream

8 ounces halloumi, cut into ½-inch slices

Steamed rice, for serving

Handful fresh cilantro, minced

1. In the 12-inch skillet over medium heat, melt 7 tablespoons of butter. Add the tomato paste, garlic, ginger, garam masala, turmeric, cumin, coriander, salt, cayenne, and paprika. Stir until fully combined.

2. Stir in the diced tomatoes and let the sauce come to a steady simmer. Reduce the heat to low and simmer for 30 minutes, stirring occasionally.

3. Using an immersion blender, puree the sauce until smooth. Simmer for 5 to 7 minutes.

4. Whisk in the cream until combined. Continue to simmer and stir for 5 to 7 minutes.

5. In the 10-inch skillet over medium heat, melt the remaining 1 tablespoon of butter. Place the halloumi into the skillet and cook for 4 to 5 minutes, flip, and cook for 2 to 3 minutes, or until browned on both sides and crisp.

6. Spoon the tomato sauce over the rice, top with halloumi and cilantro, and serve.

OVEN-COOKED, VEGETARIAN

SERVES 4

Prep time: 40 minutes | **Cook time:** 1 hour 20 minutes | **Cast iron:** 12-inch skillet

Stuffed shells are a love song to cheese, with the main event being the gooey and crisp ricotta and mozzarella. This recipe features finely chopped broccoli and carrot mixed into the ricotta so you can enjoy the decadence of the cheese while telling yourself it's a vegetable.

8 ounces large pasta shells

2 tablespoons olive oil, divided

1 white onion, chopped

4 garlic cloves, minced

1 (6-ounce) can tomato paste

1 (28-ounce) can crushed tomatoes

¼ teaspoon red pepper flakes

1 teaspoon sea salt, divided

2 cups fresh ricotta

1 large carrot, finely chopped

2 cups finely chopped broccoli florets

1 large egg

1 cup shredded low-moisture mozzarella cheese, divided

1 cup grated Parmesan cheese, divided

1 tablespoon fresh oregano leaves, divided

1. Cook the pasta according to the package directions for half the recommended time for al dente. Drain and set aside.

2. Preheat the oven to 375°F.

3. Heat 1 tablespoon of oil in the skillet over medium heat. Add the onion and garlic and cook for 3 to 5 minutes, stirring frequently, until the onion is translucent.

4. Stir in the tomato paste until well combined. Smear the paste around the skillet to brown it, then stir in the crushed tomatoes and red pepper flakes until fully combined. Add ¼ teaspoon of salt and reduce the heat to low. Simmer for 20 to 25 minutes.

5. In a medium bowl, whisk the ricotta, carrot, broccoli, egg, ½ cup of mozzarella cheese, ½ cup of Parmesan cheese, 1½ teaspoons of oregano, and ½ teaspoon of salt to combine.

CONTINUED

6. Remove the skillet from the heat and transfer half the sauce to a medium bowl.

7. Stuff the shells, one at a time, with the ricotta and vegetable mixture, then nestle them into the skillet. Top the stuffed shells with the rest of the sauce, as well as the remaining ½ cup of Parmesan, ½ cup of mozzarella, 1½ teaspoons of oregano, and ¼ teaspoon of salt.

8. Tightly cover the skillet with aluminum foil and bake for 40 minutes. Remove the foil and bake, uncovered, for 10 minutes more to brown the cheese.

TIP: If you're looking for a slightly bolder vegetable in your cheese boat, I really like to mix sautéed spinach and garlic into the ricotta.

EGGPLANT LASAGNA

OVEN-COOKED, VEGETARIAN

⊙———— SERVES 4 TO 6 ————⊙

Prep time: 20 minutes | **Cook time:** 1 hour 20 minutes | **Cast iron:** 12-inch skillet

When it comes to expressing my love for someone, there are times when the only true answer is lasagna. This is because lasagna is a) the ultimate comfort food, b) one of the rare foods that tastes amazing reheated, and c) easy to make in multiples, so I can also make one for my family at the same time.

2 tablespoons olive oil

1 white onion, chopped

4 garlic cloves, minced

1 (6-ounce) can tomato paste

1 (28-ounce) can
   diced tomatoes

½ cup water

1 teaspoon sea salt, divided

2 cups ricotta

1 large egg

1 tablespoon dried
   oregano, divided

½ teaspoon freshly ground
   black pepper, divided

1 pound dried lasagna
   noodles, divided

1 large eggplant, thinly
   sliced into rounds, divided

8 ounces fresh mozzarella
   cheese, cut into ¼-inch
   slices, divided

¼ teaspoon red pepper
   flakes

1 cup grated Parmesan
   cheese

1. Heat the oil in the skillet over medium heat.

2. Add the onion and garlic and cook for 3 to 5 minutes, stirring frequently, until the onion is translucent.

3. Add the tomato paste and mix well. Smear the paste around the skillet to brown it and cook for 1 to 2 minutes. Add the diced tomatoes with their juices and stir until the tomato paste and tomatoes are well combined. Add the water and ¼ teaspoon of salt. Reduce the heat to low and simmer for 20 to 25 minutes.

4. Remove the skillet from the heat and transfer two-thirds of the sauce to a bowl.

5. Preheat the oven to 400°F.

6. In a small bowl, whisk the ricotta, egg, 1½ teaspoons of oregano, ½ teaspoon of salt, and ¼ teaspoon of pepper to combine.

CONTINUED

7. Place a layer of dried noodles into the sauce in the skillet. Top the noodles with half the ricotta mixture, a layer of eggplant, then about a quarter of the remaining sauce.

8. Add a second layer of noodles. Top it with half of the mozzarella cheese and another quarter of the remaining sauce.

9. Add a third layer of noodles. Top it with the rest of the ricotta mixture, another layer of eggplant, and about half the remaining sauce.

10. Add a final layer of noodles. Top it with the remaining sauce, then finish with the remaining half of the mozzarella cheese, the Parmesan cheese, and the remaining ¼ teaspoon of salt, ¼ teaspoon of black pepper, and 1½ teaspoons of oregano.

11. Lightly cover the skillet with aluminum foil. Bake for 30 to 35 minutes. Remove the foil and bake, uncovered, for 10 minutes more, or until the cheese is melted and bubbling.

TIP: This recipe doubles easily, and it's as much effort to assemble one lasagna as it is two. When I'm not making lasagna for other people, I make one in my skillet and another in an aluminum pan for the freezer, where it will keep for up to 1 year.

LENTIL BOLOGNESE

VEGETARIAN

SERVES 4

Prep time: 10 minutes | **Inactive time:** 2 hours | **Cook time:** 1 hour | **Cast iron:** 12-inch skillet

I once heard a story about a Passover seder held at St. Leo the Great Roman Catholic Church in Baltimore, Maryland. The dinner was organized to bring the Catholic and Jewish communities together and was set to feature Bolognese sauce. During a kosher meal, however, meat is not eaten with dairy, which meant no Parmesan cheese. Balking at the idea, the Catholic women of Little Italy took matters into their own hands and smuggled in the cheese. This Bolognese features lentils instead of ground beef, so there are no conflicts with kashrut.

1 cup dried lentils

2 tablespoons olive oil

1 white onion, diced

1 celery stalk, diced

1 large carrot, diced

¼ cup tomato paste

½ cup whole milk

1 cup white wine

4 cups water

1 (28-ounce) can diced
   tomatoes

1 tablespoon fresh rosemary
   leaves, minced

1 teaspoon dried oregano

1 teaspoon dried thyme

1 teaspoon dried basil

1 teaspoon sea salt

Tagliatelle or fettuccine
   noodles, cooked,
   for serving

Grated Parmesan cheese,
   for serving

1. At least 2 hours before you plan to start cooking, soak the lentils in water.

2. Heat the oil in the skillet over medium heat. Add the onion, celery, and carrot. Cook for 4 to 5 minutes, stirring frequently, or until the vegetables start to brown and soften.

3. Stir in the tomato paste and cook for 2 to 3 minutes, stirring, or just long enough for the tomato paste to caramelize.

4. Whisk in the milk and cook for 15 to 20 minutes, stirring, until it has cooked down by half.

5. Drain the lentils, add them to the skillet, and stir in the wine. Cook for about 10 minutes, stirring frequently, or until the liquid has mostly cooked down.

CONTINUED

6. Stir in the water, tomatoes with their juices, rosemary, oregano, thyme, basil, and salt. Bring the sauce to a light boil. Reduce the heat to low and cook, uncovered, for 25 to 30 minutes, stirring occasionally.

7. Place the cooked noodles in a large bowl. When the lentils are cooked to your taste, spoon the sauce over the noodles, top with Parmesan cheese, and serve.

TIP: This recipe is well suited for enamelware, if you have it. If you're using a 12-inch skillet, be sure to clean, dry, and re-oil the skillet after use because the acidity of the tomatoes can be hard on the skillet's seasoning.

ENCHILADA CASSEROLE

OVEN-COOKED, VEGETARIAN

SERVES 4

Prep time: 30 minutes | **Cook time:** 1 hour 10 minutes | **Cast iron:** 12-inch skillet

The first time I made this casserole, both my husband and my son made a point of walking through the kitchen and commenting on how good it smelled. When dinner was served, my son immediately declared it was delicious, which was a total departure from his normal declaration that dinner is disgusting (before he's even tried it). Dan suggested that this recipe make it into our normal dinner rotation, which it has.

For the enchilada sauce

3 tablespoons olive oil

3 tablespoons all-purpose flour

1½ teaspoons paprika

1 teaspoon ground cumin

¾ teaspoon cayenne

½ teaspoon dried oregano

½ teaspoon salt

¼ teaspoon ground cinnamon

3 tablespoons tomato paste

3 garlic cloves, minced

2 cups vegetable broth

Juice of 1 lime

For the casserole

1 cup shredded Cheddar cheese

1 cup shredded Monterey Jack cheese

1 cup Cotija cheese

1. **To make the enchilada sauce:** In a medium saucepan over medium heat, warm the oil until it simmers. Whisk in the flour until fully incorporated.

2. While whisking, one at a time and whisking well after each, add the paprika, cumin, cayenne, oregano, salt, and cinnamon. Cook for 1 to 2 minutes, whisking, until the roux begins to brown.

3. Whisk in the tomato paste and garlic until fully incorporated.

4. Slowly whisk in the broth until the sauce is smooth. Let the sauce come to a boil, then reduce the heat to low and simmer for 10 minutes, stirring occasionally. Add the lime juice and remove from the heat.

5. **To make the casserole:** Preheat the oven to 375°F.

6. In a small bowl, stir together the Cheddar, Monterey Jack, and Cotija cheeses.

CONTINUED

12 corn tortillas, divided

1 (15-ounce) can black
beans, drained and
rinsed, divided

2 cups sweet corn kernels

1 red bell pepper, cut into
strips

1 green bell pepper, cut into
strips

Handful fresh cilantro,
minced

1 lime, cut into wedges

Fresh avocado, peeled,
halved, pitted, and sliced

7. Place 4 tortillas on the bottom of the skillet in an
even layer and coat it with a thin layer of sauce.
Spread half the beans and half the corn evenly
over the tortillas. Top with the red bell pepper and
one-third of the cheese mix.

8. Place 4 tortillas on top of the cheese, then a layer
of sauce, then the remaining beans and corn, the
green bell pepper, and one-third of the cheese.

9. Arrange the remaining 4 tortillas on top of the
cheese. Evenly spread the remaining sauce over the
tortillas. Finish with the remaining cheese.

10. Bake for 45 to 50 minutes until bubbling and
browned around the edges.

11. Let the casserole cool slightly before serving with
cilantro, lime wedges, and avocado on the side.

VEGETARIAN STIR-FRY

VEGETARIAN, WEEKDAY

SERVES 2

Prep time: 10 minutes | Cook time: 15 minutes | Cast iron: 12-inch skillet

I've never had a lot of kitchen storage, so I try to make sure that any tools I buy have as many functions as possible. My 12-inch skillet can do most of what I need from a wok, so it's a great tool for me to use for stir-fries and other wok-based dishes.

For the stir-fry sauce

⅓ cup soy sauce

¼ cup vegetable broth

1 tablespoon honey

2 teaspoons cornstarch

For the stir-fry

2 tablespoons sesame oil

1 onion, diced

1 large carrot, cut into rounds

1 cup white button mushrooms, sliced

1 red bell pepper, cut into strips

1 yellow bell pepper, cut into strips

1 cup baby corn

1 cup sugar snap peas

1 cup fresh broccoli florets

3 garlic cloves, minced

1 teaspoon peeled, minced fresh ginger

Cooked rice or noodles, for serving

Minced scallion, for garnish

1. **To make the stir-fry sauce:** In a small bowl, whisk the soy sauce, broth, honey, and cornstarch until the cornstarch dissolves.

2. **To make the stir-fry:** Heat the oil in the skillet over medium-high heat. Add the onion and cook for 1 to 2 minutes. Add the carrot and mushrooms and cook for 4 to 6 minutes. Add the red and yellow bell peppers, corn, snap peas, broccoli, garlic, and ginger. Cook for 2 to 3 minutes, stirring frequently.

3. Pour the sauce into the skillet and stir well to coat. Cook for 45 seconds to 1 minute, long enough for the sauce to thicken and coat the vegetables, then remove from the heat.

4. Serve over rice, garnished with scallion.

TIP: Water chestnuts are a popular addition to a vegetarian stir-fry. If you're a fan, add a can of water chestnuts, drained, with the other vegetables in step 2.

RICOTTA-STUFFED ZUCCHINI BOATS

OVEN-COOKED, VEGETARIAN, WEEKDAY

SERVES 4

Prep time: 10 minutes | **Cook time:** 20 minutes | **Cast iron:** 12-inch skillet

I'm of the strong opinion that cheese makes most anything better. That is especially true in this recipe, where a relatively mild vegetable becomes a vessel for gooey, salty, cheesy goodness. It's zucchini at its best.

1 cup ricotta

½ teaspoon sea salt

Juice of 1 lemon

1 tablespoon fresh
  rosemary leaves

1 tablespoon fresh
  oregano leaves

2 large zucchini, halved
  lengthwise, seeds
  scooped out

½ cup shredded
  mozzarella cheese

1. Preheat the oven to 425°F.

2. In a small bowl, stir together the ricotta, salt, lemon juice, rosemary, and oregano.

3. Arrange the zucchini halves in the skillet, cut-side up. Evenly divide the filling among the 4 zucchini halves. Top each with about 2 tablespoons of mozzarella cheese.

4. Bake for 15 to 20 minutes, or until the cheese is browned and bubbling. Let the zucchini boats cool slightly, then serve.

MACARONI AND CHEESE

CLASSIC, OVEN-COOKED, VEGETARIAN

SERVES 6

Prep time: 20 minutes | **Cook time:** 1 hour | **Cast iron:** 12-inch skillet

Dan likes to point out that despite the fact that this is my sixth cookbook, he still does 95 percent of the weekly cooking. Part of the reason for that is I've been pregnant or nursing entirely too much during the past few years. Also, he's a great cook and is happy to do it. Recently, he decided to make mac and cheese, and he went *all out*, making it cheesy and gooey with a crisp panko breading. It was decadent—an instant family favorite.

1 pound dried macaroni

6 ounces fresh mozzarella cheese, cubed

1 tablespoon olive oil

1 cup heavy (whipping) cream

1 cup whole milk

2 garlic cloves, minced

8 tablespoons (1 stick) salted butter, divided

2 tablespoons all-purpose flour

1 cup shredded Gruyère cheese

1 cup white shredded Cheddar cheese

Juice of 1 lemon

1 teaspoon sea salt, plus more for topping

1½ cups bread crumbs or panko bread crumbs

1 cup grated Parmesan cheese

½ teaspoon chipotle powder

1. Preheat the oven to 350°F.

2. In a medium saucepan, cook the macaroni according to the package directions. Drain the pasta and return it to the pan. Add the mozzarella and oil and stir to combine.

3. In a small saucepan over medium-high heat, scald the cream, milk, and garlic by bringing them almost to a boil. Remove from the heat.

4. In the skillet over medium heat, melt 4 tablespoons of butter. Slowly whisk in the flour and cook for 1 to 2 minutes, whisking, until it begins to thicken. Gradually pour in the milk mixture, whisking vigorously to prevent clumping.

5. Whisk in the Gruyère and Cheddar cheeses. Cook, whisking constantly, until the cheese melts. Remove the skillet from the heat and whisk in the lemon juice and 1 teaspoon of salt.

CONTINUED

6. Stir the pasta into the sauce, mixing well to coat the noodles.

7. In another small saucepan over medium heat, melt the remaining 4 tablespoons of butter.

8. In a medium bowl, stir together the bread crumbs, Parmesan cheese, melted butter, a pinch of salt, and chipotle powder. Spread the mixture evenly over the noodles.

9. Bake for 35 to 40 minutes until browned and bubbling.

SWEET POTATO FRITTATA

GLUTEN-FREE, OVEN-COOKED, VEGETARIAN, WEEKDAY

SERVES 6

Prep time: 10 minutes | **Cook time:** 20 minutes | **Cast iron:** 12-inch skillet

This frittata is a play on one of my favorite ways to cook sweet potatoes—in a skillet with butter and a little chipotle powder. The egg and pepper Jack cheese just extend the sweet and salty combination, which is my favorite.

6 large eggs

1 cup shredded pepper
Jack cheese

¼ cup heavy (whipping)
cream

Pinch sea salt

2 tablespoons salted butter

1 large sweet potato, peeled
and cubed

1 white onion, chopped

½ teaspoon chipotle powder

2 garlic cloves, minced

1. Preheat the oven to 400°F.

2. In a medium bowl, whisk the eggs, pepper Jack cheese, cream, and salt to combine. Set aside.

3. In the skillet over medium heat, melt the butter. Add the sweet potato, onion, and chipotle powder and stir to coat. Spread the sweet potato evenly across the skillet. Cook for 3 to 4 minutes, then flip the sweet potato and cook for 2 to 3 minutes more. Stir in the garlic.

4. Pour the egg mixture over the sweet potato and stir to combine. Cook for 1 to 2 minutes to set the eggs, then transfer the frittata to the oven.

5. Bake for 8 to 10 minutes, or until the eggs are set.

TIP: If you prefer a smoother texture, the sweet potato can be grated. Cook for 2 to 3 minutes per side and make sure to avoid letting the potatoes clump together.

SKILLET NACHOS

GLUTEN-FREE, OVEN-COOKED, VEGETARIAN, WEEKDAY

SERVES 2 TO 4

Prep time: 15 minutes | Cook time: 7 minutes | Cast iron: 12-inch skillet

The trick to great homemade nachos is layers. Nobody likes when the top layer is overwhelmed with toppings and the bottom layers are just dry chips. Layering chips and toppings creates an even distribution, which is essential, especially if you are sharing these with someone who eats faster than you do.

1 (15-ounce) can black
 beans, rinsed and drained

1 red bell pepper, diced

1 green bell pepper, diced

½ cup corn kernels

1 cup shredded Cheddar
 cheese

1 cup shredded Monterey
 Jack cheese

½ cup Cotija cheese

1 (13-ounce) bag tortilla
 chips

¼ cup pickled jalapeño
 peppers, drained

½ red onion, chopped

1 cup fresh tomato salsa,
 drained

1 avocado, peeled, halved,
 pitted, and diced

½ cup sour cream (optional)

Handful fresh cilantro,
 minced

1. Preheat the oven to 425°F.

2. In a medium bowl, stir together the black beans, red and green bell peppers, and corn. Set aside.

3. In another medium bowl, combine the Cheddar, Monterey Jack, and Cotija cheeses.

4. Spread an even layer of tortilla chips on the bottom of the skillet. Top the chips with half the black bean mixture and one-third of the cheese mixture. Add a second layer of tortilla chips, then the remaining bean mixture. Top with one-third of the cheese.

5. Add a final layer of tortilla chips. Top it with the jalapeños, onion, and the remaining cheese.

6. Bake for 6 to 7 minutes, or until the cheese melts and is bubbling.

7. Serve topped with salsa, avocado, sour cream (if using), and cilantro.

TIP: There is a next level of nachos after this one, which is to use queso dip as one of your cheeses in the mix. Simply drizzle the finished nachos with hot queso in step 7 before topping them with salsa.

CARROT AND ZUCCHINI FRITTERS

VEGETARIAN, WEEKDAY

⊖——————— SERVES 2 ———————⊖

Prep time: 15 minutes | **Inactive time:** 15 minutes
Cook time: 10 minutes | **Cast iron:** 10- or 12-inch skillet

These fritters, like their cousin the latke, are light, crisp, and delicious when dipped in sour cream. Served with a big salad, they make an easy dinner that is filling but not heavy.

2 large zucchini, shredded

1 large carrot, shredded

½ teaspoon sea salt

1 large egg

2 garlic cloves, minced

½ cup all-purpose flour

Olive oil, for greasing

Sour cream, for serving

1. In a strainer set over a bowl, combine the zucchini and carrot. Add the salt and toss to coat. Let the vegetables drain for 10 to 15 minutes. Place them on a clean towel, wrap them in the towel, and twist the towel to squeeze out any excess liquid.

2. In a large bowl, beat the egg, then mix in the zucchini and carrot until fully coated. Add the garlic and flour and stir until the flour is fully and evenly incorporated.

3. Coat the skillet with a thin layer of oil, then heat it over medium-high heat.

4. Form the zucchini mixture into patties about the size of your palm, squeezing as much moisture as you can out of them as you do this. Transfer the patties to the skillet and cook for 3 to 4 minutes, or until browned. Flip and cook for 2 to 3 minutes more, then transfer the cooked fritters to a plate while you repeat the process with the remaining vegetable mixture. Serve with a side of sour cream.

TIP: It's important to drain as much liquid out of the zucchini as possible to make the fritters light and crisp, so do not shorten the time or skip step 1.

CURRIED PEA AND MUSHROOM SHEPHERD'S PIE

OVEN-COOKED, VEGETARIAN

SERVES 4 TO 6

Prep time: 20 minutes | **Cook time:** 1 hour 10 minutes | **Cast iron:** 12-inch skillet

The first time I made this shepherd's pie, it was mostly by accident. I had been making samosas and made *significantly* more filling than I needed, which meant I was stuck with leftover curried peas and mashed potatoes. I decided to try it in a quick shepherd's pie–style dish with other odds and ends from the refrigerator, and the results were delightful.

For the potatoes

3 russet potatoes, peeled and quartered

8 tablespoons (1 stick) salted butter

½ cup mayonnaise

1 teaspoon sea salt, plus more as needed

1 teaspoon cumin seed

1 teaspoon fennel seed

1 teaspoon ground coriander

1 teaspoon curry powder

½ teaspoon garam masala

½ teaspoon cayenne

For the filling

2 tablespoons salted butter

1 white onion, minced

2 cups sliced white mushrooms

1. **To make the potatoes:** Bring a large pot of salted water to a boil. Add the potatoes and cook for 13 to 15 minutes, until tender. Drain.

2. In the bowl of a stand mixer fitted with the paddle attachment, or in a large bowl using an electric mixer, combine the cooked potatoes, butter, mayonnaise, salt, cumin seed, fennel seed, coriander, curry powder, garam masala, and cayenne. Mix on medium speed until creamy, being careful not to overmix. Taste and adjust the seasoning. Set aside.

3. **To make the filling:** In the skillet over medium heat, melt the butter. Add the onion and cook for 3 to 4 minutes, until it begins to soften. Stir in the mushrooms, spreading them evenly over the bottom of the skillet to prevent crowding. Cook for 4 to 5 minutes, stirring occasionally, or until the onion has browned. Stir in the peas, carrots, garlic, cumin, garam masala, salt, and pepper. Cook for 2 to 3 minutes, stirring once or twice.

2 cups peas, fresh or frozen and thawed

2 large carrots, chopped

3 garlic cloves, minced

1 teaspoon ground cumin

½ teaspoon garam masala

½ teaspoon sea salt

½ teaspoon freshly ground black pepper

1 tablespoon all-purpose flour

1 cup vegetable broth

4. Stir in the flour so it coats the vegetables, then stir in the broth. Cook for 5 to 7 minutes, or until the mixture comes to a steady simmer, then remove from the heat.

5. Preheat the oven to 400°F.

6. Spread the mashed potatoes in an even layer over the vegetables, making sure the potatoes kiss the side of the skillet.

7. Bake for 25 to 30 minutes, or until the potatoes are browned and bubbling.

TIP: Like the samosas that inspired this dish, this is delicious served with a drizzle of tamarind chutney, which you can find in the Asian section of the grocery store.

VEGETARIAN

SERVES 2 TO 4

Prep time: 30 minutes | **Inactive time:** 1 hour
Cook time: 30 minutes | **Cast iron:** 12-inch skillet

The namesake of my family, John Rosemond, was a Polish political refugee originally known as John Kwiatkowski. He immigrated to New York in the 1840s, changed his name, and enlisted to fight in the Mexican-American War. Unfortunately for him, and fortunately for his descendants, he got devastatingly seasick on the boat, and they dropped him off in Wilmington, North Carolina, establishing my branch of the family tree. So, every time I eat a pierogi, I tip my hat to good old John Kwiatkowski.

For the filling

2 small russet potatoes,
  quartered
1 teaspoon sea salt
½ cup shredded Cheddar
  cheese
⅓ cup mayonnaise

For the dough

2 cups all-purpose flour,
  plus more for kneading
1 teaspoon sea salt
1 large egg
½ cup sour cream
4 tablespoons (½ stick)
  unsalted butter, at
  room temperature

1. **To make the filling:** Bring a medium pot of salted water to a boil. Add the potatoes and cook for 10 to 12 minutes, until tender. Drain.

2. In the bowl of a stand mixer fitted with the paddle attachment, or in a large bowl using an electric mixer, combine the potatoes, salt, Cheddar cheese, and mayonnaise. Mix on medium speed until smooth. Set aside.

3. **To make the dough:** In a large bowl, stir together the flour and salt. One at a time and mixing after each addition, add the egg, sour cream, and butter. Knead the dough until it comes together (it will be quite sticky).

4. Flour a work surface and turn the dough out onto it. Knead the dough until smooth. Wrap the dough in plastic and refrigerate it for 1 hour.

For the assembly

1 large egg, beaten

1 tablespoon water

4 tablespoons (½ stick)
  unsalted butter

5. **To assemble the pierogis:** In a small bowl, whisk the egg and water. Set the egg wash aside.

6. Divide the dough into 2 equal parts and return 1 part to the refrigerator. Flour a work surface and roll the dough out onto it into a thin, ¼-inch-thick rectangle. Use a 3-inch cookie cutter to cut 8 or 9 dough rounds. Fill each round with 1 teaspoon of filling.

7. Brush the inside edges of each round with egg wash. Fold the rounds in half to form a half-moon shape. Using your clean fingers, crimp the edges together to seal.

8. Repeat steps 6 and 7 with the remaining dough until the filling is gone.

9. Bring a large stockpot of water to a rolling boil. Boil the pierogis in batches, taking them out of the water as soon as they float. Transfer the boiled pierogis onto a baking sheet to dry.

10. In the skillet over medium-high heat, melt 2 tablespoons of butter. Working in batches, fry the pierogis for 2 minutes per side, adding butter between batches as needed. Serve hot.

TIP: Pierogis are an excellent candidate to freeze and cook later. After step 8, freeze them flat on a baking sheet, then transfer them to a freezer-safe bag, seal, and keep frozen for up to 1 year. When ready to cook the pierogis, thaw them overnight in the refrigerator and pick up at step 9.

SPICED BUTTERY LENTILS

GLUTEN-FREE, VEGETARIAN

SERVES 4

Prep time: 20 minutes | **Inactive time:** 12 hours
Cook time: 55 minutes | **Cast iron:** 12-inch skillet

Spiced lentils over rice is one of my favorite vegetarian dinners and is a regular part of our weekly dinner rotation. This recipe is my take on one of my favorite Punjabi-inspired dishes, which features black lentils (*urad dal*) and kidney beans (*rajma*) with a creamy, buttery tomato sauce. Served over rice with fresh cilantro and a squeeze of lemon juice, it is easy to understand why this dish is a favorite in Indian restaurants.

1 cup dried black lentils

½ cup dried kidney beans

1 bay leaf

Sea salt

3 tablespoons ghee

1 white onion, minced

2 garlic cloves, minced

1 tablespoon peeled, minced fresh ginger

1 teaspoon garam masala

½ teaspoon ground cumin

¼ teaspoon cayenne

¼ teaspoon ground cinnamon

¼ teaspoon ground cloves

2 tablespoons tomato paste

1 (28-ounce) can crushed tomatoes

1 cup heavy (whipping) cream

1 cup full-fat plain Greek yogurt

1. The night before you plan to serve this dish, in a large bowl, combine the lentils and kidney beans with enough water to cover by at least 2 inches. Let them soak overnight.

2. Drain the beans and rinse them 3 or 4 times. Transfer the beans to a large pot and cover with water. Add the bay leaf and a pinch of salt. Bring to a boil over high heat. Cover the pot, reduce the heat to low, and simmer for 20 to 25 minutes, or until the lentils are al dente. Drain and set aside.

3. In the skillet over medium heat, melt the ghee. Add the onion and cook for 3 to 4 minutes, stirring occasionally. Add the garlic, ginger, 1 teaspoon of salt, garam masala, cumin, cayenne, cinnamon, and cloves. Stir until well combined, then add the tomato paste. Cook, stirring constantly until the tomato paste absorbs the ghee.

Juice of 2 lemons

Steamed rice, for serving

Handful fresh cilantro,
   minced

4. Add the crushed tomatoes, then stir in the lentils
   and kidney beans. Reduce the heat to low and
   simmer for 20 to 25 minutes, stirring frequently so
   the beans don't stick.

5. In a small bowl, whisk the cream, yogurt, and lemon
   juice to combine, then whisk the cream mixture into
   the lentils and remove them from the heat.

6. Serve over rice, topped with fresh cilantro.

TIP: Traditionally, dal makhani is finished with a step called
the *dhungar* method, which adds a smoky flavor to the dal.
To achieve this, heat a small piece of hardwood lump-charcoal
until it is hot and glowing. You can do this outside with
a torch, or in another skillet. Once it is heated, place the
charcoal in a small, heatproof bowl (or even a foil ramekin),
and pour ½ teaspoon vegetable oil on top of the coal. Place
the smoking bowl into the skillet and cover with a lid. Let
the smoking charcoal infuse the dal for 1 to 2 minutes, then
remove it and serve.

CHILES RELLENOS

OVEN-COOKED, VEGETARIAN

SERVES 4

Prep time: 30 minutes | **Inactive time:** 10 minutes
Cook time: 35 minutes | **Cast iron:** 10-inch and 12-inch skillets

Putting this meal together can feel a bit like juggling, so I recommend reading the complete recipe and preparing your mise en place as much as possible before starting. The more you have prepped, the more smoothly the cooking will go.

For the peppers

4 poblano peppers

For the sauce

3 Roma tomatoes

3 garlic cloves, peeled

Handful fresh oregano
    leaves

1 cup vegetable broth

2 tablespoons vegetable oil

1 tablespoon all-purpose
    flour

1 tablespoon tomato paste

½ teaspoon sea salt, plus
    more as needed

Pinch paprika

1. **To prepare the peppers:** Place an oven rack in the top position and set the broiler to high.

2. Arrange the poblanos in the 10-inch skillet and broil for 2 to 3 minutes per side, or until charred. Immediately transfer the peppers to a bowl and cover tightly with plastic wrap or a silicone lid. Let them sit for 10 minutes.

3. While the peppers are still warm, gently peel off the blistered skin using a knife as needed (don't puncture the chiles). Once peeled, set the peppers aside to cool.

4. **To make the sauce:** In a blender, combine the tomatoes, garlic, oregano, and broth. Blend until smooth.

5. Heat the vegetable oil in a medium saucepan over medium-high heat. Whisk in the flour and cook for 2 to 3 minutes, whisking as the roux thickens. Once thick and bubbling, whisk in the tomato mixture. Reduce the heat to medium-low and whisk in the tomato paste, salt, and paprika. Taste and adjust the seasoning, as desired. Let the sauce simmer while you prepare the remaining ingredients.

For the rice

1 tablespoon olive oil

½ white onion

2 cups cooked rice

2 garlic cloves

Pinch sea salt

For the assembly

2 large eggs, separated

1½ cups queso fresco

½ cup vegetable oil

¼ cup all-purpose flour

Handful fresh cilantro,
  chopped

6. **To make the rice:** Heat the olive oil in the 12-inch skillet over medium-high heat. Add the onion and cook for 2 to 3 minutes, or until softened. Stir in the rice, garlic, and salt until mixed well.

7. Add half the sauce to the rice and stir until incorporated. Reduce the heat to low.

8. **To assemble the chiles rellenos:** In the bowl of a stand mixer fitted with the whisk attachment, or in a large bowl using an electric mixer, whip the egg whites until stiff. Whisk the yolks slightly, then fold them into the whites.

9. Cut a slit down one side of each pepper. Use a spoon to gently scrape out the seeds. Stuff each pepper with queso fresco, taking care not to overstuff them.

10. Heat the vegetable oil to 375°F in the 10-inch skillet over medium-high heat.

11. Dust each pepper with flour, then dip into the eggs, using a spoon to thoroughly coat the pepper.

12. When the oil is hot, fry the peppers, 2 at a time, for 2 to 3 minutes, or until the batter is golden brown. Flip the peppers and fry for 2 to 3 minutes more.

13. Divide the rice among 4 plates. Add 1 chile to each plate and top it with a generous spoonful of the remaining sauce. Sprinkle with cilantro and serve.

TIP: Skip the flour and egg batter and simply put the stuffed chiles back under the broiler for a few minutes to melt the cheese.

JERK CHICKEN NAKED WINGS, PAGE 149

Chapter Seven

POULTRY

CHICKEN AND ZUCCHINI CURRY

GLUTEN-FREE, WEEKDAY
SERVES 4

Prep time: 15 minutes | **Cook time:** 40 minutes | **Cast iron:** 12-inch skillet

When I wrote this recipe, my kitchen counter was overflowing with zucchini. Later, when I made it again, I used an abundance of okra from my garden. Since then, I've made it with eggplant and with yellow summer squash. The staples of the recipe, chicken and creamy curry sauce, are there to support whatever vegetable you need to sneak into your weekly meal plan.

1 tablespoon olive oil

1 pound boneless, skinless chicken breasts

1 tablespoon salted butter

1 large yellow onion, diced

4 garlic cloves, minced

1 tablespoon peeled, minced fresh ginger

1 tablespoon curry powder

1½ teaspoons paprika

1½ teaspoons ground cumin

1½ teaspoons garam masala

¾ teaspoon ground turmeric

¾ teaspoon ground coriander

1½ cups heavy (whipping) cream

½ cup chicken broth

1 (14.5-ounce) can crushed tomatoes

1 zucchini, chopped

½ teaspoon sea salt, plus more as needed

1 teaspoon cornstarch

2 cups cooked rice

1. Heat the oil in the skillet over medium heat. Add the chicken and cook for 3 to 4 minutes. Flip the chicken and cook for 3 minutes more, or until both sides are browned. Transfer the chicken to a plate and set it aside.

2. Put the butter and onion into the skillet. Cook for 3 to 4 minutes. Add the garlic and cook for 1 minute, then add the ginger, curry powder, paprika, cumin, garam masala, turmeric, and coriander. Stir well to coat the onion.

3. Stir in the cream, broth, and crushed tomatoes. Bring the sauce to a light boil, then reduce the heat to low.

4. Roughly chop the chicken and add it to the skillet, along with the zucchini and salt. Let it simmer for 15 minutes, stirring occasionally. Taste and adjust the seasoning, if desired.

1 avocado, peeled, halved,
   pitted, and sliced

¼ cup fresh cilantro

1 lemon, cut into wedges

5. In a small bowl, stir together 2 tablespoons of sauce and the cornstarch until dissolved. Stir the slurry into the sauce, mixing well to fully incorporate. Cook for 10 minutes, stirring occasionally.

6. Serve over rice with avocado, cilantro, and a lemon wedge.

SWEET AND SOUR CHICKEN

WEEKDAY

SERVES 4

Prep time: 15 minutes | **Cook time:** 25 minutes | **Cast iron:** 12-inch skillet

The combination of salty and sweet is just about heaven, and I'm always looking for new ways to scratch that itch. Sweet and sour chicken is easy and delicious, and it comes with the added nostalgia of eating pineapple from a can like I'm in my grandma's kitchen in 1989.

⅓ cup apple cider vinegar

¼ cup ketchup

2 tablespoons soy sauce

1 tablespoon sriracha

1 tablespoon light brown sugar

1 (8-ounce) can pineapple chunks, strained, ¾ cup juice reserved, divided

2 boneless, skinless chicken breasts, cut into chunks

¼ cup cornstarch

1 teaspoon sea salt, divided

⅓ cup vegetable oil, divided

1 large white onion, minced

1 red bell pepper, cut into strips

1 green bell pepper, cut into strips

4 garlic cloves, minced

1 tablespoon peeled, minced fresh ginger

Steamed rice, for serving

1. In a small bowl, whisk the vinegar, ketchup, soy sauce, sriracha, brown sugar, and ¼ cup of reserved pineapple juice until smooth. Set aside.

2. In a medium bowl, combine the chicken, cornstarch, and ½ teaspoon of salt. Coat the chicken thoroughly with the cornstarch.

3. Heat 2 tablespoons of oil in the skillet over medium-high heat. Add the chicken and spread it evenly across the bottom of the skillet. Cook for 3 to 4 minutes, or until browned. Flip and cook for 2 to 3 minutes more. Remove the chicken from the skillet and set it on a rack to drain any excess oil.

4. Pour in the remaining oil and add the onion. Stir, making sure there is nothing sticking to the skillet, and cook for 3 to 4 minutes, or until the onion is tender.

5. Add the red and green bell peppers and cook for 1 to 2 minutes, or until slightly charred.

6. Add the pineapple chunks and cook for 1 to 2 minutes, until browned.

7. Stir in the garlic and ginger and cook for 1 minute, stirring well.

8. Return the chicken to the skillet and stir, then add the sauce. Stir well so the sauce completely coats the chicken and vegetables. Cook for 2 to 3 minutes, stirring occasionally, until the sauce thickens.

9. Serve over rice.

TIP: If you're looking for restaurant-style fried chicken, make a simple batter from ½ cup of cornstarch and 2 large eggs, beaten. Dip the chicken in the batter to coat and fry in 1 inch of hot oil for 2 to 3 minutes per side. Let the chicken drain on a rack, pour off the oil, and follow the rest of the recipe from step 4.

TURKEY BURGERS

WEEKDAY

○——————— SERVES 4 ———————○

Prep time: 15 minutes | **Cook time:** 15 minutes | **Cast iron:** 12-inch skillet

The common problem with turkey burgers is that they're often horribly dry. This recipe incorporates an egg with the turkey to help with moisture, but be sure to keep a close eye on the patties while they cook so you pull them off while they're still juicy.

1 pound ground turkey

2 garlic cloves, minced

1 large egg, beaten

2 tablespoons
  Worcestershire sauce

Pinch sea salt

2 tablespoons olive oil, plus
  more as needed

4 ounces fresh mozzarella
  cheese, sliced

2 tablespoons mayonnaise

4 hamburger buns

Handful fresh spinach

½ red onion, thinly sliced

1. In a medium bowl, mix the ground turkey, garlic, egg, Worcestershire sauce, and salt. Divide the mixture into 4 balls and shape them into patties.

2. Heat the oil in the skillet over medium heat.

3. Place the turkey patties into the skillet and cook for 5 to 6 minutes. Flip and top each burger with 1 slice of mozzarella cheese. Cook for 5 to 6 minutes more, until browned and the internal temperature reaches 165°F.

4. Spread the mayonnaise on the cut side of the buns. Layer the turkey patty, fresh spinach, and onion on the bottom bun, cover with the top bun, and serve.

TIP: If you notice the burgers have absorbed the oil during the first 5 to 6 minutes of cooking, add another tablespoon of oil to the skillet when you flip them.

MISO CHICKEN THIGHS

SERVES 2

Prep time: 5 minutes | **Cook time:** 45 minutes | **Cast iron:** 12-inch skillet

There are more than one thousand types of miso, but, generally, they can be divided into two categories: light and dark. Dark miso has a stronger flavor and is ideal for rich dishes like stews. Light miso has a lighter flavor and works well for dressings and soups. The chicken thighs in this dish can carry the flavor of dark miso without being overwhelmed.

2 tablespoons dark or
  red miso
2 tablespoons unsalted
  butter, at room
  temperature
1 tablespoon sesame oil
1 tablespoon peeled, minced
  fresh ginger
1 tablespoon minced garlic
½ teaspoon sea salt
4 boneless, skin-on
  chicken thighs

1. Preheat the oven to 400°F.

2. In a small bowl, stir together the miso, butter, oil, ginger, garlic, and salt.

3. Rub the miso and butter paste evenly over the chicken thighs, working to get it under the skin whenever possible. Arrange the thighs in the skillet, skin-side down.

4. Roast for 40 to 45 minutes, or until the chicken skin is browned and the thickest part of the thigh reaches 165°F. Let it rest for 10 minutes before serving.

TIP: For a stronger flavor, marinate the chicken in the miso and butter mixture overnight before cooking.

FRENCH ONION CHICKEN

GLUTEN-FREE, OVEN-COOKED, WEEKDAY
SERVES 2

Prep time: 15 minutes | **Cook time:** 45 minutes | **Cast iron:** 12-inch skillet

This recipe was inspired by a pregnancy craving that sprung up after watching a friend make French onion soup over a video chat. While it was definitely too hot for soup in southeastern North Carolina, I *needed* it. This variation, with the chicken cooked in an onion broth with Gruyère and parsley, hits all the flavor notes while being a totally reasonable option for hot summer days.

1 tablespoon olive oil

2 boneless, skinless chicken breasts

1 tablespoon salted butter

2 large white onions, cut into slivers

½ cup dry white wine

1½ cups chicken broth

1 tablespoon cornstarch

4 garlic cloves, minced

1 tablespoon fresh thyme leaves

1 tablespoon fresh oregano leaves

1 teaspoon sea salt

½ teaspoon freshly ground black pepper

1 cup shredded Gruyère cheese, divided

1. Preheat the oven to 400°F.

2. Heat the oil in the skillet over medium heat. Add the chicken and cook for 5 minutes per side, or until browned. Remove the chicken from the skillet and set it aside.

3. Place the butter and onions into the skillet and cook for 5 to 6 minutes, stirring frequently, or until the onions are browned

4. Pour in the wine and cook for 1 to 2 minutes, stirring.

5. Whisk in the broth and cornstarch until smooth. Add the garlic, thyme, oregano, salt, and pepper.

6. Return the chicken to the skillet, turning it once to coat in the sauce. Top each chicken breast with ¼ cup of Gruyère cheese and ¼ cup of Parmesan cheese.

7. Bake for 15 to 20 minutes, or until the chicken's internal temperature reaches 165°F.

½ cup grated Parmesan
   cheese

Handful fresh parsley
   leaves, minced

1 lemon, cut into wedges

8. Using oven mitts, remove the skillet from the oven and set the broiler to high. Top each piece of chicken with ¼ cup of the remaining Gruyère. Broil for 2 to 3 minutes, or until browned and bubbling.

9. Top with fresh parsley and lemon juice and serve.

TIP: Serve on a bed of jasmine rice, with roasted potatoes, or with Cheese and Bacon Smashed Potatoes (page 67).

OVEN-COOKED

○——————— SERVES 4 TO 6 ———————○

Prep time: 45 minutes | **Cook time:** 1 hour | **Cast iron:** 12-inch skillet

One of my favorite winter comfort foods is chicken potpie, especially topped with flakey biscuits. It says, "You may be stuck inside while it's 40°F and raining outside. Grab a plate, a blanket, and a book. It'll be okay."

For the filling

3 tablespoons salted butter

6 boneless, skinless chicken thighs, roughly chopped

1 teaspoon sea salt

1 teaspoon freshly ground black pepper

1 teaspoon smoked paprika

1 yellow onion, diced

2 garlic cloves, minced

5 medium carrots, diced

1 sweet potato, peeled and cubed

2 cups milk

1 cup heavy (whipping) cream

10 to 12 cremini mushrooms, sliced

2 cups peas

For the biscuits

2 cups all-purpose flour, plus more for working the dough

1 teaspoon baking powder

1. **To make the filling:** In the skillet over medium heat, melt the butter. Place the chicken into the skillet and cook for 3 to 4 minutes per side, or until browned. Add the salt, pepper, paprika, onion, and garlic. Cook for 2 to 3 minutes, stirring occasionally.

2. Stir in the carrots and sweet potato, fully coating them in the butter. Cook for 3 to 4 minutes.

3. Stir in the milk, cream, mushrooms, and peas. Reduce the heat to low. Let simmer for 15 minutes, stirring occasionally.

4. **To make the biscuits:** Preheat the oven to 350°F.

5. In a large bowl, combine the flour, baking powder, baking soda, and salt. Use a fork or your clean hands to work the butter into the flour mixture until the texture resembles coarse cornmeal. Stir in the buttermilk until a rough dough forms.

6. Flour a work surface and turn the dough out onto it. Pat the dough into a large rectangle. Fold the dough in half, turn it, and pat it again into a large rectangle. Repeat this process 3 or 4 times, folding and rotating the dough each time. Add flour as you work to keep the dough from sticking.

1 teaspoon baking soda

Pinch salt

8 tablespoons (1 stick) cold salted butter, cubed

1 cup buttermilk

7. Using a 3-inch cookie cutter, cut 12 biscuits, reshaping the scraps to make more biscuits.

8. **To assemble the potpie:** Remove the skillet from the heat and stir, making sure the chicken and vegetables are in an even layer in the skillet. Top with the biscuits, evenly spacing them and nestling them into the sauce.

9. Bake for 30 to 35 minutes, until the biscuits are fluffy and golden brown.

TIP: For a rolled-top variation, rather than islands of biscuits, roll the biscuit dough into a 13-inch round, place it on top of the chicken and vegetables, pressing the dough into the sides of the skillet. Cut slits in the top to vent steam.

PICKLE-BRINED FRIED CHICKEN

CLASSIC

SERVES 4 TO 6

Prep time: 20 minutes | **Inactive time:** 12 hours
Cook time: 30 minutes | **Cast iron:** 12-inch skillet

For a period of my childhood, my five siblings and I were deep into daring each other to do horrible and disgusting things, usually at the expense of my youngest brother, Ryan. One day, we dared him to drink all the juice from a gallon jar of dill pickles. Let's say he made a valiant effort, but it ended rather unfortunately for him. Thankfully, there are much better things to do with pickle juice, including using it to brine your fried chicken.

8 to 10 bone-in, skin-on chicken breasts and thighs

1 cup dill pickle brine

3 cups all-purpose flour, divided

1 tablespoon red pepper flakes, divided

1 tablespoon cayenne, divided

1 tablespoon sea salt, divided

1½ teaspoons garlic powder, divided

4 large eggs

1 cup buttermilk

2 cups bread crumbs

¼ cup yellow coarse stone-ground grits

Peanut oil, for frying

1. The night before you plan to serve the chicken, in a zip-top plastic bag or flat storage container, combine the chicken and pickle brine. Seal and refrigerate to marinate overnight.

2. On a work surface (near the stove), line up 3 small bowls. In the first bowl, stir together 1½ cups of flour, 1½ teaspoons of red pepper flakes, 1½ teaspoons of cayenne, 1½ teaspoons of salt, and ¾ teaspoon of garlic powder.

3. In the second bowl, whisk the eggs and buttermilk to blend.

4. In the third bowl (closest to the stove), combine the bread crumbs and grits, along with the remaining 1½ cups of flour, 1½ teaspoons of red pepper flakes, 1½ teaspoons of cayenne, 1½ teaspoons of salt, and ¾ teaspoon of garlic powder.

5. Heat 1 inch of oil to 375°F in the skillet over high heat.

6. Take the chicken out of the marinade and pat it dry. Working one piece at a time, dip the chicken into the flour mixture, into the wet batter, then into the bread crumb mixture.

7. Add the chicken to the hot oil and fry the breasts for 4 to 5 minutes per side and the thighs and legs for 8 to 10 minutes per side, until the internal temperature reaches 165°F and the juices run clear. Transfer the chicken to a wire rack to cool slightly before serving.

TIP: If you don't have pickle juice, marinate the chicken in buttermilk overnight.

WEEKDAY

SERVES 2

Prep time: 10 minutes | **Cook time:** 30 minutes | **Cast iron:** 12-inch skillet

A favorite weekend lunch is the quesadilla because it's easy and quick to put together and I can usually stuff it with odds and ends from the refrigerator. We usually have some leftover cooked chicken, a few bell pepper halves floating around the produce drawer, and we always have cheese and tortillas.

1 tablespoon olive oil

1 boneless, skinless chicken breast, roughly chopped

Pinch sea salt

Pinch paprika

4 flour tortillas

1 cup grated Cheddar cheese

1 bell pepper, any color, seeded and diced

2 tablespoons salted butter

Sour cream, for serving

Salsa, for serving

1. Heat the oil in the skillet over medium heat. Add the chicken, salt, and paprika. Cook for 8 to 10 minutes, stirring frequently, or until the chicken is cooked through and no longer pink. Transfer the chicken to a bowl and wipe out the skillet with a clean towel.

2. On a work surface, lay out 2 tortillas. Divide the Cheddar cheese between them, then the chicken, and finally the bell pepper. Top with the remaining 2 tortillas.

3. In the skillet over medium heat, melt the butter. Use a spatula to spread the butter around. Cook the first quesadilla for 3 to 4 minutes per side. Repeat with the second quesadilla.

4. Transfer the cooked quesadillas to a cutting board to cool slightly before slicing and serving with sour cream and salsa.

TIP: If you have black beans or corn on hand, both are wonderful when added to this quesadilla.

TURKEY AND SAGE MEATBALLS

SERVES 4

Prep time: 15 minutes | **Cook time:** 15 minutes | **Cast iron:** 12-inch skillet

When my son was first starting solids, I loved to make meatballs in bulk and store them for quick meals. We made spicy meatballs, curry meatballs, herby meatballs, and meatballs with beef and turkey. These meatballs, which fall into the "herby" category, remain a family favorite.

1 pound ground turkey

1 large egg

2 garlic cloves, minced

Handful fresh sage leaves, minced

½ teaspoon sea salt

½ teaspoon red pepper flakes

½ cup bread crumbs or panko bread crumbs

¼ cup grated Parmesan cheese

4 tablespoons (½ stick) salted butter, divided

Juice of 1 lemon

1. Preheat the oven to 400°F.

2. In a large bowl, mix the ground turkey, egg, garlic, sage, salt, red pepper flakes, bread crumbs, and Parmesan cheese well, making sure the egg and bread crumbs are evenly distributed.

3. Form the mixture into 10 to 12 meatballs the size of your palm.

4. In the skillet over medium-high heat, melt 1 tablespoon of butter. Brown the meatballs for 2 to 3 minutes per side, then remove from the heat.

5. Add the remaining 3 tablespoons of butter to the skillet and squeeze the lemon juice over the meatballs.

6. Bake for 5 to 7 minutes, until the meatballs reach an internal temperature of 165°F. Turn the meatballs a few times in the butter before serving.

CHICKEN AND GREEN BEAN STIR-FRY

WEEKDAY

○————————— SERVES 2 TO 4 —————————○

Prep time: 10 minutes | **Cook time:** 25 minutes | **Cast iron:** 12-inch skillet

Sesame green beans are one of my favorite foods. Something about crispy crunchy green beans with sesame oil and a splash of soy sauce is just heaven. Served with rice or noodles, it hits the spot.

2 tablespoons sesame oil, divided

2 boneless, skinless chicken breasts, cut into 2-inch strips

1 onion, diced

2 cups fresh green beans, trimmed

3 garlic cloves, minced

1 teaspoon peeled, grated fresh ginger

Stir-fry sauce (see Vegetarian Stir-Fry, page 115)

Rice or noodles, cooked, for serving

Sesame seeds, for garnish

1. Heat 1 tablespoon of oil in the skillet over medium-high heat. Add the chicken and cook for 6 to 8 minutes, stirring frequently, or until browned. Transfer the chicken to a plate.

2. Put the onion in the skillet, along with the remaining 1 tablespoon of oil. Cook for 3 to 4 minutes, or until the onion begins to soften.

3. Add the green beans and cook for 3 to 4 minutes, stirring frequently, or until the green beans begin to brown. Add the garlic and ginger and cook for 1 to 2 minutes.

4. Return the chicken to the skillet, pour in the stir-fry sauce, and stir so everything is coated thoroughly. Cook for 2 to 3 minutes, or until the chicken is cooked through and the sauce thickens.

5. Serve over rice and garnish with sesame seeds.

TIP: Frozen whole green beans or frozen haricots verts also work great in this recipe.

BUTTERMILK ROAST CHICKEN

CLASSIC, GLUTEN-FREE, OVEN-COOKED

SERVES 4 TO 6

Prep time: 15 minutes | **Inactive time:** 12 hours
Cook time: 1 hour | **Cast iron:** 12-inch skillet

Buttermilk is an ideal marinade for chicken because it makes it tender, moist, and flavorful. Although I generally choose buttermilk as a marinade for my fried chicken to keep it from drying out, I also love it as a marinade for roast chicken. This marinade is also garlicky and herby, which results in fall-off-the-bone chicken that has a rich flavor.

1 whole chicken

2 cups buttermilk

4 garlic cloves, smashed

1 tablespoon fresh thyme leaves

1 tablespoon fresh oregano leaves

1 tablespoon fresh rosemary leaves, plus 1 tablespoon, minced

2 teaspoons sea salt, divided

2 tablespoons olive oil, divided

4 tablespoons (½ stick) salted butter, at room temperature

1 tablespoon dried oregano

1. The night before you plan to serve the chicken, remove the innards and rinse the chicken thoroughly. Place the chicken in a gallon-size zip-top plastic bag or a large bowl and add the buttermilk, garlic, thyme, oregano, 1 tablespoon of rosemary leaves, and 1 teaspoon of salt. Turn the chicken to coat, settling it so the breasts are sitting in the marinade. Refrigerate overnight.

2. Preheat the oven to 475°F.

3. Remove the chicken from the marinade and pat it dry. Using kitchen twine, tie the legs together to promote even roasting.

4. Coat the skillet with 1 tablespoon of oil. Place the chicken into the skillet and drizzle with the remaining 1 tablespoon of oil. Sprinkle with the dried oregano, 1 tablespoon of minced rosemary, and the remaining 1 teaspoon of salt.

CONTINUED

5. Roast for 20 minutes. Reduce the oven temperature to 400°F and cook for 40 minutes more, until the internal temperature reaches 165°F and the juices run clear. Let the chicken rest for 10 minutes before serving.

TIP: If you're cooking for one or two, a whole chicken might not be practical. A nice alternative is a bone-in breast, which can be roasted in 40 minutes.

JERK CHICKEN NAKED WINGS

GLUTEN-FREE, OVEN-COOKED

SERVES 2 TO 4

Prep time: 20 minutes | **Inactive time:** 12 hours
Cook time: 50 minutes | **Cast iron:** 12-inch skillet

The jerk spice blend is originally a Jamaican method for preserving meat that could later be smoked. Thanks to modern refrigeration, we've gotten better at preserving meat, but the strong flavor profiles of jerk spices have remained an integral part of Jamaican food culture.

2 pounds chicken wings
  and drumsticks
1 tablespoon garlic powder
1 tablespoon onion powder
2 teaspoons cayenne
2 teaspoons dried thyme
2 teaspoons sea salt
1½ teaspoons red pepper
  flakes
1 teaspoon paprika
1 teaspoon ground allspice
1 teaspoon light brown
  sugar
1 teaspoon dried parsley
½ teaspoon ground nutmeg
½ teaspoon ground
  cinnamon
½ teaspoon ground cloves
½ teaspoon ground cumin
4 tablespoons olive oil,
  divided

1. The night before you plan to cook the chicken, clean it and pat it dry.

2. In a medium bowl, stir together the garlic powder, onion powder, cayenne, thyme, salt, red pepper flakes, paprika, allspice, brown sugar, parsley, nutmeg, cinnamon, cloves, and cumin to make the spice blend.

3. Place the chicken in a large shallow bowl and rub it with 2 tablespoons of oil. Sprinkle with the spice blend, adding a few tablespoons at a time and working to coat the chicken thoroughly. (You'll likely have more spice blend than you need. Leftovers can be saved in a sealed jar for another use.) Cover the chicken and refrigerate it overnight.

4. Preheat the oven to 400°F.

5. Heat the remaining 2 tablespoons of oil in the skillet over medium-high heat. Add the chicken and cook for 2 to 3 minutes per side, or until browned, then transfer the skillet to the oven.

6. Bake for 35 to 40 minutes, or until the wings are browned and crisp, and the meat, at its thickest part, reaches 165°F.

ROASTED TURKEY BREAST

CLASSIC, GLUTEN-FREE, OVEN-COOKED

○——————— SERVES 2 TO 4 ———————○

Prep time: 15 minutes | **Cook time:** 1 hour 30 minutes | **Cast iron:** 12-inch skillet

At least once a year, usually between November 20 and December 30, I declare that under absolutely no circumstances will we be traveling *at all* for the holidays the following year. I fantasize about the low key Thanksgiving of my dreams at home, featuring a roasted turkey breast, Cheese and Bacon Smashed Potatoes (page 67), homemade cranberry sauce, Garlic Butter Green Beans (page 73), and maybe a Shoofly Pie (page 206).

1 whole bone-in turkey breast

8 tablespoons (1 stick) butter, at room temperature

4 garlic cloves, minced

2 teaspoons sea salt

1 teaspoon chipotle powder

2 large onions, cut into rings

½ cup white wine

½ cup chicken broth

Juice of 2 lemons

1. Clean the turkey breast and pat it dry. Let it come to room temperature, approximately 30 minutes. Do not let it sit out for more than 2 hours.

2. Preheat the oven to 325°F.

3. In a small bowl, stir together the butter, garlic, salt, and chipotle powder. Spread the butter mixture over the turkey, really working it into and under the skin wherever possible.

4. Arrange the onions on the bottom of the skillet. Pour in the white wine and broth. Place the turkey on top of the onions.

5. Roast for 1 hour 15 minutes to 1 hour 30 minutes, or until the skin is browned and crisp, the turkey's internal temperature reaches 165°F, and the juices run clear. Let it rest for 10 minutes before carving and serving.

TIP: If you notice your turkey browning too quickly, loosely cover it with aluminum foil.

CHICKEN MARSALA

WEEKDAY
SERVES 4

Prep time: 20 minutes | Cook time: 35 minutes | Cast iron: 12-inch skillet

When I was in college, my grandparents would frequently drive to Baltimore to take me out to dinner. It was during these visits that I had my first Chicken Marsala and fell in love. This dish always reminds me of those special nights with my grandparents, feeling like such a real adult, delighting in food and company.

1½ cups chicken broth

1½ cups Marsala wine

4 boneless, skinless chicken breasts, butterflied

2 tablespoons olive oil, plus more as needed

½ cup all-purpose flour

1½ teaspoons sea salt, divided

3 tablespoons salted butter

2 cups sliced cremini mushrooms

3 garlic cloves, minced

¼ teaspoon freshly ground black pepper

1 teaspoon fresh thyme leaves, minced

1 teaspoon fresh oregano leaves, minced

¼ cup heavy (whipping) cream

1. In a medium saucepan over high heat, combine the broth and Marsala wine. Bring to a light boil, then reduce the heat to low and let simmer for 7 minutes.

2. On a cutting board and using a meat tenderizer, flatten the chicken to an even thickness.

3. Heat the oil in the skillet over medium-high heat.

4. In a shallow bowl, stir together the flour and ½ teaspoon of salt. Dredge both sides of the chicken in the flour. Place the chicken into the skillet and cook for 5 to 6 minutes, flip, and cook for 5 to 6 minutes more, adding more oil as needed. Set the chicken aside to cool.

5. In the skillet over medium heat, melt the butter. Add the mushrooms and cook for 5 to 6 minutes, stirring frequently, or until they are soft and begin to brown. Add the garlic and cook for 1 to 2 minutes, until fragrant.

CONTINUED

Cooked angel hair pasta,
for serving

Minced fresh parsley leaves,
for garnish

Lemon wedges, for garnish

6. Pour in the warm wine and broth mixture and stir in the pepper, thyme, oregano, and the remaining 1 teaspoon of salt. Cook for 2 to 3 minutes.

7. Stir in the cream and add the chicken to the skillet, flipping it once to coat. Simmer for 4 to 5 minutes, or until the sauce thickens.

8. Serve on a bed of angel hair pasta garnished with fresh parsley and a lemon wedge for squeezing.

TIP: This chicken Marsala also works well over rice or served with a side salad.

BLACKENED CHICKEN THIGHS WITH PINEAPPLE SALSA

GLUTEN-FREE, OVEN-COOKED

◦─────── SERVES 4 ───────◦

Prep time: 20 minutes | **Cook time:** 45 minutes | **Cast iron:** 12-inch skillet

For most people, pineapples bring Hawai'i to mind, but pineapples are not native to Hawai'i and weren't brought there until the 1800s. Pineapples are actually native to Brazil and Paraguay, and they are beloved in cuisines from South America, Central America, Mexico, and the Caribbean. This savory pineapple salsa beautifully balances the spicy blackened chicken—a combination of fresh, charred, hot, and sweet.

For the salsa

1 pineapple, peeled, cored, and diced

1 cup cherry tomatoes, quartered

1 green bell pepper, diced

1 jalapeño pepper, seeded and minced

½ red onion, diced

Juice of 2 limes

1 tablespoon white wine vinegar

Handful fresh cilantro, minced

Sea salt

Freshly ground black pepper

1. **To make the salsa:** In a large bowl, stir together the pineapple, tomatoes, bell pepper, jalapeño, onion, lime juice, vinegar, cilantro, and salt and pepper to taste. Set aside in the refrigerator.

2. **To make the chicken:** Preheat the oven to 450°F. Place the skillet into the oven to preheat.

3. Rinse the chicken and pat it dry.

4. In a small bowl, stir together the paprika, coriander, thyme, turmeric, cayenne, salt, and garlic. Rub the spice blend evenly over the chicken thighs, working to get it under the skin wherever possible.

5. Reduce the oven temperature to 400°F.

6. Using oven mitts, remove the skillet from the oven, place it over medium-high heat, and pour in the oil. Add the chicken and sear on both sides for 3 to 4 minutes. Transfer the skillet to the oven.

CONTINUED

For the chicken

8 boneless, skin-on
  chicken thighs

1 teaspoon smoked paprika

1 teaspoon
  ground coriander

1 teaspoon ground thyme

1 teaspoon ground turmeric

½ teaspoon cayenne

½ teaspoon sea salt

3 garlic cloves, minced

1 tablespoon sunflower oil

Cooked rice, for serving

7. Bake the chicken for 30 to 35 minutes, or until the chicken's internal temperature reaches 165°F. Let the chicken rest for 10 minutes.

8. Serve nestled in a bed of rice and topped with pineapple salsa.

TIP: If you can't find fresh pineapple, frozen and thawed is preferable to canned for this recipe.

CHICKEN BIRYANI

GLUTEN-FREE

SERVES 4

Prep time: 30 minutes | **Inactive time:** 12 hours
Cook time: 35 minutes | **Cast iron:** 12-inch skillet with lid

Chicken biryani is a rice and curry dish that originated in the Muslim community of India and is popular around the world. The foundation of the dish is meat marinated in yogurt and spices, then cooked in a tomato-based curry. This dish is an impressive centerpiece when spooned onto a serving platter.

For the marinade

½ cup full-fat Greek yogurt

3 garlic cloves, minced

1 jalapeño pepper, seeded
   and minced

1 tablespoon peeled, minced
   fresh ginger

1 teaspoon paprika

1 teaspoon garam masala

½ teaspoon ground turmeric

½ teaspoon sea salt

6 boneless, skinless chicken
   breasts

For the biryani

4 cups water

Sea salt

2 cups basmati rice, rinsed
   at least 3 times and
   drained

¼ cup ghee

½ teaspoon ground cumin

1. **To make the marinade:** The night before you plan to serve the biryani, in a large bowl, stir together the yogurt, garlic, jalapeño, ginger, paprika, garam masala, turmeric, and salt.

2. Clean the chicken and pat it dry. Coat the chicken evenly in the marinade, and then settle it in the bowl. Cover the bowl and refrigerate overnight.

3. **To make the biryani:** In a medium saucepan, bring the water and a pinch of salt to a boil. Add the rice and cook for 8 to 10 minutes, stirring occasionally. Remove from heat and drain.

4. In the skillet over medium heat, melt the ghee. Add the ground cumin, cumin seeds, cardamom, cloves, coriander, garlic, ginger, and onion to the skillet. Cook for 4 to 5 minutes, stirring frequently, or until the onion browns.

5. Stir in the tomato paste. Add the crushed tomatoes and stir to combine.

CONTINUED

½ teaspoon cumin seeds

4 green cardamom pods

1 teaspoon ground cloves

1 teaspoon ground
coriander

2 garlic cloves, minced

1 teaspoon peeled, minced
fresh ginger

1 large yellow onion, thinly
sliced

3 tablespoons tomato paste

1 (14-ounce) can crushed
tomatoes

1 cup milk

½ teaspoon saffron threads

2 tablespoons chopped
fresh mint leaves,
divided

2 tablespoons chopped
fresh cilantro, divided

6. Remove the chicken from the marinade and put it into the skillet, turning once to coat. Cook for 3 to 4 minutes, flip the chicken, and cook for 3 to 4 minutes more. Remove the skillet from the heat.

7. In a small saucepan over medium-high heat, scald the milk by bringing it almost to a boil, then add the saffron.

8. Spread half the parboiled rice over the chicken. Sprinkle 1 tablespoon of mint and 1 tablespoon of cilantro over it. Drizzle half of the saffron milk over the rice.

9. Top with the remaining rice and finish with the remaining 1 tablespoon of mint, 1 tablespoon of cilantro, and the rest of the saffron milk.

10. Tightly cover the skillet and return it to the stovetop over medium-low heat. Cook for 10 minutes, remove from the heat, and let the biryani rest for 10 minutes. Transfer to a plate to serve.

TIP: If saffron is hard to find, skip the saffron milk step, omitting the milk entirely.

BLACKENED MAHI-MAHI TACOS WITH MANGO SALSA, PAGE 165

Chapter Eight

SEAFOOD

JALAPEÑO AND SHALLOT CRAB CAKES

WEEKDAY

○———————— SERVES 4 ————————○

Prep time: 15 minutes | **Cook time:** 10 minutes | **Cast iron:** 12-inch skillet

I spent eight great years as a Marylander, and while I was there, I picked up a few tricks. Besides my ability to pull a swift Baltimore-style U-turn in the middle of the street, I also learned how to properly steam and pick crabs, and, after you've eaten all the crabs you can possibly eat, how to pick them for crab cakes.

1 pound lump blue crabmeat

½ cup bread crumbs

1 large egg, lightly beaten

Juice of 1 lemon, divided

Zest of 1 lemon, grated

1 jalapeño pepper, seeded and minced

1 shallot, finely chopped

Pinch sea salt

Freshly ground black pepper

4 tablespoons (½ stick) salted butter

1. In a large bowl, stir together the crabmeat, bread crumbs, egg, half the lemon juice, lemon zest, jalapeño, shallot, salt, and black pepper. Form 4 patties of equal size.

2. In the skillet over medium-high heat, melt the butter.

3. Place the crab cakes into the skillet and sear for 4 minutes per side, until they are crisp, browned, and hold their shape.

4. Top with the remaining lemon juice and serve.

SEARED LOBSTER TAILS

GLUTEN-FREE, WEEKDAY

SERVES 2

Prep time: 15 minutes | **Cook time:** 10 minutes | **Cast iron:** 12-inch skillet with lid

One of my forever favorite shows is *Gilmore Girls*, and it's a little embarrassing how many moments in life I immediately connect to a plot line. For instance, when I think of lobster, I think of the Gilmores' trip to Martha's Vineyard when Luke Danes declares that lobster is *delicious*. This lobster is easy to make and will make you feel as smug as Logan when you serve it to your grateful guests.

2 lobster tails, cleaned

Pinch sea salt

Pinch freshly ground black pepper

Pinch red pepper flakes

Juice of 1 lemon, divided

2 tablespoons olive oil

2 tablespoons salted butter

2 garlic cloves, minced

2 tablespoons fresh parsley leaves, minced

1. Season the meat side of the lobster with salt, black pepper, and red pepper flakes. Squeeze half of the lemon juice over the lobster.

2. Heat the oil and melt the butter in the skillet over medium-high heat. Add the garlic.

3. Put the lobster in the skillet, meat-side down, and cook for 2 to 3 minutes, or until the meat is crisp and golden brown. Flip the lobster, cover the skillet, and cook for 2 to 3 minutes more, until the lobster meat is opaque and the shells have turned red. Remove the tails from the heat.

4. Top with the remaining half of the lemon juice and the parsley and serve.

BROWN BUTTER AND GARLIC WAHOO

GLUTEN-FREE, WEEKDAY

SERVES 4

Prep time: 5 minutes | **Cook time:** 40 minutes | **Cast iron:** 12-inch skillet

Wahoo is one of our favorite fishes because it's mild in flavor and has a hearty, substantial texture. A wahoo steak makes a filling and delicious dinner, and the brown butter makes it special.

8 tablespoons (1 stick) salted butter

2 garlic cloves, minced

1 lemon, sliced

4 wahoo steaks

Pinch sea salt

1. In the skillet over medium-low heat, melt the butter.

2. Add the garlic and 3 or 4 lemon slices, and let the butter come to a simmer. Cook for 30 minutes, stirring occasionally, until the butter is golden brown.

3. Season the wahoo steaks with salt. Increase the heat under the skillet to medium-high. Sear the wahoo for 3 to 4 minutes per side.

4. Top with a squeeze of fresh lemon and serve with lemon slices on the side.

TIP: If wahoo is not available, king mackerel has a similar texture and flavor.

SHRIMP AND GRITS

CLASSIC, GLUTEN-FREE

SERVES 4

Prep time: 20 minutes | **Cook time:** 50 minutes | **Cast iron:** 12-inch skillet

Living in the coastal South, shrimp and grits is a staple. It's one of my favorite foods, and, honestly, the combination of creamy cheesy grits and salty fresh shrimp is "close your eyes and moan" good.

For the grits

4 cups water

2 cups yellow stone-ground grits

3 cups whole milk

2 teaspoons sea salt

1 teaspoon ground white pepper

1 teaspoon freshly ground black pepper

2 tablespoons salted butter

½ cup grated Parmesan cheese

Juice of 1 lemon

For the shrimp

8 ounces thick-cut bacon, roughly chopped

4 tablespoons (½ stick) salted butter

1 yellow onion, chopped

3 garlic cloves, minced

1 teaspoon red pepper flakes

1. **To make the grits:** In a medium pot over high heat, combine the water and grits. Bring to a boil, then reduce the heat to low.

2. Stir in the milk, salt, white pepper, black pepper, and butter. Simmer for 40 to 45 minutes, stirring frequently, as the grits thicken.

3. When the grits have absorbed the liquid (but still stir easily), stir in the Parmesan cheese and lemon juice. Remove from the heat.

4. **To make the shrimp:** About 20 minutes before the grits are ready, put the bacon into the skillet, place it over medium heat, and cook for 8 to 10 minutes, stirring occasionally, or until it begins to brown and crisp.

5. Add the butter, onion, garlic, red pepper flakes, and salt. Cook for 5 to 7 minutes, stirring frequently, until the onion begins to brown and soften.

CONTINUED

Pinch sea salt

1 pound shrimp, peeled and deveined

Juice of 1 lemon

¼ cup roughly chopped scallion

6. Add the shrimp to the skillet. Cook for 4 to 5 minutes, stirring frequently, until the shrimp turn pink. Sprinkle with lemon juice.

7. Fill each bowl with a heaping serving of grits, then top with a generous portion of shrimp and bacon, making sure to get some of the pan juices, and finish with scallion.

BLACKENED MAHI-MAHI TACOS WITH MANGO SALSA

WEEKDAY
SERVES 4

Prep time: 30 minutes | **Cook time:** 10 minutes | **Cast iron:** 12-inch skillet

Mahi-mahi is a mild, tender fish that holds up well to high heat and spice. This mango salsa is bright, sweet, and tangy, and the colors of the mango and cilantro echo the colors of the mahi-mahi dancing in the waves.

For the salsa

3 mangos, peeled and diced

1 cup cherry tomatoes, quartered

1 green bell pepper, diced

1 jalapeño pepper, seeded and minced

½ red onion, diced

Juice of 2 limes

1 tablespoon white wine vinegar

Handful fresh cilantro, minced

Sea salt

Freshly ground black pepper

1. **To make the salsa:** Begin by making the salsa so it has time for the flavors to blend. In a large bowl, stir together the mangos, tomatoes, bell pepper, jalapeño, onion, lime juice, vinegar, cilantro, and salt and pepper to taste. Set aside in the refrigerator.

2. **To make the tacos:** In a small bowl, stir together the oregano, black pepper, salt, paprika, cayenne, red pepper flakes, and cumin. Set aside.

3. Heat the skillet over medium-high heat.

CONTINUED

For the tacos

1 teaspoon dried oregano

1 teaspoon freshly ground
   black pepper

1 teaspoon sea salt

1 teaspoon smoked paprika

½ teaspoon cayenne

¼ teaspoon red pepper
   flakes

¼ teaspoon ground cumin

4 mahi steaks

4 tablespoons (½ stick)
   salted butter, melted

8 flour tortillas or 12 corn
   tortillas

1 cup shredded cabbage

2 limes, cut into wedges

Sour cream, for serving
   (optional)

4. Brush both sides of each fish fillet with melted butter and carefully coat both sides with the spice mixture.

5. Place the fillets in the hot skillet and cook for 2 to 3 minutes per side, until blackened and cooked through. Let the mahi rest for 2 to 3 minutes, then slice or roughly chop.

6. Layer each tortilla with mahi, cabbage, and salsa. Serve with a lime wedge and sour cream (if using).

BUTTERMILK GROUPER BITES

CLASSIC

⟡———— SERVES 2 TO 4 ————⟡

Prep time: 30 minutes | **Inactive time:** 12 hours
Cook time: 10 minutes | **Cast iron:** 12-inch skillet

After I was diagnosed with celiac disease, my family gradually made the adjustment to foods that were safe for me to eat. Once, a few years ago, my dad made a big deal about making gluten-free grouper bites (see tip) with fresh grouper he'd caught. Then, just before the grouper went into the oil, he poured a little bit of his wheat beer into the oil to see if it was ready. Thankfully, Dan caught it and I was fine, but my dad felt awful. He made it up to me with more grouper bites down the road, but I'll always think of that moment whenever we fry up a batch.

2 grouper filets, cut into bite-size pieces

1 cup buttermilk

1 tablespoon fresh oregano leaves

1 tablespoon fresh thyme leaves

1 cup mayonnaise

1 tablespoon pickle relish

1 tablespoon minced shallot

Juice of 1 lemon

1 teaspoon sea salt, plus more for seasoning

1 teaspoon freshly ground black pepper, plus more for seasoning

1 cup bread crumbs

1 cup all-purpose flour

1. The night before you plan to serve the grouper bites, in a large bowl, combine the grouper, buttermilk, oregano, and thyme. Make sure the fish is submerged, cover the bowl, and chill in the refrigerator overnight.

2. To make the tartar sauce, in a small bowl, stir together the mayonnaise, relish, shallot, and lemon juice. Season with a pinch of salt and black pepper. Cover and refrigerate.

3. When you're ready to make the grouper bites, on a work surface, lay out 2 small bowls. In the first bowl, stir together the bread crumbs, flour, cayenne, 1 teaspoon of salt, garlic powder, and 1 teaspoon of black pepper.

4. In a second bowl, whisk the eggs and hot sauce to blend.

CONTINUED

Seafood   **167**

1 teaspoon cayenne

1 teaspoon garlic powder

2 large eggs

1 tablespoon hot sauce

Peanut oil, for frying

5. Drain the buttermilk from the grouper and discard the marinade. Pat the grouper dry.

6. Heat 1 inch of oil to 375°F in the skillet over high heat.

7. Dredge the grouper bites in the egg, then fully coat them with the bread crumbs.

8. Fry the bites for 2 to 3 minutes per side, or until golden brown. Transfer to a wire rack to drain. Serve the grouper bites with a side of tartar sauce.

TIP: Make these gluten-free by swapping out the bread crumbs and flour with gluten-free products. Just don't pour beer into the oil!

SHRIMP BURGERS WITH CHIPOTLE MAYONNAISE

Prep time: 20 minutes | **Inactive time:** 25 minutes
Cook time: 10 minutes | **Cast iron:** 12-inch skillet

Something about eating a shrimp burger always makes me feel like I'm out for a vacation dinner in a beach town after a long day on the ocean. These days, I live in a beach town, and the shrimp burgers I eat are all at my house, but they still taste terrific after a long day at the beach.

1 pound shrimp, peeled
  and deveined

¼ cup bread crumbs

1 large egg, beaten

2 shallots, minced

2 garlic cloves, minced

¼ cup fresh cilantro,
  roughly chopped

Juice of 1½ lemons, divided

Sea salt

¼ cup mayonnaise

1 teaspoon chipotle powder

2 tablespoons olive oil

4 hamburger buns, toasted

Lettuce, for topping

1. Divide the shrimp into thirds. Finely mince one third, dice one third, and roughly chop one third. Put all the shrimp into a large bowl.

2. Stir in the bread crumbs, egg, shallots, garlic, cilantro, juice of 1 lemon, and a pinch of salt. Divide and form the shrimp mixture into 4 patties. Gently place the patties on a plate and chill for 25 minutes.

3. In a small bowl, stir together the mayonnaise, remaining juice of ½ lemon, the chipotle powder, and a pinch of salt. Set aside.

4. Heat the oil in the skillet over medium-high heat. Place the patties into the skillet and cook for 4 to 5 minutes, or until browned. Flip and cook for 3 to 4 minutes more.

5. Spread the chipotle mayonnaise evenly on the cut side of each bun. Top each bottom bun with a shrimp burger and lettuce, then serve.

TIP: Shrimp burgers freeze well. Lay them flat on a baking sheet in the freezer after step 2. Once frozen solid, store in a freezer-safe container for up to 1 year.

BACON-WRAPPED SCALLOPS

GLUTEN-FREE, OVEN-COOKED, WEEKDAY

SERVES 4

Prep time: 10 minutes | **Cook time:** 20 minutes | **Cast iron:** 12-inch skillet

Scallops are a wonderfully decadent food, especially when cooked well. Wrapping them with bacon and cooking them in butter only adds to the experience, resulting in a dish that is rich and succulent. These scallops are lovely served on their own, but they also work well with fresh and buttery pasta and a glass of white wine.

12 large sea scallops

6 thin-cut bacon strips, halved lengthwise

Pinch sea salt

1 tablespoon olive oil

2 tablespoons salted butter, divided

2 garlic cloves, minced

Juice of 1 lemon

1. Preheat the oven to 425°F. Place the skillet into the oven to preheat.

2. Pat the scallops dry. Wrap a halved bacon strip around each scallop, securing it with a toothpick. Season the scallops with salt.

3. Using oven mitts, remove the skillet from the oven and put the oil and 1 tablespoon of butter into the skillet. Stir or swirl the skillet to combine.

4. Place the wrapped scallops into the skillet and return it to the oven. Bake for 15 to 17 minutes.

5. Using oven mitts, remove the skillet from the oven and add the remaining 1 tablespoon of butter and the garlic and flip the scallops. Let them cook in the hot skillet for 2 to 3 minutes. Top with lemon juice and serve hot.

TIP: A sprinkle of minced fresh basil on top of these scallops is delicious.

SEARED AHI TUNA

WEEKDAY
———○——————— SERVES 2 ———————○—

Prep time: 10 minutes | **Cook time:** 5 minutes | **Cast iron:** 12-inch skillet

When we first moved to coastal North Carolina after years of living in Baltimore and Washington, DC, we were shocked to find seafood so affordable in our little town! On our first trip to the fish market, we brought home a haul, including two tuna steaks fresh from the Gulf Stream for less than what one tuna steak would have cost us in a restaurant. Years later, I love bringing visiting friends from big cities to the fish market and encouraging them to go wild.

Juice of 1 lime

2 tablespoons soy sauce

1 tablespoon sesame oil, plus 1 teaspoon

1 teaspoon honey

2 tablespoons minced garlic

1 tablespoon peeled, grated fresh ginger

1 tablespoon minced scallion

2 tuna steaks

1 tablespoon white sesame seeds

1 tablespoon black sesame seeds

Pinch sea salt

1 teaspoon vegetable oil

1. In a small bowl, whisk the lime juice, soy sauce, 1 tablespoon of sesame oil, honey, garlic, ginger, and scallion to combine. Set the sauce aside.

2. Pat the tuna dry and sprinkle both sides with white and black sesame seeds and salt.

3. Heat the vegetable oil and the remaining 1 teaspoon of sesame oil in the skillet over high heat. Sear the tuna for 1 to 2 minutes per side for rare and 2 to 3 minutes per side for medium. Remove the tuna from the heat and let it rest on a cutting board for 5 minutes.

4. Slice the tuna, put it on plates, and drizzle sauce over the top.

TIP: When serving tuna rare, it's important to buy sushi- or sashimi-grade tuna.

LOBSTER MAC AND CHEESE

OVEN-COOKED

○———— SERVES 6 ————○

Prep time: 15 minutes | Cook time: 55 minutes | Cast iron: 12-inch skillet

This recipe features *not only* the most luxurious crustacean in the sea but also heavy cream, four cheeses, and a healthy serving of butter. It's mac and cheese at its finest.

1 pound dried cavatappi pasta or elbow macaroni

6 ounces fresh mozzarella cheese, cubed

1 tablespoon olive oil

1 cup heavy (whipping) cream

1 cup whole milk

2 garlic cloves, minced

4 tablespoons (½ stick) salted butter

2 tablespoons all-purpose flour

1 cup shredded Gruyère cheese

1 cup shredded white Cheddar cheese

4 ounces cream cheese, cubed

Juice of 1 lemon

1 teaspoon Old Bay seasoning

Sea salt

2 cups cooked lobster meat, diced

1. Preheat the oven to 350°F.

2. Bring a large pot of salted water to a boil. Cook the pasta according to the package directions. Drain the pasta and return it to the pot. Add the mozzarella and oil and stir well.

3. In a small saucepan over medium-high heat, scald the cream, milk, and garlic by bringing it almost to a boil. Remove from the heat.

4. In the skillet over medium heat, melt the butter. Slowly whisk in the flour. Cook for 1 to 2 minutes, whisking, until the roux begins to thicken. Gradually pour the milk mixture into the roux and whisk vigorously to prevent clumping.

5. Add the Gruyère, Cheddar, and cream cheeses to the sauce, whisking constantly until the cheeses melt. Remove the skillet from the heat and whisk in the lemon juice, Old Bay, and salt to taste.

6. Stir the pasta into the cheese sauce, mixing well to coat the noodles.

7. Add the lobster, stirring to evenly distribute the meat throughout the noodles.

8. Bake for 35 to 40 minutes, or until browned and bubbling.

SALMON CAKES

OVEN-COOKED

○———————— SERVES 4 TO 6 ————————○

Prep time: 20 minutes | **Inactive time:** 40 minutes
Cook time: 25 minutes | **Cast iron:** 12-inch skillet

Salmon cakes are a versatile way to incorporate more salmon into your weekly rotation. We love them as burgers, topping a salad, or shaped into mini patties and served as part of an appetizer spread.

1 pound fresh salmon fillets

3 tablespoons olive oil, divided

2 garlic cloves, minced

2 shallots, minced

1 large egg, beaten

¾ cup bread crumbs

Juice of 2 lemons, divided

3 tablespoons fresh dill, chopped, divided

½ cup mayonnaise

Pinch red pepper flakes

Sea salt

1 cup full-fat plain Greek yogurt

1. Preheat the oven to 350°F.

2. Place the salmon into the skillet, skin-side down, and drizzle with 1 tablespoon of oil.

3. Bake for 15 minutes, or until the salmon begins to brown. Using oven mitts, remove from the oven. Remove the salmon and let cool to room temperature for about 30 minutes. Wipe out the skillet, making sure there are no pieces of skin stuck to the surface.

4. Flake off the salmon from the skin and transfer the flesh to a medium bowl. Add the garlic, shallots, egg, bread crumbs, juice of 1 lemon, 1 tablespoon of dill, mayonnaise, red pepper flakes, and a pinch of salt. Mix until well combined. Form the mixture into 6 patties the size of your palm. Place them on a plate and chill in the refrigerator for 10 minutes.

5. In a small bowl, whisk the yogurt, the remaining 2 tablespoons of dill and juice of 1 lemon, and a pinch of salt. Chill the dill sauce in the refrigerator.

6. Heat the remaining 2 tablespoons of oil in the skillet over medium-high heat. Cook the patties for 3 to 4 minutes per side, until firm, crisp, and browned. Serve with dill sauce for dipping.

SHRIMP AND SCALLOP SCAMPI

WEEKDAY

SERVES 4

Prep time: 10 minutes | **Cook time:** 15 minutes | **Cast iron:** 12-inch skillet

Living at the beach, we frequently have out of town guests who hope to eat as much seafood as possible. Scampi is one of my favorite dishes to serve on these occasions because it's simple and delicious and really lets the seafood shine.

1 pound angel hair pasta

6 tablespoons salted butter, divided

1 pound shrimp, peeled and deveined

3 garlic cloves, minced, divided

Pinch sea salt

8 to 12 fresh sea scallops

½ cup dry white wine

Juice of 1 lemon

Handful fresh basil leaves

1. Bring a large pot of salted water to a boil. Cook the angel hair pasta according to the package directions.

2. Meanwhile, in the skillet over medium heat, melt 2 tablespoons of butter. Put the shrimp, half of the garlic, and salt into the skillet. Cook the shrimp for 4 to 5 minutes, stirring occasionally, until the shrimp are pink. Remove from the skillet and set aside.

3. Add 2 tablespoons of butter to the skillet to melt. Put the scallops and the remaining garlic into the skillet. Sprinkle the scallops with salt and cook for 2 minutes. Flip and cook for 1 minute.

4. Return the shrimp to the skillet and pour in the wine and lemon juice. Cook for 2 minutes, stir in the basil, then remove from the heat.

5. Drain the pasta, return it to the pot, and toss it with the remaining 2 tablespoons of butter. Stir in the shrimp, scallops, and garlic butter from the skillet. Toss well and serve.

SWEET AND SPICY CATFISH

GLUTEN-FREE, WEEKDAY

SERVES 4

Prep time: 10 minutes | **Cook time:** 10 minutes | **Cast iron:** 12-inch skillet

If all that comes to mind when you think of catfish is that episode of *Hillbilly Handfishin'* you caught late at night, I encourage you to delve a little deeper into this wonderful fish. It has a nice texture and mild flavor, and I think it particularly shines when you go with a sweet and spicy flavor blend.

1 tablespoon light brown sugar

1 teaspoon paprika

1 teaspoon dried oregano

1 teaspoon garlic powder

1 teaspoon ground cumin

½ teaspoon onion powder

½ teaspoon sea salt

¼ teaspoon cayenne

4 catfish fillets

1 tablespoon salted butter

1. In a small bowl, stir together the brown sugar, paprika, oregano, garlic powder, cumin, onion powder, salt, and cayenne. Coat the catfish on both sides with the spice mixture.

2. In the skillet over medium-high heat, melt the butter. Cook the catfish for 3 to 4 minutes, flip, and cook for 3 to 4 minutes, or until browned and opaque.

TIP: Catfish is also one of the best fishes to fry. Follow the method for frying fish laid out with Buttermilk Grouper Bites (page 167).

MAPLE-GLAZED SALMON

OVEN-COOKED, WEEKDAY

SERVES 2

Prep time: 10 minutes | **Cook time:** 20 minutes | **Cast iron:** 12-inch skillet

It took me a while to love salmon. The slow process began with my introduction to lox and built as I tried this distinctly flavored fish with different spices and served different ways. A maple glaze, fortified with fresh ginger and lime juice, gives a bright sweetness that complements the flavor of the salmon beautifully.

2 tablespoons soy sauce

1 tablespoon maple syrup

2 garlic cloves, minced

1 tablespoon peeled, minced fresh ginger

Juice of 1 lime

¼ teaspoon paprika

1 tablespoon olive oil

2 (4-ounce) salmon fillets

1. In a small bowl, whisk the soy sauce, maple syrup, garlic, ginger, lime juice, and paprika to combine.

2. Preheat the oven to 375°F.

3. Spread the oil evenly over the bottom of the skillet. Place the salmon into the skillet, skin-side down. Reserve 2 tablespoons of the sauce, then spoon what remains over the salmon.

4. Bake for 15 minutes, or until the salmon begins to brown and the flesh is opaque.

5. Using oven mitts, remove the salmon from the oven. Set the broiler to high.

6. Spoon the reserved sauce over the salmon. Return the salmon to the oven and broil for 2 to 3 minutes, or until a golden crust forms on the salmon. Remove from the oven and serve.

TIP: For a similar style but slightly different flavor, substitute honey for the maple syrup.

SEAFOOD JAMBALAYA

GLUTEN-FREE

SERVES 4

Prep time: 20 minutes | **Inactive time:** 10 minutes
Cook time: 45 minutes | **Cast iron:** 12-inch skillet with lid

Jambalaya is a wonderful base recipe with well-spiced rice, bell peppers, and a light tomato sauce. This seafood version—with sausage, shrimp, and catfish—is full of flavor and one I love to pull out for those special summer occasions when fresh seafood abounds.

1 tablespoon olive oil

1 pound andouille sausage, cut into ½-inch slices

3 celery stalks, roughly chopped

1 green bell pepper, chopped

1 white onion, chopped

2 teaspoons Cajun seasoning

½ teaspoon sea salt

8 ounces catfish, diced

4 Roma tomatoes, chopped

3 garlic cloves, minced

1 cup long-grain white rice, rinsed

2 cups chicken broth or seafood broth

1 pound shrimp, peeled and deveined

Handful fresh cilantro, minced

2 lemons, cut into wedges

1. Heat the oil in the skillet over medium heat. Cook the sausage for 3 to 4 minutes per side, until it begins to brown. Add the celery, bell pepper, and onion. Cook for 7 to 9 minutes, stirring frequently, until the vegetables begin to caramelize.

2. Stir in the Cajun seasoning, salt, catfish, tomatoes, and garlic. Cook for 2 to 3 minutes.

3. Stir in the rice, then add the broth. Bring to a boil, then reduce the heat to low, cover the skillet, and simmer for 20 to 25 minutes, or until the rice absorbs most of the liquid. Stir in the shrimp. Cook for 3 to 4 minutes. Remove from heat and uncover. Stir and let rest for 10 minutes.

4. Top with cilantro and serve with lemon wedges.

TIP: Jambalaya traditionally includes chicken, so you can add a chicken breast (diced and cooked with the andouille) or swap it for the catfish.

STEAK WITH GRILLED FENNEL SALAD, PAGE 180

Chapter Nine

BEEF, PORK, AND LAMB

STEAK WITH GRILLED FENNEL SALAD

GLUTEN-FREE, WEEKDAY
SERVES 4

Prep time: 20 minutes | **Cook time:** 20 minutes | **Cast iron:** 12-inch skillet

This recipe is a tribute to late spring, with fresh fennel, herbs, radishes, and the first early tomatoes. The salad pairs beautifully with the rich and juicy steak.

1 head fennel, bulb, stalk, and fronds

2 garlic cloves, minced

Handful fresh cilantro, minced

Handful fresh parsley leaves, minced

Handful fresh mint leaves, minced

2 or 3 radishes, thinly sliced

2 large tomatoes, diced

Juice of 1 lemon

1 teaspoon honey

2 tablespoons olive oil

½ cup crumbled feta cheese

3 tablespoons salted butter, divided

1 pound strip steak, 1 inch thick, at room temperature, and patted dry

Sea salt

Freshly ground black pepper

1. Separate the fennel bulb from the greens, setting the bulb aside. Remove the fronds from the stalk. Reserve a handful of the fronds. Mince the rest of the fronds and the stalk, quarter the fennel bulb, and set them aside.

2. Put the reserved fronds in a large bowl along with the garlic, cilantro, parsley, mint, radishes, tomatoes, lemon juice, honey, oil, and feta cheese. Toss thoroughly and set aside.

3. In the skillet over medium heat, melt 1 tablespoon of butter. Cook the fennel for 4 to 5 minutes, stirring occasionally, or until it has browned around the edges, then add it to the salad.

4. Season each side of the steak with salt and pepper.

5. In the skillet over medium-high heat, melt the remaining 2 tablespoons of butter. Put the steak into the skillet. Cook for 5 minutes, then flip. For a rare steak, cook for 3 to 5 minutes more, or until the internal temperature reaches 135°F (5 to 7 minutes more to 140°F for medium).

6. Transfer the steak to a cutting board and let it rest for 5 minutes. Thinly slice the steak and serve topped with fennel salad.

BACON AND KOHLRABI OVER CREAMY GRITS

GLUTEN-FREE, WEEKDAY

SERVES 4

Prep time: 15 minutes | **Cook time:** 1 hour | **Cast Iron:** 12-inch skillet

Kohlrabi is a frequent flyer in our springtime CSA box, and it can be tricky to find recipes that incorporate both the bulb and the green. I've found that bacon is a perfect companion for the slightly bitter greens, especially with a splash of acidity to brighten the flavor.

4 cups water

2 cups yellow stone-ground grits

3 cups whole milk

2 teaspoons sea salt, plus a pinch

1 teaspoon ground white pepper

1 teaspoon freshly ground black pepper

3 tablespoons salted butter, divided

½ cup grated Parmesan cheese

Juice of 1 lemon

8 ounces thick-cut bacon, roughly chopped

1 white onion, minced

1 kohlrabi bulb, peeled and roughly chopped

Pinch red pepper flakes

1. In a medium pot over high heat, combine the water and grits. Bring to a boil, then reduce the heat to low.

2. Stir in the milk, 2 teaspoons of salt, white pepper, black pepper, and 2 tablespoons of butter. Simmer for 40 to 45 minutes, stirring frequently, or until the grits thicken.

3. When the grits have absorbed the liquid (but still stir easily), stir in the Parmesan cheese and lemon juice. Remove from the heat.

4. While the grits cook, in the skillet over medium heat, cook the bacon for 5 to 6 minutes, stirring frequently, or until browned.

5. Add the remaining 1 tablespoon of butter, the onion, kohlrabi bulb, remaining pinch of salt, and red pepper flakes. Cook for 8 to 10 minutes, or until the kohlrabi is tender.

CONTINUED

1 cup kohlrabi greens,
   roughly chopped
3 garlic cloves, minced
Handful garlic scapes or
   scallions, minced

6. Stir in the kohlrabi greens, making sure to coat them in the butter and bacon drippings. Cook for 4 to 5 minutes, stirring frequently, until tender. Add the garlic and cook for 1 to 2 minutes.

7. Plate the grits and top them with the bacon and kohlrabi mixture. Serve garnished with a sprinkling of garlic scapes.

TIP: I prefer stone-ground grits, especially for recipes like these. They are coarser, which makes them heartier and thicker, so they hold up to the vegetables and bacon.

HERB AND GARLIC MEATLOAF

CLASSIC, GLUTEN-FREE, OVEN-COOKED

SERVES 4

Prep time: 20 minutes | **Cook time:** 1 hour | **Cast iron:** 12-inch skillet

Meatloaf is a classic dish, and everyone should have a solid recipe. I think of it as a dinner that is equally suitable for a cold winter's night with just our family, a hot dish I can bring to someone I want to comfort with food, and a satisfying dinner I can happily serve to company. There is never a time when meatloaf is unwelcome.

For the sauce

½ cup apple cider vinegar

½ cup tomato paste

1 tablespoon fresh rosemary leaves, minced

1 tablespoon fresh oregano leaves, minced

1 tablespoon fresh thyme leaves, minced

2 garlic cloves, minced

1. Preheat the oven to 350°F.

2. **To make the sauce:** In a small bowl, whisk the vinegar, tomato paste, rosemary, oregano, thyme, and garlic until smooth. Set aside.

3. **To make the meatloaf:** In a large bowl, mix the ground beef, onion, bread crumbs, tomato paste, milk, garlic, eggs, oregano, rosemary, thyme, basil, salt, garlic powder, and paprika. Mix well so all the ingredients are fully incorporated, then press the meat mixture into skillet in an even layer.

CONTINUED

For the meatloaf

2 pounds 85% lean
ground beef
1 white onion, minced
1 cup bread crumbs
½ cup tomato paste
½ cup whole milk
4 garlic cloves, minced
2 large eggs, lightly beaten
1 tablespoon dried oregano
1 tablespoon dried rosemary
1 tablespoon dried thyme
1 tablespoon dried basil
1 teaspoon sea salt
1 teaspoon garlic powder
1 teaspoon smoked paprika

4. Brush half the sauce over the meatloaf.

5. Bake for 1 hour, until browned, bubbling, and the internal temperature reaches 160°F.

6. Brush the top of the meatloaf with the remaining sauce, then let the meatloaf rest for 10 minutes before serving.

LONDON BROIL WITH SPRING ONION PESTO

GLUTEN-FREE, OVEN-COOKED, WEEKDAY

⊙——————— SERVES 4 ———————⊙

Prep time: 20 minutes | **Cook time:** 15 minutes | **Cast iron:** 12-inch skillet

This spring onion pesto is bright and fresh and uses both the bulb and greens of the onions. London broil is one of my favorite cuts of beef because it manages to sound sophisticated while being easy to prepare. A London broil is also usually a cut that can easily feed four, which means it makes an impressive centerpiece.

For the pesto

2 spring onions, bulbs and
  greens, roughly chopped
1 cup shelled
  sunflower seeds
4 garlic cloves, smashed
½ teaspoon sea salt
3 to 4 tablespoons olive oil

For the steak

2 pounds London broil
  steak, patted dry
2 tablespoons olive oil
1 teaspoon sea salt
1 tablespoon freshly ground
  black pepper

1. **To make the pesto:** In a food processor, combine the spring onions, sunflower seeds, garlic, and salt. Pulse a few times, then turn on the processor. Slowly drizzle the olive oil through the feed tube. Blend until the ingredients form a finely chopped paste.

2. **To make the steak:** Preheat the broiler to high. Place the skillet on the middle rack in the oven for 10 minutes while the broiler heats.

3. Rub the steak on both sides with the oil, salt, and pepper.

4. Using oven mitts, remove the skillet from the oven and place the steak into the skillet. Broil for 5 to 7 minutes and flip. For a rare steak, cook for 5 minutes more, or until the internal temperature reaches 135°F (6 minutes more to 140°F for medium, and 7 minutes more to 150°F for medium well). Remove the steak from the skillet and let it rest for 5 minutes.

5. Slice the steak and serve it topped with pesto.

CLASSIC LAMB SHEPHERD'S PIE

CLASSIC, GLUTEN-FREE, OVEN-COOKED

○———— SERVES 6 ————○

Prep time: 20 minutes | **Cook time:** 1 hour 30 minutes | **Cast iron:** 12-inch skillet

Shepherd's pie, a classic English dish, traditionally consists of two layers. The bottom layer is spiced ground lamb and vegetables with a tomato base, and the top layer is whipped mashed potatoes. It's a deeply comforting dish that is a lovely blend of textures, where each forkful offers meat, vegetable, and creamy potatoes.

For the mashed potatoes

2 Yukon gold potatoes, quartered

6 tablespoons salted butter

¾ cup mayonnaise

Sea salt

Freshly ground black pepper

For the lamb and vegetables

1 tablespoon salted butter

1 pound ground lamb

2 carrots, chopped

1 cup frozen peas

1 white onion, chopped

1 cup frozen corn kernels

3 garlic cloves, minced

1 teaspoon red pepper flakes

1 teaspoon Worcestershire sauce

1. **To make the mashed potatoes:** In a medium saucepan, combine the potatoes and enough water to cover. Place the pan over high heat and boil the potatoes for about 20 minutes, or until soft. Drain and transfer to a large bowl.

2. Add the butter, mayonnaise, and a pinch of salt and pepper to the potatoes. Using an electric mixer, mix at medium speed until the potatoes are mashed.

3. **To make the lamb and vegetables:** Preheat the oven to 350°F.

4. In the skillet over medium heat, melt the butter.

5. Add the ground lamb and cook for 7 to 9 minutes, or until browned. Stir in the carrots, peas, onion, corn, garlic, red pepper flakes, rosemary, thyme, and Worcestershire sauce. Cook for 10 to 12 minutes, stirring frequently.

6. Stir in the tomato paste. Add the broth and stir again. Cook for 3 to 4 minutes, then remove from the heat.

2 tablespoons tomato paste

1 cup chicken broth

1 tablespoon fresh rosemary
leaves, minced

1 tablespoon fresh thyme
leaves, minced

7. Spoon the mashed potatoes over the filling in the skillet, making sure the potatoes kiss the edge of the skillet.

8. Bake for 45 minutes, or until browned and bubbling.

TIP: Lamb is not for everyone. If you're not a fan of lamb, try this with ground beef instead.

ONE-SKILLET STEAK AND POTATOES

GLUTEN-FREE, WEEKDAY

SERVES 2

Prep time: 10 minutes | **Cook time:** 25 minutes | **Cast iron:** 12-inch skillet

Every once in a while, I have a deep desire for a good steak and cannot be satisfied by any other meal. Of course, the craving is never *just* for steak, it's for the whole package: steak, potatoes, and a glass of red wine. If you're going to go for it, go big. This one-skillet dish is the full package, just add wine.

1 pound strip steak

1 to 2 teaspoons sea salt

½ teaspoon freshly ground black pepper

4 tablespoons (½ stick) salted butter, divided

1 teaspoon red pepper flakes

2 pounds baby potatoes, halved

2 garlic cloves, minced

1. Pat the steak dry and season each side with salt and pepper.

2. In the skillet over medium-high heat, melt 1 tablespoon of butter.

3. Put the steak into the skillet and cook for 2 minutes per side. Remove the steak from the skillet.

4. Reduce the heat to medium. Put 1 tablespoon of butter, the red pepper flakes, and the potatoes, cut-side down, into the skillet. Cook for 8 to 10 minutes, or until the cut-side of the potatoes is brown and crisp. Flip the potatoes and add 1 tablespoon of butter. Cook for 5 minutes.

5. Return the steak to the skillet, along with the remaining 1 tablespoon of butter and the garlic. Cook for 2 to 3 minutes, flip the steak, and cook for 2 to 3 minutes. Let the steak rest for 5 minutes before serving.

TIP: I always serve this dish with Garlic Butter Green Beans (page 73).

HERB-CRUSTED PORK LOIN

CLASSIC, GLUTEN-FREE, OVEN-COOKED, WEEKDAY

SERVES 4

Prep time: 10 minutes | **Cook time:** 20 minutes | **Cast iron:** 12-inch skillet

Pork loin is a cut that is affordable, tender, and carries flavor well. Roasting pork tenderloin helps it retain moisture and stay tender. I particularly love roasting it in the skillet because it allows the meat to form a nice crust on the bottom as it cooks.

1 tablespoon dried oregano

1 tablespoon dried rosemary

1 tablespoon dried thyme

1 tablespoon dried basil

1 teaspoon sea salt

½ teaspoon red pepper flakes

1 boneless pork loin, patted dry

1 tablespoon salted butter, at room temperature

2 tablespoons olive oil

Juice of 1 lemon

1. Preheat the oven to 400°F.

2. In a small bowl, stir together the oregano, rosemary, thyme, basil, salt, and red pepper flakes. Spread the mixture onto a plate.

3. Rub the pork with butter, then roll it in the herb mixture, coating all sides.

4. Drizzle the oil into the skillet and place the tenderloin into the skillet.

5. Roast for 18 to 20 minutes, or until the pork's internal temperature reaches 145°F. Let it rest for 5 minutes, then slice and serve with a squeeze of lemon juice over the top.

OVEN-ROASTED RIBS

GLUTEN-FREE, OVEN-COOKED

SERVES 4

Prep time: 15 minutes | **Cook time:** 2 hours 15 minutes | **Cast iron:** 12-inch skillet with lid

When you're craving ribs, there is no substitute. This version—dry rubbed with a spice blend that is hot and sweet and brushed with a sauce that has notes of brown sugar, tomato, and cayenne—scratches the itch perfectly.

2¼ cups packed light brown sugar, divided

3 tablespoons chipotle powder, divided

2 tablespoons cayenne, plus 1 teaspoon

1 tablespoon garlic powder

1 tablespoon sea salt

1 teaspoon ground ginger

1 (1½- to 2-pound) rack of ribs, halved and patted dry

1 tablespoon olive oil

2 cups fresh Roma tomato puree or canned tomato puree

Juice of 1 lemon

1. Preheat the oven to 350°F.

2. In a small bowl, stir together 2 cups of brown sugar, 2 tablespoons of chipotle powder, 2 tablespoons of cayenne, the garlic powder, salt, and ginger. Rub the spice mixture into the ribs, coating all sides.

3. Heat the oil in the skillet over medium heat. Brown the ribs for 2 to 3 minutes per side. Turn off the heat.

4. Cover the skillet with a lid or aluminum foil and transfer it to the oven. Bake for 2 hours, or until the ribs are bubbling, browned, and the meat is falling off the bone.

5. When the ribs have about 20 minutes of cooking time left, in a small saucepan over low heat, combine the tomato puree and lemon juice, along with the remaining ¼ cup of brown sugar, 1 tablespoon of chipotle powder, and 1 teaspoon of cayenne. Simmer, stirring occasionally, until the ribs are done.

6. Remove the ribs from the oven, brush with the sauce, and return to the oven for 5 minutes. Brush the ribs a second time with sauce and let them rest for 5 minutes before serving.

PORK-STUFFED BELL PEPPERS

GLUTEN-FREE, OVEN-COOKED, WEEKDAY

SERVES 4

Prep time: 20 minutes | Cook time: 40 minutes | Cast iron: 10-inch skillet

Dan and I have a tendency to fall *deeply* in love with a dish, eat it all the time for a few months, and then burn out on it for a while only to rediscover it later and follow the same pattern. Pork-stuffed bell peppers will always remind me of our first apartment together; it was one of the first dishes we fell fully into, and one that has come back into the rotation a few times over the years.

4 tablespoons olive
   oil, divided

1 pound ground pork

1 small white onion, minced

4 garlic cloves, minced

½ cup fresh parsley leaves,
   roughly chopped

1 tablespoon fresh oregano
   leaves, minced

1 teaspoon red
   pepper flakes

½ teaspoon sea salt

¼ teaspoon freshly ground
   black pepper

2 cups long-grain white
   or brown rice, cooked
   al dente

1 tablespoon salted butter,
   at room temperature

4 red bell peppers

½ cup grated
   Parmesan cheese

1. Preheat the oven to 400°F.

2. Heat 2 tablespoons of oil in the skillet over medium heat. Add the ground pork and cook for 5 to 6 minutes, stirring occasionally. Add the onion, garlic, parsley, oregano, red pepper flakes, salt, and black pepper. Cook for 2 to 3 minutes to soften the onion. Transfer to a large bowl and stir in the cooked rice and butter.

3. Cut the tops off each bell pepper and scoop out the seeds. Stuff the peppers with the pork and rice mixture, then place them into the skillet so they stand upright, supported by the side of the skillet.

4. Top each pepper with 2 tablespoons of Parmesan cheese and drizzle with the remaining 2 tablespoons of oil.

5. Bake for 30 minutes, until browned and the internal temperature reaches 160°F. Serve hot.

TIP: This recipe works just as well in the 12-inch skillet, but take care not to tip the peppers as you put them into the oven.

APPLE CIDER VINEGAR PORK CHOPS

CLASSIC, GLUTEN-FREE, OVEN-COOKED

○————————— SERVES 2 —————————○

Prep time: 10 minutes | **Inactive time:** 45 minutes
Cook time: 25 minutes | **Cast iron:** 12-inch skillet

Name a more iconic duo than pork and vinegar—I'll wait. I'm from North Carolina, which means I only eat barbecue slow cooked in apple cider vinegar. But my love of this combination doesn't stop there. I feel strongly that pork in all forms—from bacon to pork chops—are only improved with a splash of vinegar.

2 bone-in pork chops

2 tablespoons apple cider vinegar

1 teaspoon red pepper flakes

2 garlic cloves, minced

½ teaspoon sea salt

½ teaspoon freshly ground black pepper

1 tablespoon olive oil

1. Pat the pork chops dry and place them in a medium bowl with the vinegar, red pepper flakes, garlic, salt, and black pepper. Turn to coat. Chill in the refrigerator for 45 minutes.

2. Preheat the oven to 375°F.

3. Heat the oil in the skillet over medium-high heat. Put the pork chops into the skillet and cook for 4 to 5 minutes per side. Transfer the skillet to the oven and cook for 10 to 12 minutes, or until the internal temperature reaches 145°F. Let it rest for 5 minutes before serving.

ROASTED SAUSAGE AND POTATOES WITH CHIPOTLE CREAM SAUCE

GLUTEN-FREE, OVEN-COOKED, WEEKDAY

SERVES 2

Prep time: 15 minutes | **Cook time:** 30 minutes | **Cast iron:** 12-inch skillet

When I was training as a Montessori teacher, I spent a few weeks away from my family in an Airbnb, where I was fully immersed in work. I spent those weeks cooking only for myself and doing what I pleased with my free time. This was one of my favorite meals to make during that time because it made a perfect, easy dinner and provided enough leftovers for lunch the next day.

2 links cooked andouille sausage, cut into ½-inch slices

15 to 20 baby potatoes, halved

4 shallots, cut into slivers

2 tablespoons olive oil

Sea salt

Freshly ground black pepper

1 cup plain Greek yogurt

Juice of 1 lemon

½ teaspoon chipotle powder

1 avocado, peeled, halved, pitted, and cut into chunks

10 to 12 cherry tomatoes, halved

Handful fresh cilantro, minced

1. Preheat the oven to 375°F.

2. Arrange the sausage, potatoes, and shallots in the skillet in a single layer. Drizzle with oil and season with salt and pepper.

3. Bake for 25 to 30 minutes, or until the potatoes are cooked through.

4. Meanwhile, in a small bowl, whisk the yogurt, lemon juice, and chipotle powder to combine.

5. Serve the sausage and potatoes topped with avocado, tomatoes, cilantro, and a drizzle of yogurt sauce.

TIP: If you're a fan of sauerkraut (or beet sauerkraut), throw a scoop on top of this dish.

BREADED PORK MEDALLIONS

WEEKDAY

SERVES 4

Prep time: 15 minutes | **Cook time:** 20 minutes | **Cast iron:** 12-inch skillet

I love pork tenderloin with a simple breading lightly pan-fried in butter and oil. Slicing the pork into medallions, then flattening them makes them easier to fry, and—pro tip—telling your child you're eating medallions for dinner makes for a slam-dunk meal.

1 pork tenderloin, cut into 1-inch-thick slices

1 cup all-purpose flour

1 teaspoon red pepper flakes, divided

1 teaspoon sea salt, divided

1 teaspoon garlic powder, divided

2 large eggs

2 tablespoons apple cider vinegar

¼ cup spicy brown mustard

1 cup bread crumbs

1 tablespoon olive oil, plus more as needed

1 tablespoon salted butter, plus more as needed

1. Using a meat tenderizer, pound the pork slices until they're about ¾ inch thick.

2. On a work surface near the stove, lay out 3 small bowls. In the first bowl, stir together the flour, ½ teaspoon of red pepper flakes, ½ teaspoon of salt, and ½ teaspoon of garlic powder.

3. In the second bowl, whisk the eggs, vinegar, and mustard to combine.

4. In the third bowl, combine the bread crumbs with the remaining ½ teaspoon of red pepper flakes, ½ teaspoon of salt, and ½ teaspoon of garlic powder.

5. Dip 3 or 4 medallions into the flour mixture, into the egg mixture, and into the bread crumbs, coating all sides of each medallion.

6. Heat the oil and melt the butter in the skillet over medium heat. Working in batches, fry the medallions for 2 to 3 minutes per side, then transfer to drain slightly. Add more butter and oil to the skillet, as needed, between batches.

TIP: Try these pork medallions with Turmeric Roasted Beets (page 74) and Cheese and Bacon Smashed Potatoes (page 67).

LAMB CHOPS WITH HERB BUTTER

GLUTEN-FREE, WEEKDAY

SERVES 2

Prep time: 15 minutes | **Cook time:** 15 minutes | **Cast iron:** 12-inch skillet

Homemade herb butter is one of the easiest ways to add a punch of flavor to a dish, and it can be made in advance and used in many different dishes. This recipe calls for enough herb butter to accompany the lamb chops, but feel free to double (or triple) the recipe and keep it refrigerated to kick up any meal.

4 lamb chops

Sea salt

1 teaspoon fresh thyme
leaves, minced, plus
1 tablespoon

6 tablespoons salted butter,
room temperature,
divided

1 tablespoon fresh rosemary
leaves, minced

1 tablespoon fresh oregano
leaves, minced

2 garlic cloves, minced

1. Season the lamb chops with salt to taste and 1 teaspoon of thyme. Let the lamb rest while you make the herb butter.

2. In a small bowl, thoroughly combine 4 tablespoons of butter, the remaining 1 tablespoon of thyme, the rosemary, oregano, and garlic.

3. In the skillet over medium-high heat, melt the remaining 2 tablespoons of butter. Cook the lamb for 5 to 6 minutes, flip, and cook it for 5 to 6 minutes more, or until the internal temperature reaches 145°F. Let the lamb rest for 5 minutes.

4. Serve each chop with a dollop of herb butter on top.

TIP: Leftover herbed butter can be stored in an airtight container in the refrigerator for up to 6 months.

SEARED SHORT RIBS WITH LIME CABBAGE SLAW

GLUTEN-FREE, WEEKDAY

SERVES 4

Prep time: 20 minutes | **Cook time:** 10 minutes | **Cast iron:** 12-inch skillet

My usual go-to preparation of short ribs is slow cooked in a braise and served over grits, but I've recently become a convert to short ribs cooked hot and fast and served very thinly sliced. This recipe lets the taste and texture of the rib come forward. The slaw has a fresh flavor and crunch, which is the perfect accompaniment to the tender, succulent ribs.

For the lime cabbage slaw

2 cups shredded green
  cabbage
2 cups shredded red
  cabbage
½ red onion, thinly sliced
2 garlic cloves, minced
½ teaspoon sea salt
1 tablespoon mayonnaise
Juice of 2 limes
2 tablespoons fresh cilantro

For the short ribs

2 tablespoons olive oil
1 pound boneless beef
  short ribs, 1-inch thick, at
  room temperature
Pinch sea salt
Pinch freshly ground
  black pepper

1. **To make the lime cabbage slaw:** In a medium bowl, combine the green and red cabbage, onion, garlic, salt, mayonnaise, lime juice, and cilantro. Mix thoroughly and chill in the refrigerator.

2. **To make the short ribs:** Heat the oil in the skillet over medium-high heat.

3. Season the ribs with salt and pepper.

4. Cook the ribs for 3 to 4 minutes per side, or until nicely browned. Let them rest for 5 minutes.

5. Thinly slice the ribs and serve with the slaw.

PORK BELLY AND KIMCHI BOWL

GLUTEN-FREE, WEEKDAY

○ ─────── SERVES 2 ─────── ○

Prep time: 10 minutes | **Cook time:** 20 minutes | **Cast iron:** 12-inch skillet

Gochujang is a Korean red chili paste that is both savory and sweet. Made from fermented chile powder, rice, soy bean, barley powder, and salt, the paste brings a spicy kick and umami flavor to this dish. In my limited experience cooking with Korean flavors, I've found that gochujang and pork belly are an amazing combination, and this bowl allows both to shine.

8 ounces pork belly, cut into thin strips

1 teaspoon sea salt

2 tablespoons vegetable oil, divided

1 yellow onion, minced

2 garlic cloves, minced

1 cup kimchi

1 tablespoon gochujang

2 cups cooked rice, white or brown

1 scallion, green parts only, finely chopped

1. Season the pork belly with salt.

2. Heat 1 tablespoon of oil in the skillet over medium-high heat. Add the pork belly and cook for 4 to 5 minutes per side, until cooked through and crisp. Transfer the pork belly to a plate and set it aside.

3. Reduce the heat to medium and add the remaining 1 tablespoon of oil and the onion to the skillet. Cook for 2 to 3 minutes, or until the onion begins to soften. Stir in the garlic, kimchi, and gochujang. Cook for 2 to 3 minutes, stirring frequently.

4. Add the pork belly to the skillet and cook for 1 to 2 minutes, stirring to coat the pork in gochujang.

5. Serve the pork belly and kimchi mixture over rice and topped with scallion greens.

THAI BASIL BEEF

WEEKDAY

SERVES 4

Prep time: 25 minutes | Cook time: 15 minutes | Cast iron: 12-inch skillet

In our herb garden this year, I planted Thai basil. The flavor has notes of anise or licorice and is slightly spicy. It's an addition to my herb garden I've appreciated and one I'll plant year after year.

1 tablespoon vegetable oil

1 pound ground beef

1 white onion, diced

5 garlic cloves, minced

Pinch sea salt

1 red bell pepper, seeded
   and thinly sliced

1 red chile, seeded and
   thinly sliced

1 carrot, shredded

2 tablespoons soy sauce

1 tablespoon fish sauce

Juice of 1 lime

2 cups fresh Thai
   basil leaves

2 cups basmati rice, cooked

1 scallion, green parts only,
   roughly chopped

1. Heat the oil in the skillet over medium-high heat. Add the ground beef and cook for 2 to 3 minutes, stirring frequently. Add the onion, garlic, and salt and cook for 2 to 3 minutes, stirring frequently, until the beef begins to brown.

2. Stir in the bell pepper, red chile, carrot, soy sauce, fish sauce, and lime juice. Cook for 2 to 3 minutes. Stir in the basil and cook for 1 to 2 minutes, or until the basil just wilts.

3. Serve over rice and topped with scallion greens.

TIP: To make this dish gluten-free, substitute tamari for the soy sauce.

GARLIC LAMB AND VEGETABLE PASTA

WEKDAY

SERVES 4

Prep time: 15 minutes | Cook time: 15 minutes | Cast iron: 12-inch skillet

A good friend of mine, Jolyane, is the mother of the happiest child I have ever had the pleasure of meeting, Charlie. Charlie has severe food allergies, which has forced his mom to learn on her feet as she navigates feeding him. This recipe is her base recipe for Charlie's diet. It's also a delicious pasta dish that lets the flavors of the lamb and vegetables shine.

Sea salt

1 pound penne pasta

2 tablespoons olive oil, plus more for the pasta

1 pound ground lamb

1 large carrot, thinly sliced into circles

3 garlic cloves, minced

2 cups sliced baby portabella mushrooms

1 tablespoon fresh oregano leaves, minced

4 cups fresh spinach

Grated Parmesan cheese, for serving

1. Bring a large pot of salted water to a boil. Cook the penne according to the package directions. Drain and drizzle with oil.

2. Meanwhile, heat the oil in the skillet over medium heat. Brown the ground lamb for 4 to 5 minutes, stirring occasionally. Stir in the carrot, garlic, mushrooms, a pinch of salt, and the oregano and cook for 4 to 5 minutes.

3. Stir in the spinach and cook for 2 to 3 minutes, or until the spinach wilts.

4. In a large serving bowl, toss together the pasta and lamb mixture. Serve topped with Parmesan cheese.

TIP: For easy leftovers, double the ingredients, cooking only half the pasta. Refrigerate in an airtight container for up to 1 week and serve with freshly cooked pasta.

BEEF RAGÙ WITH PAPPARDELLE

CLASSIC

○——————— SERVES 4 ———————○

Prep time: 20 minutes | **Cook time:** 1 hour | **Cast iron:** 12-inch skillet

Ragù is heartier than a classic tomato sauce but simple enough to make. There is absolutely nothing better than the smell of a ragù simmering on the stovetop, especially with a glass of red wine to enjoy while you make it.

1 tablespoon salted butter

1 pound 85% lean ground beef

4 ounces pancetta, finely chopped

2 tablespoons olive oil

1 white onion, diced

1 celery stalk, diced

1 large carrot, peeled and diced

¼ cup tomato paste

1 cup red wine

1 cup whole milk

1 cup beef broth

1 (28-ounce) can diced tomatoes

1 teaspoon dried oregano

1 teaspoon dried thyme

1 teaspoon dried basil

1 tablespoon fresh rosemary leaves, minced

1 teaspoon sea salt, plus more as needed

1 pound cooked pappardelle noodles

Grated Parmesan cheese, for serving

1. In the skillet over medium heat, combine the butter, ground beef, and pancetta. Cook for 10 to 12 minutes, or until the meat begins to brown.

2. Add the oil, onion, celery, and carrot. Cook for 4 to 5 minutes, stirring frequently, or until the vegetables start to brown and soften.

3. Stir in the tomato paste and cook for 2 to 3 minutes, stirring, or just long enough for the paste to caramelize. Whisk in the wine.

4. Pour in the milk and broth and cook for about 10 minutes, stirring, or until the sauce has cooked down.

5. Stir in the tomatoes with their juices, oregano, thyme, basil, rosemary, and salt. Let the sauce come to a light boil, then reduce the heat to low and cook for 25 to 30 minutes, stirring occasionally.

6. Taste and adjust the seasoning, if desired. Serve over pappardelle and topped with Parmesan cheese.

CARNE ASADA TACOS

GLUTEN-FREE, WEEKDAY

SERVES 4

Prep time: 10 minutes | **Inactive time:** 15 minutes
Cook time: 15 minutes | **Cast iron:** 12-inch skillet

I am far from alone in my love and devotion to tacos. They are a perfect food, and we are all indebted to the people of Mexico for bringing them into our lives. My favorite, hands down, is the carne asada taco. It's just *chef's kiss* perfection.

1 teaspoon ground cumin

1 teaspoon chili powder

1 teaspoon ground
   coriander

¼ teaspoon ground
   cinnamon

¼ teaspoon sea salt

1 pound skirt steak

1 tablespoon olive oil

8 corn tortillas

½ white onion, minced

Handful fresh
   cilantro, minced

2 limes, cut into wedges

1. In a small bowl, stir together the cumin, chili powder, coriander, cinnamon, and salt.

2. Pat the steak dry and thoroughly rub the spice mixture over both sides. Let the steak rest for 15 minutes.

3. Heat the oil in the skillet over medium-high heat. Cook the steak for 5 to 6 minutes per side, or until the steak has a crisp crust and reaches 145°F. Remove from the skillet and let it rest for 5 minutes.

4. Thinly slice the skirt steak and serve with tortillas, onion, cilantro, and lime wedges.

CHIPOTLE BEEF TOSTADA

GLUTEN-FREE, WEEKDAY

SERVES 4

Prep time: 20 minutes | Cook time: 20 minutes | Cast iron: 10-inch and 12-inch skillets

When Dan and I first moved in together and realized how fun it was to cook and eat together, we became obsessed with fried tortillas for a while, both in the form of tostadas and sopapillas. Tostadas are delicious served hot and eaten quickly.

12 cherry tomatoes, halved

½ red onion, minced

Juice of 2 limes

½ cup fresh cilantro, minced

2 garlic cloves, minced

Sea salt

1 tablespoon olive oil

1 tablespoon salted butter

1½ white onions, minced, divided

8 ounces 85% lean ground beef

1 teaspoon chipotle powder

½ cup vegetable oil

4 corn tortillas

¼ cup shredded Cheddar cheese

¼ cup shredded Monterey Jack cheese

1 cup shredded romaine lettuce

1 avocado, peeled, halved, pitted, and sliced

Salsa, for serving

1. In a medium bowl, combine the tomatoes, red onion, lime juice, cilantro, garlic, and a pinch of salt. Set aside.

2. Heat the olive oil and melt the butter in the 12-inch skillet over medium heat. Add 1 minced white onion and cook for 2 to 3 minutes. Add the ground beef, a pinch of salt, and the chipotle powder. Using a wooden spoon, break up the ground beef and stir to combine it with the onion. Cook for 7 to 10 minutes, stirring occasionally, until the beef is cooked through and no longer pink.

3. Meanwhile, heat the vegetable oil to 375°F in the 10-inch skillet over medium-high heat.

4. Fry the tortillas, one at a time, for 45 seconds to 1 minute per side, until crisp and golden brown. Transfer to a rack, sprinkle with salt, and let them cool.

5. Place each tortilla on a plate and layer it with beef, Cheddar cheese, Monterey Jack cheese, romaine, avocado, the remaining ½ minced white onion, and salsa.

MOUNTAIN PIE, PAGE 214

Chapter Ten

DESSERTS

SHOOFLY PIE

CLASSIC, OVEN-COOKED, VEGETARIAN
○————————— SERVES 6 —————————○

Prep time: 30 minutes | **Inactive time:** 1 hour
Cook time: 40 minutes | **Cast iron:** 12-inch skillet

Shoofly Pie is a dish that Dan brought into our marriage— something he grew up eating in Pennsylvania. Named so because it is so sweet you have to shoo the flies away from it (a winning endorsement and kind of gross name all at the same time), the foundation of the pie is blackstrap molasses. It has a brown sugar crumble on top that gives it a bit of texture, and the result is delightful.

For the crust

2½ cups all-purpose flour, plus more for rolling the dough

1 cup (2 sticks) cold salted butter, cubed

¼ cup packed light brown sugar

Pinch sea salt

¼ cup cold water

For the filling

1 teaspoon baking soda

¾ cup boiling water

1 cup blackstrap molasses

1 large egg

1 teaspoon vanilla extract

1. **To make the crust:** In a food processor, combine the flour, butter, brown sugar, and salt. Pulse until the texture resembles coarse cornmeal. Add the cold water, a few tablespoons at a time, pulsing until a ball forms. Wrap the dough in plastic wrap and chill in the refrigerator for 1 hour.

2. **To make the filling:** In a large bowl, combine the baking soda and boiling water. Add the molasses and whisk vigorously to combine.

3. Whisk in the egg and vanilla and set aside.

4. Preheat the oven to 375°F.

5. **To make the topping:** In the food processor, combine the flour, butter, brown sugar, and cinnamon. Pulse until just combined. Mix ⅓ of this brown sugar crumble into the filling. Set aside the remaining topping.

For the topping

1 cup all-purpose flour

8 tablespoons (1 stick) salted butter

½ cup packed light brown sugar

Pinch ground cinnamon

For the assembly

1 large egg

2 cups heavy (whipping) cream

½ cup granulated sugar

1 teaspoon vanilla extract

6. **To assemble the pie:** Flour a work surface and place the crust on it. Roll the crust into a 15-inch round. Press the crust into the bottom and sides of the skillet.

7. Pour the filling over the crust. Top with the remaining brown sugar crumble.

8. In a small bowl, whisk the egg and brush the visible crust with egg wash.

9. Bake for 40 minutes, or until the crust is golden brown and the filling has mostly set. Cool completely before serving.

10. In a large bowl, combine the cream, granulated sugar, and vanilla. Using an electric mixer, whip the cream until stiff peaks form. Serve atop the room-temperature pie.

CHOCOLATE-STRAWBERRY BREAD PUDDING

OVEN-COOKED, VEGETARIAN

⊖ ———————— **SERVES 4 TO 6** ———————— ⊖

Prep time: 20 minutes | **Cook time:** 45 minutes | **Cast iron:** 12-inch skillet

Chocolate and strawberries go hand in hand, a pairing so classic it cannot be questioned. I particularly love the combination in bread pudding because the strawberries impart moistness and the chocolate brings creaminess, both of which are a lovely contrast to the crusty bread.

1 tablespoon salted butter

1 loaf French bread, preferably day-old, broken into 1-inch pieces

1 cup chocolate chips

2 cups fresh strawberries, quartered

5 large eggs

2 cups whole milk

1 cup heavy (whipping) cream

½ cup sugar

¼ teaspoon ground ginger

¼ teaspoon vanilla extract

2 cups dehydrated straw-berries, crushed (optional)

Vanilla ice cream, for serving

1. Preheat the oven to 350°F.

2. Grease the skillet with butter and evenly arrange the bread inside. Sprinkle with chocolate chips and fresh strawberries.

3. In a large bowl, whisk the eggs, milk, cream, sugar, ginger, and vanilla to combine. Evenly pour the cus-tard over the bread. Do not mix. Top with an even layer of dehydrated strawberries (if using).

4. Bake for 45 minutes. Remove from the oven and cool, letting the filling set before serving with a scoop of vanilla ice cream.

TIP: Substitute blackberries and white chocolate for the strawberries and chocolate chips.

BLOOD ORANGE RHUBARB CRUMBLE

OVEN-COOKED, VEGETARIAN

⊖————————— SERVES 4 —————————⊖

Prep time: 20 minutes | **Cook time:** 45 minutes | **Cast iron:** 10-inch skillet

This is an adventurous crumble, a step outside your classic Baked Apple Crisp (page 220). Rhubarb and blood orange bring big tangy flavors, and the result is a bright dessert best served with a scoop of ice cream.

For the filling

5 or 6 rhubarb stalks, diced
1 tablespoon grated
   orange zest
2 blood oranges, peeled,
   cleaned of membranes,
   and roughly chopped
3 tablespoons cornstarch
¼ cup granulated sugar

For the topping

8 tablespoons (1 stick)
   salted butter, melted
1 cup all-purpose flour
½ cup old-fashioned
   rolled oats
¼ cup packed light brown
   sugar
1 tablespoon honey
1 teaspoon baking powder
½ teaspoon ground cinnamon
1 tablespoon grated
   orange zest
Vanilla ice cream, for serving

1. Preheat the oven to 375°F.

2. **To make the filling:** In a medium bowl, stir together the rhubarb, orange zest, oranges, cornstarch, and granulated sugar. Mix well. Spread the filling in the skillet in an even layer.

3. **To make the topping:** In a small bowl, stir together the melted butter, flour, oats, brown sugar, honey, baking powder, cinnamon, and orange zest. Spread the topping over the filling.

4. Bake for 45 minutes, or until bubbling. Let it set for 5 minutes before serving with a scoop of ice cream.

CLASSIC, OVEN-COOKED, VEGETARIAN

SERVES 4 TO 6

Prep time: 20 minutes | **Inactive time:** 1 hour
Cook time: 1 hour | **Cast iron:** 12-inch skillet

Buttermilk pie is a classic Southern dish, one of the many variations of chess pie. The filling of a chess pie starts with butter, sugar, and eggs. There are dozens of variations and additions to the basic chess pie, from chocolate to vinegar, but the buttermilk pie is my favorite because of its creaminess.

For the crust

1¼ cups all-purpose flour,
   plus more for rolling
   the dough
8 tablespoons (1 stick)
   salted butter, cubed
½ cup sugar
¼ cup shortening
Pinch sea salt
Pinch ground ginger
Pinch ground cinnamon
½ cup cold water

For the filling

¾ cup salted butter, melted
1½ cups sugar
1 teaspoon vanilla extract
3 large eggs
3 tablespoons all-purpose
   flour
Pinch sea salt
1 cup buttermilk

1. **To make the crust:** In a food processor, combine the flour, butter, sugar, shortening, salt, ginger, and cinnamon. Pulse until the texture resembles coarse cornmeal. Add the water, a few tablespoons at a time, pulsing until a ball forms. Wrap the dough in plastic wrap and chill in the refrigerator for 1 hour.

2. Preheat the oven to 400°F.

3. **To make the filling:** In a large bowl, stir together the melted butter, sugar, and vanilla.

4. One at time, using an electric mixer, beat in the eggs. Mix in the flour and salt. Slowly stir in the buttermilk until a batter forms.

5. **To assemble the pie:** Flour a work surface and place the crust on it. Roll the dough into a 15-inch round. Press the dough into the bottom and sides of the skillet.

6. Pour the buttermilk filling into the crust.

7. Bake for 10 minutes. Reduce the oven temperature to 350°F and bake the pie for 50 minutes more. Let the pie cool completely (about 2 hours) to set before serving.

CRISPY MARSHMALLOW BARS

VEGETARIAN, WEEKDAY

SERVES 2 TO 4

Prep time: 10 minutes | **Cook time:** 5 minutes | **Cast iron:** 12-inch skillet

Besides crispy chicken sandwiches, green tea mochi, and Cheeseburgers (page 93), one of my most consistent pregnancy cravings was crispy marshmallow bars. And let me tell you, when it comes to pregnancy and marshmallow bars, it's hard to control myself. They're just a gooey, crunchy, sweet, and a little salty slice of heaven.

4 tablespoons (½ stick) salted butter, divided

1 tablespoon sugar

1 (16-ounce) bag mini marshmallows

1 tablespoon ground cinnamon

½ teaspoon ground nutmeg

3 cups puffed rice cereal

1. In the skillet over medium heat, melt 2 tablespoons of butter. Add the sugar and marshmallows. Cook for 3 to 5 minutes, stirring frequently, as the marshmallows melt and begin to toast. Stir in the cinnamon and nutmeg.

2. In a large bowl, combine the melted marshmallows and cereal. Stir well so the cereal is fully coated.

3. Clean the skillet and grease it with the remaining 2 tablespoons of butter. Press the marshmallow-cereal mixture into the skillet. Let it cool completely before serving.

TIP: Once the marshmallow and cereal are combined, it can be transferred into any dish to cool. For the sake of a one-skillet recipe, I suggest putting it back into the skillet. It can also be transferred to a lined baking pan or even into muffin tins.

PEAR AND PECAN PIE

OVEN-COOKED, VEGETARIAN

○———————— SERVES 6 ————————○

Prep time: 25 minutes | **Inactive time:** 1 hour
Cook time: 1 hour 5 minutes | **Cast iron:** 12-inch skillet

A pear pie should be a blend of underripe, slightly firm pears and pears that are ripe and beginning to soften. The ripe pears bring a rich flavor, while the slightly underripe pears offer texture and stability to the filling.

For the crust

2½ cups all-purpose flour, plus more for rolling the dough

12 tablespoons (1½ sticks) salted butter, cubed, plus more for greasing

3 tablespoons granulated sugar

¼ teaspoon sea salt

¼ cup cold water

1 large egg, beaten

For the filling

4 tablespoons (½ stick) salted butter

6 pears, peeled and cut into ¼-inch slices

⅔ cup packed light brown sugar

¼ teaspoon ground ginger

¼ teaspoon ground cinnamon

1. **To make the crust:** In a food processor, combine the flour, butter, granulated sugar, and salt. Pulse until the texture resembles coarse cornmeal. Add the cold water, a few tablespoons at a time, pulsing until a ball forms. Wrap the dough in plastic wrap and chill in the refrigerator for 1 hour.

2. **To make the filling:** In the skillet over medium heat, melt the butter. Add the pears, brown sugar, ginger, and cinnamon. Scrape the seeds from the vanilla bean into the skillet. Simmer the filling for 20 minutes, stirring, until the pears have softened and most of the liquid has cooked down. Remove from the heat, stir in the flour and pecans, and transfer the filling to a bowl.

3. **To assemble the pie:** Clean out the skillet and set it aside to cool.

4. Preheat the oven to 375°F.

5. Divide the crust dough in half. Flour a work surface and place the crust on it. Roll half the dough into a 15-inch round. Press the dough round into the bottom and sides of the skillet.

1 vanilla bean (see tip)

2 tablespoons all-purpose
flour

1 cup fresh pecans,
roughly chopped

1 large egg, beaten

6. Scoop the filling into the crust.

7. Roll the remaining dough into a 13-inch round. Lay it flat over the pear filling, pinching the edges to seal. Brush the visible pie dough with the beaten egg. Cut 5 or 6 slits in the top crust for ventilation.

8. Bake for 45 minutes, or until the crust is golden brown. Let it cool before serving.

TIP: Use the point of the knife to cut a slit in the vanilla bean lengthwise. Using your fingers, open it wide so the seeds can easily be scraped out.

MOUNTAIN PIE

OVEN-COOKED, VEGETARIAN

⊙———— SERVES 4 TO 6 ————⊙

Prep time: 20 minutes | **Cook time:** 1 hour | **Cast iron:** 12-inch skillet

Mountain pie is what my grandma called a cake-based cobbler. I've also heard it called a dump cobbler or a batter cobbler, but for whatever reason, it was introduced to her as mountain pie, and the name stuck. One thing these all have in common is that the fruit filling is nestled in the batter without being mixed, and the batter is left to rise like a delicious cakey cloud.

8 tablespoons (1 stick) salted butter

1 cup all-purpose flour

1 cup sugar

½ cup plain Greek yogurt

½ cup water

1 teaspoon vanilla extract

1½ teaspoons baking powder

½ teaspoon sea salt

1 cup sliced peaches

1 cup raspberries

1. Preheat the oven to 350°F. Put the butter into the skillet, then put the skillet into the oven.

2. In a large bowl, stir together the flour, sugar, yogurt, water, vanilla, baking powder, and salt.

3. When the butter has melted, pour the batter into the butter. Do not mix. Put the peaches and raspberries right into the middle of the batter, but do not mix.

4. Bake for 50 to 60 minutes, or until the batter has risen and is golden brown and bubbling. Let it cool slightly before serving.

TIP: Mountain pie is a favorite family recipe and can be made with many different summer fruits, from cherries to blueberries.

CARAMEL FRIED GREEN TOMATOES AND ICE CREAM

VEGETARIAN, WEEKDAY

SERVES 2 TO 4

Prep time: 20 minutes | **Cook time:** 25 minutes | **Cast iron:** 12-inch skillet

Okay, I know—this one sounds like a stretch—but trust me. Green tomatoes are unexpectedly perfect as a dessert. They have a mild, sweet flavor and a nice crisp texture that holds up well when fried. A sweet batter and the addition of caramel sauce and ice cream makes this a winner during late summer and early fall.

For the caramel sauce

1 cup sugar

⅓ cup water

½ cup heavy (whipping) cream

4 tablespoons (½ stick) salted butter

1 teaspoon vanilla extract

For the fried tomatoes

½ cup all-purpose flour

4 tablespoons sugar, divided

¼ teaspoon ground cinnamon, divided

¼ teaspoon ground nutmeg, divided

2 large eggs

½ teaspoon vanilla extract

1 cup crushed graham crackers

¼ cup cornmeal

1. **To make the caramel sauce:** In the skillet over medium-high heat, combine the sugar and water. Cook, stirring, until the sugar dissolves and the liquid is clear. Continue cooking for 10 to 12 minutes, or until the caramel darkens to an amber color.

2. Remove the caramel from the heat and stir in the cream. Whisk vigorously as the caramel sauce bubbles.

3. Add the butter and continue to whisk until the caramel smooths out. Whisk in the vanilla. Let the caramel cool for 10 to 15 minutes, then transfer it to a glass jar.

4. **To make the fried tomatoes:** Clean out the skillet.

5. On a work surface (near the stove), line up 3 small bowls. In first bowl, stir together the flour, 2 tablespoons of sugar, ⅛ teaspoon of cinnamon, and ⅛ teaspoon of nutmeg.

CONTINUED

Vegetable oil, for frying

1 whole green tomato, halved, then cut into ¼-inch slices

Vanilla ice cream, for serving

6. In the second bowl, whisk the eggs and vanilla to blend.

7. In the third bowl (closest to the skillet), stir together the graham crackers and cornmeal, along with the remaining 2 tablespoons of sugar, ⅛ teaspoon of cinnamon, and ⅛ teaspoon of nutmeg.

8. Heat ½ inch of oil to 375°F in the skillet over medium-high heat.

9. Dip the tomato slices into the flour mixture, into the egg mixture, and into the graham cracker mixture.

10. Working in batches, fry the tomatoes for 2 to 3 minutes per side, or until golden brown.

11. To serve, spoon the ice cream into bowls, top with tomato slices, and a drizzle of caramel sauce.

BOURBON WHITE PEACH AND NECTARINE PIE

OVEN-COOKED, VEGETARIAN

○────────── SERVES 6 ──────────○

Prep time: 25 minutes | **Inactive time:** 1 hour
Cook time: 50 minutes | **Cast iron:** 12-inch skillet

The only thing better than biting into a fresh peach is peach pie. This recipe uses both white peaches and nectarines with a splash of bourbon.

For the crust

2½ cups all-purpose flour,
plus more for rolling
the dough

12 tablespoons (1½ sticks)
salted butter, cubed, plus
more for greasing

3 tablespoons granulated
sugar

¼ teaspoon sea salt

¼ cup cold water

For the filling

5 white peaches, peeled and
thinly sliced

2 nectarines, peeled and
thinly sliced

¼ cup all-purpose flour

½ cup packed light brown
sugar

2 tablespoons bourbon

1 teaspoon vanilla extract

1 large egg, beaten

1. **To make the crust:** In a food processor, combine the flour, butter, granulated sugar, and salt. Pulse until the texture resembles coarse cornmeal. Add the cold water, a few tablespoons at a time, pulsing until a ball forms. Wrap the dough in plastic wrap and chill in the refrigerator for 1 hour.

2. Preheat the oven to 400°F.

3. **To make the filling:** In a large bowl, stir together the peaches, nectarines, flour, brown sugar, bourbon, and vanilla. Set the filling aside.

4. **To assemble the pie:** Divide the dough in half. Flour a work surface and place the dough on it. Roll half the dough into a 15-inch round. Press the dough round into the bottom and sides of the skillet.

5. Scoop the filling into the dough.

6. Roll the remaining dough into a 13-inch round. Use a pie dough wheel or a knife to cut the dough into 1-inch strips. Weave the strips into a lattice and transfer it to the pie. Press the edges together and discard any extra dough. Brush the visible dough with the beaten egg.

7. Bake for 45 to 50 minutes, or until the crust is golden brown. Let it cool to set.

APPLE CIDER DONUTS

CLASSIC, VEGETARIAN

— SERVES 6 TO 8 —

Prep time: 30 minutes | **Inactive time:** 3 hours 10 minutes
Cook time: 45 minutes | **Cast iron:** 12-inch skillet

Nothing says fall like an apple cider donut. They are light, fluffy, and best eaten wandering around a fall festival. Since living in the muggy Southeast leaves fall mostly a fantasy for me, I generally accept I'll be eating my donuts wandering around my air-conditioned house in a tank top and shorts, but with the spirit of fall held closely in my heart.

1¼ cups apple cider, divided

4 tablespoons (½ stick) salted butter, plus more for greasing

2 teaspoons active dry yeast

½ cup buttermilk

2 large eggs

1 teaspoon vanilla extract

4 cups all-purpose flour, plus more for kneading

½ cup granulated sugar

1 tablespoon baking soda

1 teaspoon baking powder

1 teaspoon ground cinnamon

1 teaspoon ground nutmeg

Pinch sea salt

Vegetable oil, for frying

2 cups powdered sugar

1. In a medium saucepan over medium-low heat, simmer 1 cup of apple cider for about 30 minutes, until it reduces by half. Remove from the heat and stir in the butter. Let it cool to room temperature. Stir in the yeast, buttermilk, eggs, and vanilla. Cover and set aside for 10 minutes.

2. In a large bowl, stir together the flour, granulated sugar, baking soda, baking powder, cinnamon, nutmeg, and salt.

3. Using a wooden spoon, fold the wet ingredients into the dry ingredients until a loose dough forms.

4. Grease a medium bowl with butter and turn the dough into it. Loosely cover the dough with a towel and let it rise for 2 hours.

5. Line a baking sheet with wax paper and set aside.

6. Flour a work surface and turn the dough out onto it. Coat the dough with flour until it is no longer sticky. Knead the dough by stretching it, folding it on itself, and turning it. Repeat this process for 10 minutes.

7. Using a donut cutter (or 4-inch round and 1-inch round cookie cutters), cut 8 to 10 donuts out of the dough. Transfer them to the prepared baking sheet and refrigerate for 1 hour.

8. Heat 1½ inches of oil to 375°F in the skillet over high heat.

9. In a medium bowl, pour the remaining ¼ cup of apple cider. Stir in the powdered sugar, a little at a time, until the glaze is thick enough to coat the back of a spoon but still easy to pour.

10. Working in batches, fry the donuts for 2 minutes per side, until golden brown and puffed. As the donuts come out of the skillet, let the oil drip off, then dip them into the glaze, turning to coat both sides. Transfer to a drying rack to cool before serving.

BAKED APPLE CRISP

SERVES 4

Prep time: 15 minutes | **Cook time:** 40 minutes | **Cast iron:** 10-inch skillet

A baked apple crisp is sweet, simple, and completely comforting. It's the kind of dessert that feels like a hug, and I love to put one together for a cozy weekend at home with my family.

8 tablespoons (1 stick) salted butter, melted, plus 1 tablespoon

6 apples, peeled and cut into ¼-inch-thick slices

1 teaspoon ground cinnamon, divided

2 cups old-fashioned rolled oats

½ cup packed light brown sugar

¼ cup all-purpose flour

1. In the skillet over medium heat, melt 1 tablespoon of butter. Add the apples and ½ teaspoon of cinnamon. Stir to coat the apples in the butter and cinnamon. Cook for 5 to 6 minutes, or until the apples begin to soften. Remove from the heat.

2. Preheat the oven to 350°F.

3. In a medium bowl, stir together the oats, melted butter, remaining ½ teaspoon of cinnamon, brown sugar, and flour. Spread the oat mixture evenly over the apples.

4. Bake for 35 minutes, or until bubbling. Cool slightly before serving.

BEIGNETS

CLASSIC, VEGETARIAN

SERVES 6

Prep time: 20 minutes | **Inactive time:** 6 hours
Cook time: 15 minutes | **Cast iron:** 12-inch skillet

My sister Lauren lives in New Orleans. Visiting her and her family is a treat both because I love my sister and because she lives in a place with a rich history and culture. From the Audubon Zoo (my son's favorite) to beignets in City Park, there is so much to do and love about the city. Beignets are a tasty reminder of the place we love when we can't be there in person.

Vegetable oil, for frying and greasing

1 tablespoon active dry yeast

½ cup hot water

2 tablespoons salted butter

½ cup whole milk

½ cup heavy (whipping) cream

2 large eggs

1 teaspoon vanilla extract

¾ cup granulated sugar

1 teaspoon baking powder

4 cups all-purpose flour, plus more for kneading

Powdered sugar, for topping

1. Grease a large bowl with oil.

2. In another large bowl, stir together the yeast and hot water. Set aside.

3. In a medium saucepan over medium-high heat, scald the butter, milk, and cream by bringing the mixture almost to a boil, then pour it into the yeast mixture.

4. Stir in the eggs, one at a time, then stir in the vanilla, granulated sugar, baking powder, and 2 cups of flour, stirring until a loose dough forms.

5. Knead in the remaining 2 cups of flour, then transfer the dough to a floured surface. Knead the dough by stretching it, folding it on itself, and turning it. Repeat this process for 10 minutes. Transfer the dough to the oiled bowl, cover tightly, and refrigerate for at least 6 hours.

CONTINUED

6. Flour a work surface and turn the dough out onto it. Roll the dough until it is ½ inch thick. Cut the dough into 3-by-3-inch squares.

7. Heat 1½ inches of oil to 375°F in the skillet over medium-high heat.

8. Working in batches, fry the beignets for 2 minutes per side, then transfer to a rack to cool slightly.

9. Coat the beignets with powdered sugar while they are still hot.

TIP: Beignets are best enjoyed warm with an iced cafe au lait made with chicory coffee.

CARROT CAKE WITH WHIPPED CREAM CHEESE FROSTING

OVEN-COOKED, VEGETARIAN

SERVES 6

Prep time: 15 minutes | **Cook time:** 55 minutes | **Cast iron:** 12-inch skillet

Dan loves cake, but carrot cake and red velvet cake are his two favorites. I'm more of a pie person, but because I am a loving and devoted partner, I try to work a few cakes in each year. This recipe is a favorite not just for Dan but also the whole family.

For the pecan topping

1 tablespoon salted butter

1 cup pecans

For the cake

4 large eggs

¾ cup vegetable oil

¾ cup olive oil

1 teaspoon vanilla extract

3 cups shredded carrot
  (6 to 8 medium carrots)

2 cups all-purpose flour

1 cup granulated sugar

2 teaspoons baking soda

½ teaspoon ground
  cinnamon

½ teaspoon ground ginger

½ teaspoon ground nutmeg

Pinch sea salt

1. **To make the pecan topping:** In the skillet over medium heat, melt the butter. Add the pecans and toast for 3 to 4 minutes, stirring frequently. Transfer to a bowl and set aside.

2. **To make the cake:** In a large bowl, whisk the eggs, vegetable oil, olive oil, and vanilla. Stir in the carrots until incorporated.

3. In another large bowl, combine the flour, granulated sugar, baking soda, cinnamon, ginger, nutmeg, and salt. Fold the dry ingredients into the wet ingredients.

4. Preheat the oven to 350°F.

5. Pour the batter into the skillet and smooth the surface so it's even.

6. Bake for 50 minutes, or until cooked through.

7. You can ice and serve the cake in the skillet or transfer it to a rack and plate it before serving. Let the cake cool completely before icing.

CONTINUED

For the cream cheese frosting

6 tablespoons (¾ stick) salted butter, at room temperature

8 ounces cream cheese, at room temperature

2 cups powdered sugar

1 teaspoon vanilla extract

Juice of 1 lemon

8. **To make the cream cheese frosting:** While the cake cools, in the bowl of a stand mixer fitted with the paddle attachment, or in a large bowl using an electric mixer, cream the butter and cream cheese. Slowly add the powdered sugar until it is fully whipped in. Mix in the vanilla and lemon juice.

9. Spread the icing over the cooled cake and top with toasted pecans. Slice and serve.

ICED LEMON POUND CAKE

CLASSIC, OVEN-COOKED, VEGETARIAN

SERVES 6

Prep time: 25 minutes | **Cook time:** 1 hour 15 minutes | **Cast iron:** 12-inch skillet

This pound cake recipe is from my great-grandmother, Flossie. Traditionally made in a Bundt pan, it adapts well to the skillet because the edges crisp up beautifully. With a bright lemon icing, it is as well suited for the brunch table as it is the dessert spread.

For the cake

2 cups (4 sticks) salted
   butter, plus 1 tablespoon
2½ cups granulated sugar
6 large eggs
1 teaspoon vanilla extract
3½ cups cake flour
2 teaspoons baking powder
1 teaspoon sea salt
¼ teaspoon ground mace
1 cup whole milk

For the icing

1 cup powdered sugar
Juice of 1 lemon

1. **To make the cake:** Preheat the oven to 325°F. Grease the skillet with 1 tablespoon of butter.

2. In the bowl of a stand mixer fitted with the paddle attachment, or in a large bowl using an electric mixer, cream the butter until light and fluffy. Add the granulated sugar and continue beating. Mix in the eggs, one at a time, until fully incorporated. Mix in the vanilla.

3. In a large bowl, combine the flour, baking powder, salt, and mace. Add the dry ingredients to the wet ingredients, a little at a time, alternating with milk, until fully incorporated. Pour the batter into the skillet.

4. Bake for 1 hour 15 minutes, until browned on top and a toothpick inserted into the center comes out clean. Let the cake cool to room temperature.

5. **To make the icing:** In a small bowl, whisk the powdered sugar and lemon juice until smooth. Drizzle the icing over the pound cake before serving.

GOOEY CHOCOLATE SKILLET CAKE

OVEN-COOKED, WEEKDAY

SERVES 4 TO 6

Prep time: 25 minutes | **Cook time:** 35 minutes | **Cast iron:** 12-inch skillet

When I was in college, I was known for two things: quesadillas packed with toppings made in my quesadilla maker, and very gooey chocolate cake. The trick to a deeply gooey chocolate cake is to poke holes in the cake as soon as it comes out of the oven and immediately apply icing. The icing melts into the cake and makes it outrageously moist. We admittedly ate more quesadillas and chocolate cake than likely would have been recommended in college, but it was only because they were so good. No regrets.

For the cake

- 4 tablespoons (½ stick) salted butter, at room temperature, plus more for greasing
- 2½ cups all-purpose flour
- 1 cup unsweetened cocoa powder
- 2 teaspoons baking powder
- 1 teaspoon baking soda
- 1 teaspoon sea salt
- 1½ cups granulated sugar
- 3 large eggs
- ¼ cup vegetable oil
- 2 teaspoons vanilla extract
- 1 cup buttermilk
- 1 cup chocolate chips

1. **To make the cake:** Preheat the oven to 350°F. Grease the skillet with butter.

2. In a large bowl, sift together the flour, cocoa powder, baking powder, baking soda, and salt.

3. In the bowl of a stand mixer fitted with the paddle attachment, or in a large bowl using an electric mixer, cream the butter and granulated sugar.

4. In a small bowl, whisk the eggs, oil, vanilla, and buttermilk to combine.

5. While the mixer is running, add ⅓ of the dry ingredients to the butter mixture. When it is fully combined, add ⅓ of the wet ingredients and mix well. Continue, alternating wet and dry ingredients until combined. Scrape the bottom of the bowl, add the chocolate chips, and mix for 2 to 3 minutes. Pour the batter into the skillet.

For the icing

8 tablespoons (1 stick) salted butter, at room temperature

3 cups powdered sugar

½ cup unsweetened cocoa powder, sifted

1 teaspoon vanilla extract

¼ cup heavy (whipping) cream

6. Bake for 30 to 35 minutes, or until cooked through.

7. **To make the icing:** In the bowl of a stand mixer fitted with the whisk attachment, or in a large bowl using an electric mixer, slowly whip the butter, powdered sugar, cocoa powder, and vanilla while slowly adding the cream. Once the cream is fully incorporated, chill the icing in the refrigerator.

8. When the cake is done, use a fork to poke holes throughout the cake and spread the icing over the hot cake. The icing will melt into the cake. Slice and serve.

STRAWBERRY AND GOAT MILK COBBLER

OVEN-COOKED, VEGETARIAN

○────── SERVES 4 TO 6 ──────○

Prep time: 15 minutes | **Cook time:** 1 hour | **Cast iron:** 12-inch skillet

This cobbler is a spin-off on my family's classic Mountain Pie (page 214), with the addition of goat's milk, adding a beautiful tangy complement to the strawberries. With this recipe, I also spread the strawberries throughout the cobbler instead of dumping them in the middle, which makes the texture slightly cakier.

8 tablespoons (1 stick) salted butter

1 cup all-purpose flour

1 cup sugar

¾ cup goat's milk

1 teaspoon vanilla extract

1½ teaspoons baking powder

½ teaspoon sea salt

3 cups halved fresh strawberries

1. Preheat the oven to 350°F. Put the butter into the skillet, then put the skillet into the oven.

2. In a large bowl, stir together the flour, sugar, goat's milk, vanilla, baking powder, and salt.

3. When the butter has melted, pour the batter into the butter. Do not mix. Distribute the strawberries throughout the batter, but do not mix.

4. Bake for 50 to 60 minutes, or until the batter has risen and is golden brown and bubbling. Serve warm.

TIP: If goat's milk is not readily available, use cow's milk or a fifty-fifty mix of plain Greek yogurt and water.

ICED CRANBERRY AND ORANGE CAKE

CLASSIC, OVEN-COOKED, VEGETARIAN, WEEKDAY

⊝———————— SERVES 6 TO 8 ————————⊙

Prep time: 20 minutes | **Cook time:** 40 minutes | **Cast iron:** 12-inch skillet

The combination of cranberries and oranges is such a classic for the holidays. This cake is well suited to any holiday table in fall or winter, and it is easy enough to throw together that it won't add any stress to your all-day cooking marathons.

For the cake

10 tablespoons (1¼ sticks) salted butter, at room temperature, plus more for greasing

1 cup granulated sugar

3 large eggs

1 teaspoon vanilla extract

1½ cups all-purpose flour

1¼ teaspoons baking powder

½ teaspoon baking soda

½ teaspoon sea salt

1 cup plain Greek yogurt

1 cup dried cranberries

1 tablespoon grated orange zest

For the icing

Juice of 1 orange

2 cups powdered sugar

1. **To make the cake:** Preheat the oven to 350°F. Grease the skillet with butter.

2. In the bowl of a stand mixer fitted with the paddle attachment, or in a large bowl using an electric mixer, cream the butter and granulated sugar. Mix in the eggs, one at a time, until fully incorporated. Mix in the vanilla.

3. In another large bowl, stir together the flour, baking powder, baking soda, and salt. While mixing, add ⅓ of the dry ingredients to the wet ingredients. Follow with ⅓ cup of yogurt. Repeat with remaining dry ingredients and yogurt, alternating, until mixed. Scrape the bottom of the bowl and mix for 1 to 2 minutes more.

4. Fold in the cranberries and orange zest. Gently pour the batter into the skillet.

5. Bake for 35 to 40 minutes, or until cooked through and golden brown. Let the cake cool completely.

6. **To make the icing:** Pour the orange juice into a small bowl. Whisk in the powdered sugar, a little at a time, until the icing is thick enough to coat the back of a spoon but still able to be poured. Pour the icing over the cake and serve.

CHOCOLATE CHIP SKILLET COOKIE

OVEN-COOKED, VEGETARIAN

SERVES 4 TO 6

Prep time: 20 minutes | **Inactive time:** 1 hour
Cook time: 25 minutes | **Cast iron:** 12-inch skillet

There is something about a giant chocolate chip cookie that brings out the inner five-year-old in me, causing such joy and elation. I know, logically, a slice of a giant cookie is the same as eating an individual cookie, but *how cool is a giant cookie?* The coolest.

2¾ cups all-purpose flour

1⅔ teaspoons cream of tartar

1 teaspoon baking soda

½ teaspoon sea salt

1 cup (2 sticks) salted butter, at room temperature

1 cup sugar

2 large eggs

1 teaspoon vanilla extract

1½ cups chocolate chips

1. In a large bowl, whisk the flour, cream of tartar, baking soda, and salt to combine.

2. In the bowl of a stand mixer fitted with the paddle attachment, or in a large bowl using an electric mixer, cream the butter and sugar at medium-high speed. Mix in the eggs, one at a time, until fully incorporated. Mix in the vanilla.

3. Reduce the mixer speed to low and slowly add the flour mixture to the butter mixture, mixing until fully combined. Fold in the chocolate chips. Cover the dough and chill in the refrigerator for 1 hour.

4. Preheat the oven to 375°F.

5. Press the dough into the skillet.

6. Bake for 20 to 25 minutes, or until cooked through. Cool before cutting into wedges and serving.

CHOCOLATE-PEPPERMINT BROWNIES

OVEN-COOKED, VEGETARIAN, WEEKDAY

SERVES 4 TO 6

Prep time: 20 minutes | **Cook time:** 30 minutes | **Cast iron:** 12-inch skillet

Chocolate-peppermint brownies scream winter the same way Bourbon White Peach and Nectarine Pie (page 217) screams summer. These brownies are minty, fresh, rich, and celebratory. Adding a crushed candy cane to the top makes it just a little fancy.

8 tablespoons (1 stick) salted butter, at room temperature

1 cup packed light brown sugar

4 large eggs, lightly beaten

2 teaspoons peppermint extract

1 teaspoon vanilla extract

¼ cup buttermilk

1½ cups unsweetened cocoa powder

⅔ cup all-purpose flour

¼ teaspoon baking soda

1 candy cane, crushed

1. Preheat the oven to 350°F.

2. In a medium bowl, stir together the butter, brown sugar, eggs, peppermint extract, and vanilla. Stir in the buttermilk.

3. In another medium bowl, gently whisk the cocoa powder, flour, and baking soda to combine. Fold the flour mixture into the butter mixture.

4. Spoon the batter into the skillet and top with the crushed candy cane.

5. Bake for 25 to 30 minutes, or until cooked through. Let it cool slightly before serving.

GINGERBREAD CAKE

OVEN-COOKED, VEGETARIAN, WEEKDAY

SERVES 4 TO 6

Prep time: 20 minutes | **Cook time:** 35 minutes | **Cast iron:** 12-inch skillet

There are so many wonderful ways to enjoy gingerbread, from crisp snaps to cheesecake to decadent fancy lattes. Gingerbread cake has fewer bells and whistles, but its rich ginger flavor is a wonderful companion to the moist and soft cake.

4 tablespoons (½ stick) salted butter, at room temperature, plus more for greasing

1½ cups all-purpose flour

1 teaspoon ground ginger

1 teaspoon ground cinnamon

½ teaspoon baking soda

½ teaspoon ground cloves

¼ teaspoon sea salt

½ cup packed light brown sugar

1 large egg

½ cup molasses

½ cup plain Greek yogurt

¼ cup crystallized ginger, roughly chopped

1. Preheat the oven to 350°F. Grease the skillet with butter.

2. In a medium bowl, combine the flour, ginger, cinnamon, baking soda, cloves, and salt.

3. In the bowl of a stand mixer fitted with the paddle attachment, or in a large bowl using an electric mixer, cream the butter and brown sugar. Mix in the egg, molasses, yogurt, and crystallized ginger.

4. Slowly add the dry ingredients to the wet ingredients, mixing until well combined. Pour the batter into the skillet.

5. Bake for 30 to 35 minutes, or until cooked through. Let it cool before serving.

MEASUREMENT CONVERSIONS

VOLUME EQUIVALENTS	U.S. Standard	U.S. Standard (ounces)	Metric (approximate)
LIQUID	2 tablespoons	1 fl. oz.	30 mL
	¼ cup	2 fl. oz.	60 mL
	½ cup	4 fl. oz.	120 mL
	1 cup	8 fl. oz.	240 mL
	1½ cups	12 fl. oz.	355 mL
	2 cups or 1 pint	16 fl. oz.	475 mL
	4 cups or 1 quart	32 fl. oz.	1 L
	1 gallon	128 fl. oz.	4 L
DRY	⅛ teaspoon	—	0.5 mL
	¼ teaspoon	—	1 mL
	½ teaspoon	—	2 mL
	¾ teaspoon	—	4 mL
	1 teaspoon	—	5 mL
	1 tablespoon	—	15 mL
	¼ cup	—	59 mL
	⅓ cup	—	79 mL
	½ cup	—	118 mL
	⅔ cup	—	156 mL
	¾ cup	—	177 mL
	1 cup	—	235 mL
	2 cups or 1 pint	—	475 mL
	3 cups	—	700 mL
	4 cups or 1 quart	—	1 L
	½ gallon	—	2 L
	1 gallon	—	4 L

OVEN TEMPERATURES

Fahrenheit	Celsius (approximate)
250°F	120°C
300°F	150°C
325°F	165°C
350°F	180°C
375°F	190°C
400°F	200°C
425°F	220°C
450°F	230°C

WEIGHT EQUIVALENTS

U.S. Standard	Metric (approximate)
½ ounce	15 g
1 ounce	30 g
2 ounces	60 g
4 ounces	115 g
8 ounces	225 g
12 ounces	340 g
16 ounces or 1 pound	455 g

INDEX

A

Andouille and Bell Pepper
    Breakfast Hash, 19
Appetizers
    Boudin Balls, 66
    Buffalo Wings, 62
    Fried Pickles, 70
    Goat Cheese and Bacon
        Stuffed Mushrooms, 61
    Sausage and Cheddar Balls, 60
    Spinach and Artichoke Dip, 63
    Vegetable Tempura, 64
Apple Cider Donuts, 218–219
Apple Cider Vinegar
        Pork Chops, 192
Apple Crisp, Baked, 220
Artichokes
    Roasted Artichokes, 80
    Spinach and Artichoke Dip, 63
Arugula
    Bacon, Arugula, Tomato, and
        Pesto Sandwiches, 88
    Fig, Prosciutto, and
        Arugula Pizza, 101
Avocado, Bacon, Tomato, and
        a Runny Egg, Sourdough
        Toast with, 89–90

B

Bacon
    Bacon, Arugula, Tomato, and
        Pesto Sandwiches, 88
    Bacon and Kohlrabi Over
        Creamy Grits, 181–182

Bacon-Wrapped Scallops, 170
    Cheese and Bacon Smashed
        Potatoes, 67–68
    Goat Cheese and Bacon
        Stuffed Mushrooms, 61
    Shrimp and Grits, 163–164
    Sourdough Toast with
        Avocado, Bacon, Tomato,
        and a Runny Egg, 89–90
Baked Apple Crisp, 220
Bananas
    Banana Nut Bread, 45
    Bananas Foster Dutch
        Baby, 16–17
Beans
    Enchilada Casserole, 113–114
    Skillet Nachos, 120
Beef
    Beef and Mint Lettuce
        Wraps, 84
    Beef Ragù with
        Pappardelle, 200
    Carne Asada Tacos, 201
    Cheeseburgers, 93
    Chipotle Beef Tostada, 202
    Herb and Garlic
        Meatloaf, 183–184
    London Broil with Spring
        Onion Pesto, 185
    One-Skillet Steak and
        Potatoes, 188
    Seared Short Ribs with Lime
        Cabbage Slaw, 196
    Steak with Grilled
        Fennel Salad, 180
    Thai Basil Beef, 198

Beets
    Beet and Goat Cheese
        Pizza, 96–97
    Turmeric Roasted Beets, 74
Beignets, 221–222
Bell peppers
    Andouille and Bell Pepper
        Breakfast Hash, 19
    Pork-Stuffed Bell Peppers, 191
    Roasted Red Pepper and
        Goat Cheese Frittata, 23
    Seafood Jambalaya, 177
    Sweet and Sour
        Chicken, 134–135
    Vegetarian Stir-Fry, 115
Berries
    Blueberry Pancakes, 12
    Blueberry Scones, 41
    Chocolate-Strawberry
        Bread Pudding, 208
    French Toast with Strawberry
        Compote, 13
    Iced Cranberry and
        Orange Cake, 229
    Mountain Pie, 214
    Strawberry and Goat
        Milk Cobbler, 228
    Walnut and Cranberry
        Baked Oatmeal, 25
Biscuits
    Biscuit-Topped Chicken
        Potpie, 140–141
    Fried Chicken Biscuits, 86–87
    Ham and Cheese Stuffed
        Biscuits, 46

Jalapeño-Cheddar Drop
    Biscuits, 40
Rosemary Buttermilk
    Biscuits, 33–34
Blackened Chicken Thighs with
    Pineapple Salsa, 153–154
Blackened Mahi-Mahi Tacos with
    Mango Salsa, 165–166
Blood Orange Rhubarb
    Crumble, 209
Blueberries
    Blueberry Pancakes, 12
    Blueberry Scones, 41
Bologna and Egg Sandwich,
    Fried, 22
Bolognese, Lentil, 111–112
Boudin Balls, 66
Bourbon White Peach and
    Nectarine Pie, 217
Braided Cinnamon Bread, 53–54
Breaded Pork Medallions, 194
Bread Pudding,
    Chocolate-Strawberry, 208
Breads
    Banana Nut Bread, 45
    Blueberry Scones, 41
    Braided Cinnamon
        Bread, 53–54
    Buttered Dinner Rolls, 38–39
    Caramelized Onion and
        Tomato Focaccia, 47–48
    Caramel-Pecan Cinnamon
        Rolls, 42–43
    Chocolate Zucchini Bread, 32
    Green Chile Corn Bread with
        Whipped Honey Butter, 44
    Ham and Cheese Stuffed
        Biscuits, 46
    Irish Soda Bread with
        Marmalade, 51–52
    Jalapeño-Cheddar Drop
        Biscuits, 40
    Mozzarella-Stuffed Garlic
        Knots, 49–50
    Rosemary Buttermilk
        Biscuits, 33–34

Sourdough Bread, 35–37
Swirled Herb Bread, 55–56
Broccoli
    Broccoli and Carrot Stuffed
        Shells, 107–108
    Vegetarian Stir-Fry, 115
Brown Butter and Garlic
    Wahoo, 162
Brownies,
        Chocolate-Peppermint, 231
Brussels Sprouts, Sriracha, 71
Buffalo Wings, 62
Burgers
    Cheeseburgers, 93
    Shrimp Burgers with Chipotle
        Mayonnaise, 169
    Turkey Burgers, 136
Butter
    Brown Butter and Garlic
        Wahoo, 162
    Buttered Dinner Rolls, 38–39
    Butter Halloumi, 106
    Garlic Butter Green
        Beans, 73
    Green Chile Corn Bread
        with Whipped
        Honey Butter, 44
    Herb Butter Roasted
        Pattypan, 77
    Lamb Chops with Herb
        Butter, 195
    Spiced Buttery Lentils, 126–127
Buttermilk
    Biscuit-Topped Chicken
        Potpie, 140–141
    Buttermilk Fried Okra, 76
    Buttermilk Grouper
        Bites, 167–168
    Buttermilk Pie, 210
    Buttermilk Roast
        Chicken, 147–148
    Fried Chicken Biscuits, 86–87
    Ham and Cheese Stuffed
        Biscuits, 46
    Jalapeño-Cheddar Drop
        Biscuits, 40

Pickle-Brined Fried
    Chicken, 142–143
Rosemary Buttermilk
    Biscuits, 33–34

C

Cabbage Lime Slaw, Seared
    Short Ribs with, 196
Cakes
    Carrot Cake with Whipped
        Cream Cheese
        Frosting, 223–224
    Gingerbread Cake, 232
    Gooey Chocolate Skillet
        Cake, 226–227
    Iced Cranberry and
        Orange Cake, 229
    Iced Lemon Pound Cake, 225
Calzone, Skillet, 94
Caramel
    Caramel Fried Green Tomatoes
        and Ice Cream, 215–216
    Caramel-Pecan Cinnamon
        Rolls, 42–43
Caramelized Cream-Fried Eggs
    over Parmesan Grits, 21
Caramelized Onion and Tomato
    Focaccia, 47–48
Carne Asada Tacos, 201
Carrots
    Biscuit-Topped Chicken
        Potpie, 140–141
    Broccoli and Carrot Stuffed
        Shells, 107–108
    Carrot and Zucchini Fritters, 121
    Carrot Cake Pancakes with
        Cream Cheese Frosting, 29
    Carrot Cake with Whipped
        Cream Cheese
        Frosting, 223–224
    Classic Lamb Shepherd's
        Pie, 186–187
    Garlic Lamb and Vegetable
        Pasta, 199
    Vegetarian Stir-Fry, 115

Casseroles
  Enchilada Casserole, 113–114
  French Toast Casserole, 24
  Spinach and Mushroom
    Breakfast Casserole, 26
Cast-iron skillets
  buying, 2–3
  care and cleaning, 6
  cooking rules, 9
  enameled, 3
  history of, 2
  re-seasoning, 4–5
  restoring, 7
  seasoning, 3–4
Catfish
  Seafood Jambalaya, 177
  Sweet and Spicy Catfish, 175
Cauliflower, Roasted, 72
Charred Zucchini, 79
Cheddar cheese
  Cheese and Bacon Smashed
    Potatoes, 67–68
  Cheeseburgers, 93
  Chicken Quesadillas, 144
  Chipotle Beef Tostada, 202
  Enchilada Casserole, 113–114
  Ham and Cheese Stuffed
    Biscuits, 46
  Jalapeño-Cheddar Drop
    Biscuits, 40
  Lobster Mac and Cheese, 172
  Macaroni and Cheese, 117–118
  Potato and Cheese
    Pierogis, 124–125
  Sausage and Cheddar Balls, 60
  Skillet Nachos, 120
  Turkey Melt, 85
Cheese. See also Cream cheese
  Beet and Goat Cheese
    Pizza, 96–97
  Broccoli and Carrot Stuffed
    Shells, 107–108
  Butter Halloumi, 106
  Caramelized Cream-Fried Eggs
    over Parmesan Grits, 21

Cheese and Bacon Smashed
    Potatoes, 67–68
Cheeseburgers, 93
Chicken Quesadillas, 144
Chiles Rellenos, 128–129
Chipotle Beef Tostada, 202
Croque Madame, 27–28
Croque Monsieur, 91–92
Eggplant Lasagna, 109–110
Enchilada Casserole, 113–114
Fig, Prosciutto, and
    Arugula Pizza, 101
French Onion Chicken, 138–139
Goat Cheese and Bacon
    Stuffed Mushrooms, 61
Ham and Cheese Stuffed
    Biscuits, 46
Hot Italian Sandwich, 95
Jalapeño-Cheddar Drop
    Biscuits, 40
Lobster Mac and Cheese, 172
Macaroni and Cheese, 117–118
Mozzarella-Stuffed Garlic
    Knots, 49–50
Panzanella, 78
Pepperoni Pizza with
    Hot Honey, 98–99
Pesto and Sausage Pizza, 100
Potato and Cheese
    Pierogis, 124–125
Ricotta-Stuffed Zucchini
    Boats, 116
Roasted Red Pepper and
    Goat Cheese Frittata, 23
Sausage and Cheddar Balls, 60
Skillet Calzone, 94
Skillet Nachos, 120
Sweet Potato Frittata, 119
Turkey Melt, 85
Cheeseburgers, 93
Chicken
  Biscuit-Topped Chicken
    Potpie, 140–141
  Blackened Chicken Thighs with
    Pineapple Salsa, 153–154

Buffalo Wings, 62
Buttermilk Roast
    Chicken, 147–148
Chicken and Green Bean
    Stir-Fry, 146
Chicken and Zucchini
    Curry, 132–133
Chicken Biryani, 155–156
Chicken Marsala, 151–152
Chicken Quesadillas, 144
French Onion Chicken, 138–139
Fried Chicken Biscuits, 86–87
Jerk Chicken Naked Wings, 149
Miso Chicken Thighs, 137
Pickle-Brined Fried
    Chicken, 142–143
Sweet and Sour
    Chicken, 134–135
Chickpeas, Crispy Chipotle, 65
Chiles Rellenos, 128–129
Chipotle Beef Tostada, 202
Chipotle Cream Sauce,
    Roasted Sausage and
    Potatoes with, 193
Chipotle Mayonnaise, Shrimp
    Burgers with, 169
Chocolate
  Chocolate Chip Skillet
    Cookie, 230
  Chocolate-Peppermint
    Brownies, 231
  Chocolate-Strawberry
    Bread Pudding, 208
  Chocolate Zucchini Bread, 32
  Gooey Chocolate Skillet
    Cake, 226–227
Cinnamon Rolls,
    Caramel-Pecan, 42–43
Classic
  Andouille and Bell Pepper
    Breakfast Hash, 19
  Apple Cider Donuts, 218–219
  Apple Cider Vinegar
    Pork Chops, 192
  Baked Apple Crisp, 220

Beef Ragù with
    Pappardelle, 200
Beignets, 221–222
Blueberry Pancakes, 12
Buttered Dinner Rolls, 38–39
Buttermilk Grouper
    Bites, 167–168
Buttermilk Pie, 210
Buttermilk Roast
    Chicken, 147–148
Cheeseburgers, 93
Classic Lamb Shepherd's
    Pie, 186–187
Herb and Garlic
    Meatloaf, 183–184
Herb-Crusted Pork Loin, 189
Iced Cranberry and
    Orange Cake, 229
Iced Lemon Pound Cake, 225
Kohlrabi and Potato
    Hash, 20
Macaroni and Cheese, 117–118
Pickle-Brined Fried
    Chicken, 142–143
Roasted Turkey Breast, 150
Sausage and Cheddar
    Balls, 60
Shoofly Pie, 206–207
Shrimp and Grits, 163–164
Skillet Greens, 69
Sourdough Bread, 35–37
Cleaning cast iron, 6
Cobblers
    Mountain Pie, 214
    Strawberry and Goat
        Milk Cobbler, 228
Collard greens
    Skillet Greens, 69
Cookie, Chocolate Chip
    Skillet, 230
Corn
    Classic Lamb Shepherd's
        Pie, 186–187
    Enchilada Casserole, 113–114
    Vegetarian Stir-Fry, 115

Corn Bread, Green Chile, with
    Whipped Honey Butter, 44
Cotija cheese
    Enchilada Casserole, 113–114
    Skillet Nachos, 120
Crab Cakes, Jalapeño
    and Shallot, 160
Cranberries, dried
    Iced Cranberry and
        Orange Cake, 229
    Walnut and Cranberry
        Baked Oatmeal, 25
Cream cheese
    Carrot Cake Pancakes with
        Cream Cheese Frosting, 29
    Carrot Cake with Whipped
        Cream Cheese
        Frosting, 223–224
    Lobster Mac and Cheese, 172
    Spinach and Artichoke
        Dip, 63
Crispy Chipotle Chickpeas, 65
Crispy Marshmallow Bars, 211
Croque Madame, 27–28
Croque Monsieur, 91–92
Crumble, Blood Orange
    Rhubarb, 209
Curried Pea and Mushroom
    Shepherd's Pie, 122–123
Curry, Chicken and
    Zucchini, 132–133

D

Desserts
    Apple Cider Donuts, 218–219
    Beignets, 221–222
    Blood Orange Rhubarb
        Crumble, 209
    Bourbon White Peach and
        Nectarine Pie, 217
    Buttermilk Pie, 210
    Caramel Fried Green Tomatoes
        and Ice Cream, 215–216

Carrot Cake with Whipped
    Cream Cheese
    Frosting, 223–224
Chocolate Chip Skillet
    Cookie, 230
Chocolate-Peppermint
    Brownies, 231
Chocolate-Strawberry
    Bread Pudding, 208
Crispy Marshmallow Bars, 211
Gingerbread Cake, 232
Gooey Chocolate Skillet
    Cake, 226–227
Iced Cranberry and
    Orange Cake, 229
Iced Lemon Pound Cake, 225
Mountain Pie, 214
Pear and Pecan Pie, 212–213
Shoofly Pie, 206–207
Strawberry and Goat
    Milk Cobbler, 228
Donuts, Apple Cider, 218–219

E

Eggplants
    Eggplant Lasagna, 109–110
    Vegetable Tempura, 64
Eggs
    Caramelized Cream-Fried Eggs
        over Parmesan Grits, 21
    Croque Madame, 27–28
    Fried Bologna and Egg
        Sandwich, 22
    Roasted Red Pepper and
        Goat Cheese Frittata, 23
    Sourdough Toast with
        Avocado, Bacon, Tomato,
        and a Runny Egg, 89–90
    Spinach and Mushroom
        Breakfast Casserole, 26
    Sweet Potato Frittata, 119
Enameled cast-iron skillets, 3
Enchilada Casserole, 113–114
Equipment, 5

F

Fennel Salad, Grilled,
    Steak with, 180
Fig, Prosciutto, and
    Arugula Pizza, 101
Fish and seafood
    Bacon-Wrapped Scallops, 170
    Blackened Mahi-Mahi Tacos
        with Mango Salsa, 165–166
    Brown Butter and Garlic
        Wahoo, 162
    Buttermilk Grouper
        Bites, 167–168
    Jalapeño and Shallot
        Crab Cakes, 160
    Lobster Mac and Cheese, 172
    Maple-Glazed Salmon, 176
    Salmon Cakes, 173
    Seared Ahi Tuna, 171
    Seared Lobster Tails, 161
    Shrimp and Grits, 163–164
    Shrimp and Scallop
        Scampi, 174
    Shrimp Burgers with Chipotle
        Mayonnaise, 169
    Sweet and Spicy Catfish, 175
Focaccia, Caramelized Onion
    and Tomato, 47–48
Four-Ingredient Pancakes, 18
French Onion Chicken, 138–139
French Toast Casserole, 24
French Toast with Strawberry
    Compote, 13
Fried Bologna and Egg
    Sandwich, 22
Fried Chicken Biscuits, 86–87
Fried Pickles, 70
Frittatas
    Roasted Red Pepper and
        Goat Cheese Frittata, 23
    Sweet Potato Frittata, 119
Fritters, Carrot and Zucchini, 121

G

Garlic
    Brown Butter and Garlic
        Wahoo, 162
    Garlic Butter Green Beans, 73
    Garlic Lamb and Vegetable
        Pasta, 199
    Herb and Garlic
        Meatloaf, 183–184
    Mozzarella-Stuffed Garlic
        Knots, 49–50
Gingerbread Cake, 232
Gluten-free
    Andouille and Bell Pepper
        Breakfast Hash, 19
    Apple Cider Vinegar
        Pork Chops, 192
    Bacon and Kohlrabi Over
        Creamy Grits, 181–182
    Bacon-Wrapped Scallops, 170
    Blackened Chicken Thighs with
        Pineapple Salsa, 153–154
    Boudin Balls, 66
    Brown Butter and Garlic
        Wahoo, 162
    Butter Halloumi, 106
    Buttermilk Roast
        Chicken, 147–148
    Caramelized Cream-Fried Eggs
        over Parmesan Grits, 21
    Carne Asada Tacos, 201
    Charred Zucchini, 79
    Cheese and Bacon Smashed
        Potatoes, 67–68
    Chicken and Zucchini
        Curry, 132–133
    Chicken Biryani, 155–156
    Chipotle Beef Tostada, 202
    Classic Lamb Shepherd's
        Pie, 186–187
    Crispy Chipotle Chickpeas, 65
    French Onion Chicken, 138–139
    Garlic Butter Green Beans, 73
    Goat Cheese and Bacon
        Stuffed Mushrooms, 61
    Hasselback Potatoes, 75
    Herb and Garlic
        Meatloaf, 183–184
    Herb Butter Roasted
        Pattypan, 77
    Herb-Crusted Pork Loin, 189
    Jerk Chicken Naked Wings, 149
    Kohlrabi and Potato Hash, 20
    Lamb Chops with Herb
        Butter, 195
    London Broil with Spring
        Onion Pesto, 185
    One-Skillet Steak and
        Potatoes, 188
    Oven-Roasted Ribs, 190
    Pork Belly and Kimchi
        Bowl, 197
    Pork-Stuffed Bell Peppers, 191
    Roasted Artichokes, 80
    Roasted Cauliflower, 72
    Roasted Red Pepper and
        Goat Cheese Frittata, 23
    Roasted Sausage and
        Potatoes with Chipotle
        Cream Sauce, 193
    Roasted Turkey Breast, 150
    Seafood Jambalaya, 177
    Seared Lobster Tails, 161
    Seared Short Ribs with Lime
        Cabbage Slaw, 196
    Shrimp and Grits, 163–164
    Skillet Greens, 69
    Skillet Nachos, 120
    Spiced Buttery Lentils, 126–127
    Spinach and Artichoke Dip, 63
    Spring Pea and Mushroom
        Risotto, 104–105
    Steak with Grilled
        Fennel Salad, 180
    Sweet and Spicy Catfish, 175
    Sweet Potato Frittata, 119
    Turmeric Roasted Beets, 74

Goat cheese
  Beet and Goat Cheese
    Pizza, 96–97
  Goat Cheese and Bacon
    Stuffed Mushrooms, 61
  Roasted Red Pepper and
    Goat Cheese Frittata, 23
Goat Milk and Strawberry
  Cobbler, 228
Gooey Chocolate Skillet
  Cake, 226–227
Green beans
  Chicken and Green Bean
    Stir-Fry, 146
  Garlic Butter Green Beans, 73
Green Chile Corn Bread with
  Whipped Honey Butter, 44
Green Tomatoes, Caramel Fried,
  and Ice Cream, 215–216
Grits
  Bacon and Kohlrabi Over
    Creamy Grits, 181–182
  Caramelized Cream-Fried
    Eggs over Parmesan
    Grits, 21
  Shrimp and Grits, 163–164
Grouper Bites,
  Buttermilk, 167–168
Gruyère cheese
  Croque Madame, 27–28
  Croque Monsieur, 91–92
  French Onion Chicken, 138–139
  Macaroni and Cheese, 117–118

H

Halloumi, Butter, 106
Ham. *See also* Prosciutto
  Croque Madame, 27–28
  Croque Monsieur, 91–92
  Ham and Cheese Stuffed
    Biscuits, 46
  Hot Italian Sandwich, 95

Hash
  Andouille and Bell Pepper
    Breakfast Hash, 19
  Kohlrabi and Potato Hash, 20
Hasselback Potatoes, 75
Herb and Garlic Meatloaf, 183–184
Herb Butter Roasted Pattypan, 77
Herb-Crusted Pork Loin, 189
Honey
  Green Chile Corn Bread with
    Whipped Honey Butter, 44
  Pepperoni Pizza with
    Hot Honey, 98–99
Hot Italian Sandwich, 95

I

Ice Cream, Caramel Fried Green
  Tomatoes and, 215–216
Iced Cranberry and
  Orange Cake, 229
Iced Lemon Pound Cake, 225
Irish Soda Bread with
  Marmalade, 51–52

J

Jalapeño peppers
  Jalapeño and Shallot
    Crab Cakes, 160
  Jalapeño-Cheddar Drop
    Biscuits, 40
  Jerk Chicken Naked
    Wings, 149

K

Kimchi and Pork Belly Bowl, 197
Kohlrabi
  Bacon and Kohlrabi Over
    Creamy Grits, 181–182
  Kohlrabi and Potato Hash, 20

L

Lamb
  Classic Lamb Shepherd's
    Pie, 186–187
  Garlic Lamb and Vegetable
    Pasta, 199
  Lamb Chops with Herb
    Butter, 195
Lentils
  Lentil Bolognese, 111–112
  Spiced Buttery Lentils, 126–127
Lettuce Wraps, Beef and Mint, 84
Lime Cabbage Slaw, Seared
  Short Ribs with, 196
Lobster
  Lobster Mac and Cheese, 172
  Seared Lobster Tails, 161
London Broil with Spring
  Onion Pesto, 185

M

Macaroni and Cheese, 117–118
Mahi-Mahi, Blackened, Tacos
  with Mango Salsa, 165–166
Mango Salsa, Blackened
  Mahi-Mahi Tacos
  with, 165–166
Maple-Glazed Salmon, 176
Marmalade, Irish Soda
  Bread with, 51–52
Marshmallow Bars, Crispy, 211
Meatballs
  Boudin Balls, 66
  Turkey and Sage Meatballs, 145
Meatloaf, Herb and
  Garlic, 183–184
Mint and Beef Lettuce Wraps, 84
Miso Chicken Thighs, 137
Molasses
  Gingerbread Cake, 232
  Shoofly Pie, 206–207

Monterey Jack cheese
  Chipotle Beef Tostada, 202
  Enchilada Casserole, 113–114
  Skillet Nachos, 120
Mountain Pie, 214
Mozzarella cheese
  Broccoli and Carrot Stuffed
    Shells, 107–108
  Eggplant Lasagna, 109–110
  Fig, Prosciutto, and
    Arugula Pizza, 101
  Lobster Mac and Cheese, 172
  Macaroni and Cheese, 117–118
  Mozzarella-Stuffed Garlic
    Knots, 49–50
  Panzanella, 78
  Pepperoni Pizza with
    Hot Honey, 98–99
  Pesto and Sausage Pizza, 100
  Ricotta-Stuffed Zucchini
    Boats, 116
  Skillet Calzone, 94
Mushrooms
  Biscuit-Topped Chicken
    Potpie, 140–141
  Chicken Marsala, 151–152
  Curried Pea and Mushroom
    Shepherd's Pie, 122–123
  Garlic Lamb and Vegetable
    Pasta, 199
  Goat Cheese and Bacon
    Stuffed Mushrooms, 61
  Spinach and Mushroom
    Breakfast Casserole, 26
  Spring Pea and Mushroom
    Risotto, 104–105
  Vegetable Tempura, 64
  Vegetarian Stir-Fry, 115

N

Nachos, Skillet, 120
Nectarine and White Peach
  Pie, Bourbon, 217

Nuts
  Banana Nut Bread, 45
  Caramel-Pecan Cinnamon
    Rolls, 42–43
  Carrot Cake Pancakes with
    Cream Cheese Frosting, 29
  Carrot Cake with Whipped
    Cream Cheese
    Frosting, 223–224
  Pear and Pecan Pie, 212–213
  Walnut and Cranberry
    Baked Oatmeal, 25

O

Oatmeal, Walnut and
    Cranberry Baked, 25
Oats
  Baked Apple Crisp, 220
  Blood Orange Rhubarb
    Crumble, 209
  Walnut and Cranberry
    Baked Oatmeal, 25
Okra, Buttermilk Fried, 76
One-Skillet Steak and
    Potatoes, 188
Onions
  Caramelized Onion and
    Tomato Focaccia, 47–48
  French Onion Chicken, 138–139
  London Broil with Spring
    Onion Pesto, 185
Oranges
  Blood Orange Rhubarb
    Crumble, 209
  Iced Cranberry and
    Orange Cake, 229
  Irish Soda Bread with
    Marmalade, 51–52
Oven-cooked
  Apple Cider Vinegar
    Pork Chops, 192
  Bacon-Wrapped Scallops, 170
  Baked Apple Crisp, 220

Banana Nut Bread, 45
Bananas Foster Dutch
  Baby, 16–17
Beet and Goat Cheese
  Pizza, 96–97
Biscuit-Topped Chicken
  Potpie, 140–141
Blackened Chicken Thighs with
  Pineapple Salsa, 153–154
Blood Orange Rhubarb
  Crumble, 209
Blueberry Scones, 41
Bourbon White Peach and
  Nectarine Pie, 217
Braided Cinnamon
  Bread, 53–54
Broccoli and Carrot Stuffed
  Shells, 107–108
Buttered Dinner Rolls, 38–39
Buttermilk Pie, 210
Buttermilk Roast
  Chicken, 147–148
Caramelized Onion and
  Tomato Focaccia, 47–48
Caramel-Pecan Cinnamon
  Rolls, 42–43
Carrot Cake with Whipped
  Cream Cheese
  Frosting, 223–224
Charred Zucchini, 79
Cheese and Bacon Smashed
  Potatoes, 67–68
Chiles Rellenos, 128–129
Chocolate Chip Skillet
  Cookie, 230
Chocolate-Peppermint
  Brownies, 231
Chocolate-Strawberry
  Bread Pudding, 208
Chocolate Zucchini Bread, 32
Classic Lamb Shepherd's
  Pie, 186–187
Croque Madame, 27–28
Croque Monsieur, 91–92

Curried Pea and Mushroom
    Shepherd's Pie, 122–123
Eggplant Lasagna, 109–110
Enchilada Casserole, 113–114
Fig, Prosciutto, and
    Arugula Pizza, 101
French Onion Chicken, 138–139
French Toast Casserole, 24
Fried Chicken Biscuits, 86–87
Gingerbread Cake, 232
Goat Cheese and Bacon
    Stuffed Mushrooms, 61
Gooey Chocolate Skillet
    Cake, 226–227
Green Chile Corn Bread with
    Whipped Honey Butter, 44
Ham and Cheese Stuffed
    Biscuits, 46
Hasselback Potatoes, 75
Herb and Garlic
    Meatloaf, 183–184
Herb Butter Roasted
    Pattypan, 77
Herb-Crusted Pork Loin, 189
Hot Italian Sandwich, 95
Iced Cranberry and
    Orange Cake, 229
Iced Lemon Pound Cake, 225
Irish Soda Bread with
    Marmalade, 51–52
Jalapeño-Cheddar Drop
    Biscuits, 40
Jerk Chicken Naked Wings, 149
Lobster Mac and Cheese, 172
London Broil with Spring
    Onion Pesto, 185
Macaroni and Cheese, 117–118
Maple-Glazed Salmon, 176
Miso Chicken Thighs, 137
Mountain Pie, 214
Mozzarella-Stuffed Garlic
    Knots, 49–50
Oven-Roasted Ribs, 190
Pear and Pecan Pie, 212–213

Pepperoni Pizza with
    Hot Honey, 98–99
Pesto and Sausage Pizza, 100
Pork-Stuffed Bell Peppers, 191
Ricotta-Stuffed Zucchini
    Boats, 116
Roasted Cauliflower, 72
Roasted Red Pepper and
    Goat Cheese Frittata, 23
Roasted Sausage and
    Potatoes with Chipotle
    Cream Sauce, 193
Roasted Turkey Breast, 150
Rosemary Buttermilk
    Biscuits, 33–34
Salmon Cakes, 173
Sausage and Cheddar Balls, 60
Savory Dutch Baby, 14–15
Shoofly Pie, 206–207
Skillet Calzone, 94
Skillet Nachos, 120
Sourdough Bread, 35–37
Spinach and Artichoke Dip, 63
Spinach and Mushroom
    Breakfast Casserole, 26
Sriracha Brussels Sprouts, 71
Strawberry and Goat
    Milk Cobbler, 228
Sweet Potato Frittata, 119
Swirled Herb Bread, 55–56
Turkey and Sage Meatballs, 145
Turkey Melt, 85
Turmeric Roasted Beets, 74
Walnut and Cranberry
    Baked Oatmeal, 25
Oven-Roasted Ribs, 190

P

Pancakes
    Bananas Foster Dutch
        Baby, 16–17
    Blueberry Pancakes, 12

Carrot Cake Pancakes with
    Cream Cheese Frosting, 29
Four-Ingredient Pancakes, 18
Savory Dutch Baby, 14–15
Panzanella, 78
Parmesan Grits, Caramelized
    Cream-Fried Eggs over, 21
Pasta
    Beef Ragù with
        Pappardelle, 200
    Broccoli and Carrot Stuffed
        Shells, 107–108
    Eggplant Lasagna, 109–110
    Garlic Lamb and Vegetable
        Pasta, 199
    Lobster Mac and Cheese, 172
    Macaroni and Cheese, 117–118
    Shrimp and Scallop Scampi, 174
Pattypan, Herb Butter
    Roasted, 77
Peaches
    Bourbon White Peach and
        Nectarine Pie, 217
    Mountain Pie, 214
Pear and Pecan Pie, 212–213
Peas
    Biscuit-Topped Chicken
        Potpie, 140–141
    Classic Lamb Shepherd's
        Pie, 186–187
    Curried Pea and Mushroom
        Shepherd's Pie, 122–123
    Spring Pea and Mushroom
        Risotto, 104–105
    Vegetarian Stir-Fry, 115
Pecans
    Caramel-Pecan Cinnamon
        Rolls, 42–43
    Carrot Cake with Whipped
        Cream Cheese
        Frosting, 223–224
    Pear and Pecan Pie, 212–213
Peppermint-Chocolate
    Brownies, 231

Pepperoni
  Hot Italian Sandwich, 95
  Pepperoni Pizza with
    Hot Honey, 98–99
Pesto
  Bacon, Arugula, Tomato, and
    Pesto Sandwiches, 88
  London Broil with Spring
    Onion Pesto, 185
  Pesto and Sausage Pizza, 100
Pickle-Brined Fried
  Chicken, 142–143
Pickles, Fried, 70
Pierogis, Potato and
  Cheese, 124–125
Pies, savory
  Biscuit-Topped Chicken
    Potpie, 140–141
  Classic Lamb Shepherd's
    Pie, 186–187
  Curried Pea and Mushroom
    Shepherd's Pie, 122–123
Pies, sweet
  Bourbon White Peach and
    Nectarine Pie, 217
  Buttermilk Pie, 210
  Mountain Pie, 214
  Pear and Pecan Pie, 212–213
  Shoofly Pie, 206–207
Pineapple
  Blackened Chicken Thighs with
    Pineapple Salsa, 153–154
  Sweet and Sour
    Chicken, 134–135
Pizzas
  Beet and Goat Cheese
    Pizza, 96–97
  Fig, Prosciutto, and
    Arugula Pizza, 101
  Pepperoni Pizza with
    Hot Honey, 98–99
  Pesto and Sausage Pizza, 100
  Skillet Calzone, 94
Poblano peppers
  Chiles Rellenos, 128–129

Pork. *See also* Bacon;
  Ham; Sausage
  Apple Cider Vinegar
    Pork Chops, 192
  Boudin Balls, 66
  Breaded Pork Medallions, 194
  Herb-Crusted Pork Loin, 189
  Oven-Roasted Ribs, 190
  Pork Belly and Kimchi
    Bowl, 197
  Pork-Stuffed Bell Peppers, 191
Potatoes. *See also* Sweet potatoes
  Andouille and Bell Pepper
    Breakfast Hash, 19
  Cheese and Bacon Smashed
    Potatoes, 67–68
  Classic Lamb Shepherd's
    Pie, 186–187
  Curried Pea and Mushroom
    Shepherd's Pie, 122–123
  Hasselback Potatoes, 75
  Kohlrabi and Potato Hash, 20
  One-Skillet Steak and
    Potatoes, 188
  Potato and Cheese
    Pierogis, 124–125
  Roasted Sausage and
    Potatoes with Chipotle
    Cream Sauce, 193
Prosciutto, Fig, and
  Arugula Pizza, 101
Provolone cheese
  Hot Italian Sandwich, 95

Q

Queso fresco
  Chiles Rellenos, 128–129

R

Raspberries
  Mountain Pie, 214
Recipes, about, 8

Rhubarb Blood Orange
  Crumble, 209
Rice
  Chicken Biryani, 155–156
  Chiles Rellenos, 128–129
  Pork-Stuffed Bell Peppers, 191
  Seafood Jambalaya, 177
  Spring Pea and Mushroom
    Risotto, 104–105
Ricotta-Stuffed Zucchini
  Boats, 116
Roasted Artichokes, 80
Roasted Cauliflower, 72
Roasted Red Pepper and Goat
  Cheese Frittata, 23
Roasted Sausage and
  Potatoes with Chipotle
  Cream Sauce, 193
Roasted Turkey Breast, 150
Rolls
  Buttered Dinner Rolls, 38–39
  Caramel-Pecan Cinnamon
    Rolls, 42–43
Rosemary Buttermilk
  Biscuits, 33–34
Rules, 9
Rust, 7

S

Salads
  Panzanella, 78
  Seared Short Ribs with Lime
    Cabbage Slaw, 196
  Steak with Grilled
    Fennel Salad, 180
Salmon
  Maple-Glazed Salmon, 176
  Salmon Cakes, 173
Sandwiches. *See also* Burgers
  Bacon, Arugula, Tomato, and
    Pesto Sandwiches, 88
  Beef and Mint Lettuce
    Wraps, 84

Chicken Quesadillas, 144
Croque Madame, 27–28
Croque Monsieur, 91–92
Fried Bologna and Egg
    Sandwich, 22
Fried Chicken Biscuits, 86–87
Hot Italian Sandwich, 95
Skillet Calzone, 94
Sourdough Toast with
    Avocado, Bacon, Tomato,
    and a Runny Egg, 89–90
Turkey Melt, 85
Sausage
    Andouille and Bell Pepper
        Breakfast Hash, 19
    Beet and Goat Cheese
        Pizza, 96–97
    Pesto and Sausage Pizza, 100
    Roasted Sausage and
        Potatoes with Chipotle
        Cream Sauce, 193
    Sausage and Cheddar Balls, 60
    Seafood Jambalaya, 177
Savory Dutch Baby, 14–15
Scallops
    Bacon-Wrapped Scallops, 170
    Shrimp and Scallop Scampi, 174
Scones, Blueberry, 41
Seafood Jambalaya, 177
Seared Ahi Tuna, 171
Seared Lobster Tails, 161
Seared Short Ribs with Lime
    Cabbage Slaw, 196
Shallot and Jalapeño
    Crab Cakes, 160
Shellfish. See Fish and seafood
Shoofly Pie, 206–207
Shrimp
    Seafood Jambalaya, 177
    Shrimp and Grits, 163–164
    Shrimp and Scallop Scampi, 174
    Shrimp Burgers with Chipotle
        Mayonnaise, 169
Skillet Calzone, 94
Skillet Greens, 69

Skillet Nachos, 120
Sourdough Bread, 35–37
Sourdough Toast with Avocado,
    Bacon, Tomato, and a
    Runny Egg, 89–90
Spiced Buttery Lentils, 126–127
Spinach
    Garlic Lamb and Vegetable
        Pasta, 199
    Spinach and Artichoke Dip, 63
    Spinach and Mushroom
        Breakfast Casserole, 26
Spring Pea and Mushroom
    Risotto, 104–105
Sriracha Brussels Sprouts, 71
Steak with Grilled Fennel
    Salad, 180
Stir-fries
    Chicken and Green Bean
        Stir-Fry, 146
    Vegetarian Stir-Fry, 115
Strawberries
    Chocolate-Strawberry
        Bread Pudding, 208
    French Toast with Strawberry
        Compote, 13
    Strawberry and Goat
        Milk Cobbler, 228
Sweet and Sour Chicken, 134–135
Sweet and Spicy Catfish, 175
Sweet potatoes
    Biscuit-Topped Chicken
        Potpie, 140–141
    Sweet Potato Frittata, 119
    Vegetable Tempura, 64
Swirled Herb Bread, 55–56

T
Tacos
    Blackened Mahi-Mahi Tacos
        with Mango Salsa, 165–166
    Carne Asada Tacos, 201
Thai Basil Beef, 198

Tomatoes
    Bacon, Arugula, Tomato, and
        Pesto Sandwiches, 88
    Beef Ragù with
        Pappardelle, 200
    Blackened Chicken Thighs with
        Pineapple Salsa, 153–154
    Blackened Mahi-Mahi Tacos
        with Mango Salsa, 165–166
    Caramel Fried Green Tomatoes
        and Ice Cream, 215–216
    Caramelized Onion and
        Tomato Focaccia, 47–48
    Panzanella, 78
    Sourdough Toast with
        Avocado, Bacon, Tomato,
        and a Runny Egg, 89–90
Tools, 5
Tostada, Chipotle Beef, 202
Tuna, Seared Ahi, 171
Turkey
    Roasted Turkey Breast, 150
    Turkey and Sage Meatballs, 145
    Turkey Burgers, 136
    Turkey Melt, 85
Turmeric Roasted Beets, 74

V
Vegan
    Charred Zucchini, 79
    Crispy Chipotle Chickpeas, 65
    Roasted Artichokes, 80
    Roasted Cauliflower, 72
    Skillet Greens, 69
    Sourdough Bread, 35–37
    Turmeric Roasted Beets, 74
Vegetable Tempura, 64
Vegetarian. See also Vegan
    Apple Cider Donuts, 218–219
    Baked Apple Crisp, 220
    Banana Nut Bread, 45
    Bananas Foster Dutch
        Baby, 16–17

Vegetarian (*continued*)

Beignets, 221–222

Blood Orange Rhubarb
Crumble, 209

Blueberry Pancakes, 12

Blueberry Scones, 41

Bourbon White Peach and
Nectarine Pie, 217

Braided Cinnamon
Bread, 53–54

Broccoli and Carrot Stuffed
Shells, 107–108

Buttered Dinner Rolls, 38–39

Butter Halloumi, 106

Buttermilk Fried Okra, 76

Buttermilk Pie, 210

Caramel Fried Green Tomatoes
and Ice Cream, 215–216

Caramelized Cream-Fried Eggs
over Parmesan Grits, 21

Caramelized Onion and
Tomato Focaccia, 47–48

Caramel-Pecan Cinnamon
Rolls, 42–43

Carrot and Zucchini Fritters, 121

Carrot Cake Pancakes with
Cream Cheese Frosting, 29

Carrot Cake with Whipped
Cream Cheese
Frosting, 223–224

Chiles Rellenos, 128–129

Chocolate Chip Skillet
Cookie, 230

Chocolate-Peppermint
Brownies, 231

Chocolate-Strawberry
Bread Pudding, 208

Chocolate Zucchini Bread, 32

Crispy Marshmallow Bars, 211

Curried Pea and Mushroom
Shepherd's Pie, 122–123

Eggplant Lasagna, 109–110

Enchilada Casserole, 113–114

Four-Ingredient Pancakes, 18

French Toast Casserole, 24

French Toast with Strawberry
Compote, 13

Fried Pickles, 70

Garlic Butter Green Beans, 73

Gingerbread Cake, 232

Green Chile Corn Bread with
Whipped Honey Butter, 44

Hasselback Potatoes, 75

Herb Butter Roasted
Pattypan, 77

Iced Cranberry and
Orange Cake, 229

Iced Lemon Pound Cake, 225

Irish Soda Bread with
Marmalade, 51–52

Jalapeño-Cheddar Drop
Biscuits, 40

Kohlrabi and Potato Hash, 20

Lentil Bolognese, 111–112

Macaroni and Cheese, 117–118

Mountain Pie, 214

Mozzarella-Stuffed Garlic
Knots, 49–50

Panzanella, 78

Pear and Pecan Pie, 212–213

Potato and Cheese
Pierogis, 124–125

Ricotta-Stuffed Zucchini
Boats, 116

Roasted Red Pepper and
Goat Cheese Frittata, 23

Rosemary Buttermilk
Biscuits, 33–34

Shoofly Pie, 206–207

Skillet Nachos, 120

Spiced Buttery Lentils, 126–127

Spinach and Artichoke Dip, 63

Spinach and Mushroom
Breakfast Casserole, 26

Spring Pea and Mushroom
Risotto, 104–105

Sriracha Brussels Sprouts, 71

Strawberry and Goat
Milk Cobbler, 228

Sweet Potato Frittata, 119

Swirled Herb Bread, 55–56

Vegetable Tempura, 64

Vegetarian Stir-Fry, 115

Walnut and Cranberry
Baked Oatmeal, 25

W

Wahoo, Brown Butter
and Garlic, 162

Walnuts

Banana Nut Bread, 45

Carrot Cake Pancakes with
Cream Cheese Frosting, 29

Walnut and Cranberry
Baked Oatmeal, 25

Weekday

Andouille and Bell Pepper
Breakfast Hash, 19

Bacon, Arugula, Tomato, and
Pesto Sandwiches, 88

Bacon and Kohlrabi Over
Creamy Grits, 181–182

Bacon-Wrapped Scallops, 170

Baked Apple Crisp, 220

Bananas Foster Dutch
Baby, 16–17

Beef and Mint Lettuce
Wraps, 84

Blackened Mahi-Mahi Tacos
with Mango Salsa, 165–166

Blueberry Pancakes, 12

Blueberry Scones, 41

Boudin Balls, 66

Breaded Pork Medallions, 194

Brown Butter and Garlic
Wahoo, 162

Buffalo Wings, 62

Buttermilk Fried Okra, 76

Caramel Fried Green Tomatoes
and Ice Cream, 215–216

Caramelized Cream-Fried Eggs
over Parmesan Grits, 21

Carne Asada Tacos, 201

Carrot and Zucchini Fritters, 121
Carrot Cake Pancakes with
    Cream Cheese Frosting, 29
Charred Zucchini, 79
Cheeseburgers, 93
Chicken and Green Bean
    Stir-Fry, 146
Chicken and Zucchini
    Curry, 132–133
Chicken Marsala, 151–152
Chicken Quesadillas, 144
Chipotle Beef Tostada, 202
Chocolate-Peppermint
    Brownies, 231
Crispy Chipotle Chickpeas, 65
Crispy Marshmallow Bars, 211
Croque Madame, 27–28
Croque Monsieur, 91–92
Fig, Prosciutto, and
    Arugula Pizza, 101
Four-Ingredient Pancakes, 18
French Onion Chicken, 138–139
French Toast Casserole, 24
French Toast with Strawberry
    Compote, 13
Fried Bologna and Egg
    Sandwich, 22
Fried Chicken Biscuits, 86–87
Fried Pickles, 70
Garlic Butter Green Beans, 73
Garlic Lamb and Vegetable
    Pasta, 199
Gingerbread Cake, 232
Goat Cheese and Bacon
    Stuffed Mushrooms, 61
Gooey Chocolate Skillet
    Cake, 226–227
Green Chile Corn Bread with
    Whipped Honey Butter, 44

Ham and Cheese Stuffed
    Biscuits, 46
Herb Butter Roasted
    Pattypan, 77
Herb-Crusted Pork Loin, 189
Hot Italian Sandwich, 95
Iced Cranberry and
    Orange Cake, 229
Jalapeño and Shallot
    Crab Cakes, 160
Jalapeño-Cheddar Drop
    Biscuits, 40
Kohlrabi and Potato Hash, 20
Lamb Chops with Herb
    Butter, 195
London Broil with Spring
    Onion Pesto, 185
Maple-Glazed Salmon, 176
Miso Chicken Thighs, 137
One-Skillet Steak and
    Potatoes, 188
Panzanella, 78
Pork Belly and Kimchi
    Bowl, 197
Pork-Stuffed Bell Peppers, 191
Ricotta-Stuffed Zucchini
    Boats, 116
Roasted Cauliflower, 72
Roasted Sausage and
    Potatoes with Chipotle
    Cream Sauce, 193
Rosemary Buttermilk
    Biscuits, 33–34
Sausage and Cheddar Balls, 60
Savory Dutch Baby, 14–15
Seared Ahi Tuna, 171
Seared Lobster Tails, 161
Seared Short Ribs with Lime
    Cabbage Slaw, 196

Shrimp and Scallop Scampi, 174
Shrimp Burgers with Chipotle
    Mayonnaise, 169
Skillet Calzone, 94
Skillet Greens, 69
Skillet Nachos, 120
Sourdough Toast with
    Avocado, Bacon, Tomato,
    and a Runny Egg, 89–90
Spinach and Artichoke Dip, 63
Sriracha Brussels Sprouts, 71
Steak with Grilled
    Fennel Salad, 180
Sweet and Sour
    Chicken, 134–135
Sweet and Spicy Catfish, 175
Sweet Potato Frittata, 119
Thai Basil Beef, 198
Turkey and Sage Meatballs, 145
Turkey Burgers, 136
Turkey Melt, 85
Vegetable Tempura, 64
Vegetarian Stir-Fry, 115
Walnut and Cranberry
    Baked Oatmeal, 25

Z

Zucchini
    Carrot and Zucchini Fritters, 121
    Charred Zucchini, 79
    Chicken and Zucchini
        Curry, 132–133
    Chocolate Zucchini Bread, 32
    Ricotta-Stuffed Zucchini
        Boats, 116
    Vegetable Tempura, 64

ACKNOWLEDGMENTS

This book was the whirlwind summer project intended to take my mind off the fact that I was enormously pregnant during a pandemic. It worked! This book is a testament to the phenomenon where every day in late pregnancy lasts about two years.

It would not be possible for me to have written any cast-iron cookbooks, let alone three, without my father, James Kenneth Rosemond. He taught me that cast iron is a companion—a tool that treats you as well as you treat it. He showed me how to carefully restore, care for, and cook with my cast iron, and it's barely an exaggeration to say that without his influence, I wouldn't be writing this.

Thank you to the incredible group of recipe testers who helped me shape these recipes and provided honest feedback and constructive criticism. Special thanks to Jobi Zink (a forever superstar) and Brandy Dykhuizen.

A very special forever thank you to my sweet Brit Carlson, who came to help with the birth and ended up staying for two weeks. Thank you for cleaning my house so I could write recipes, encouraging me to write recipes when I just wanted to lay around and complain about how I was going to be pregnant forever, and gently reminding me 100 times a day that I wasn't going to be pregnant forever. You're amazing.

Finally, thank you forever to my boys. Sam, thank you for waiting until I was finished writing the recipes to make your debut, and thank you for being generally reasonable about me propping the laptop up on your back so I could finish editing while you nursed. Everett, thank you for being patient with me as I worked, even when you would have vastly preferred I be doing puzzles with you. And Dan, the best of the best, thank you for supporting me as I decided to binge write a cookbook in a matter of weeks, thank you for giving measured and helpful feedback as I tested recipes, and thank you for loving me always.

ABOUT THE AUTHOR

 **Elena Rosemond-Hoerr**, originally from Durham, North Carolina, is a food writer, photographer, and Montessori educator. She lives in coastal North Carolina with her husband, Dan, and their children, Everett and Sam.

Elena started the Southern food blog, *Biscuits and Such* (BiscuitsAndSuch.com) in 2008 while living in Maryland and feeling homesick. Twelve years and six cookbooks later, Elena still can't manage to make pancakes properly.

CPSIA information can be obtained
at www.ICGtesting.com
Printed in the USA
JSHW011436281221
21596JS00001B/1

9 781646 117635